CATHERINE CASTRO & QUENTIN ZUTTION

CALL ME NATHAN

Translated by Evan McGorray

SELF MADE HERO

In this book, the main character is fictional, identifies as male and goes through surgery. CW: trans healthcare, transphobia, self-harm, surgery, nudity, crude language

First published in English in 2022
by SelfMadeHero
139–141 Pancras Road
London NW1 1UN
www.selfmadehero.com

Written by Catherine Castro and drawn by Quentin Zuttion
Translated by Evan McGorray

The graphic novel APPELEZ-MOI NATHAN
by Catherine Castro and Quentin Zuttion
was published in 2018 by Éditions Payot et Rivages.
© Éditions Payot et Rivages

Song lyrics on pages 28, 29 and 30:
"The Other Side" written by Emily Warren Schwartz & Scott Harris Friedman
© Published by Where Da Kasz At / Hipgnosis Songs Fund Limited
Administered by Kobalt Music Publishing Ltd
"The Other Side" words and music by Warren Felder / Scott Harris / Emily Warren
© 2017 Reproduced by permission of Crows Publishing / Sony ATV Songs LLC,
London W1T 3LP

Publishing Director: Emma Hayley
Editorial & Production Director: Guillaume Rater
Publishing Assistant: Stefano Mancin
Designer: Txabi Jones
Publicist: Paul Smith
With thanks to: Dan Lockwood and Léo C Guillemin

A CIP record for this book is available from the British Library

ISBN: 978-1-914224-01-0

10 9 8 7 6 5 4 3 2 1

Printed and bound in China

PREFACE

Some books take ages to come into the world. They mature for a long time, months, years. *Call Me Nathan* was born in the blink of an eye one afternoon in the countryside, at a party among family and friends. I was introduced to someone I had once seen as a baby in similar circumstances: family, friends, etc. The being that this baby had become was standing in front of me. Radiant and anxious, anchored and floating, determined and uncertain. It was Lucas, though at that time he was only named 'Lucas' in the secret recesses of his body and soul. He was 14 years old. I don't remember exactly what we talked about, but we met one another as the music of Abba and Bob Marley brought a spark to us all on that patch of grass, the most natural of dancefloors. Back in Paris, I thought again about Lucas-whose-name-was-not-yet-Lucas. He was a rock star. Someone you don't tell what to do or not to do, someone ready to pay the price for being free. Freedom has its cost, taking the plunge and persevering, ready to fail, to make mistakes, to break up, to be judged, to catch fire, it's vital, there's no stopping it. Lucas wanted to be himself. It wasn't a dream, it was a necessity.

Lucas and I met each other again with his parents. I told the three of them that I wanted to tell the story of this blossoming in a protagonist-driven style rather than a documentarian one. At that time, five years ago, questions of transness were seldom discussed. And when they were, they caused quite a bit of controversy and misunderstanding in the public space and drama in private. Lucas was a boy trapped in a girl's body by biology. While other teens spent their time on social media checking out sneakers that would give them a sense of style that they mistook for identity, Lucas surfed forums to understand who he was. He already had style, and he came to understand his identity intimately. We are not born ourselves, we become them; this can take a lifetime, and we still don't always end up understanding who we are. Lucas was a man in the making. That is the story I wanted to tell. What he was going through took on a universal dimension. Becoming oneself is a whole life's work, a work that concerns us all, no matter our gender, our refusal to be limited to a gender or our sexuality. For Lucas, becoming himself was achieved through physical discovery and the (de)construction and conquest of his place in society.

He showed me the muscles that he'd discovered over the course of his injections. His path would be difficult but illuminating. For his family, too, providing unconditional support, the path was difficult, often painful. For each of them, the transition was a hard, disarming, totally unexpected journey. Through these meetings, the character of Nathan and the true fiction of his life were born. Several passages are pure fiction, in fact. But what wasn't made up is the love that flows from every page. Meeting with Lucas and his family was deeply emotional every time. What they experienced alongside one another had a name: love. Love alone can do anything. On the path that Lucas, Nathan and so many others are on, that makes such a difference.

Catherine Castro

I could tell you about the day I wore a dress to make my mother happy.

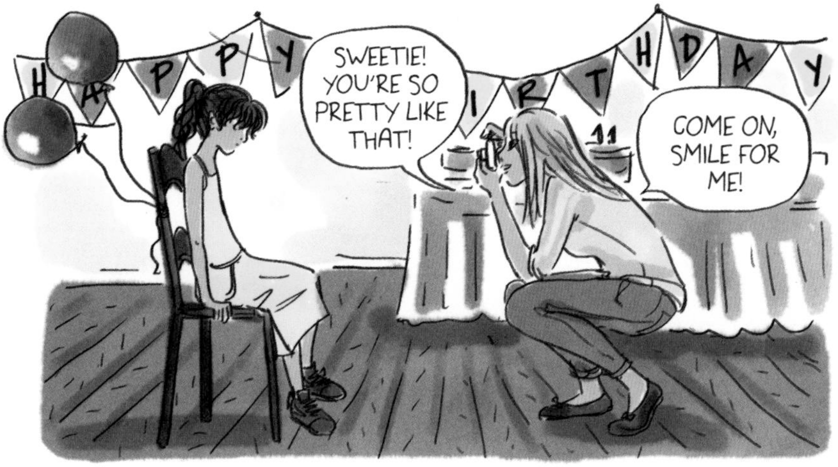
SWEETIE! YOU'RE SO PRETTY LIKE THAT!
COME ON, SMILE FOR ME!

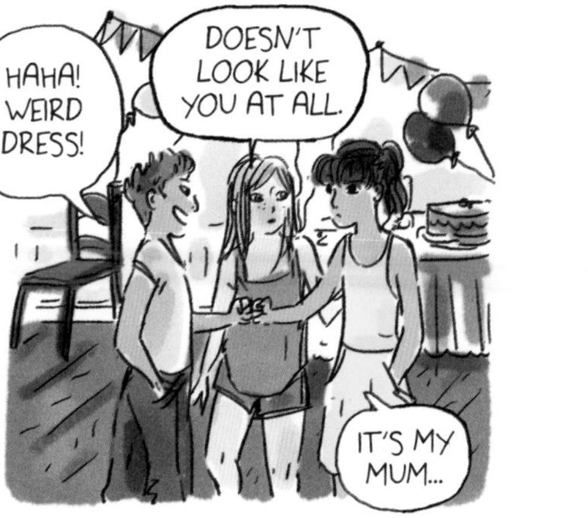
HAHA! WEIRD DRESS!
DOESN'T LOOK LIKE YOU AT ALL.
IT'S MY MUM...

That lasted 5 minutes.

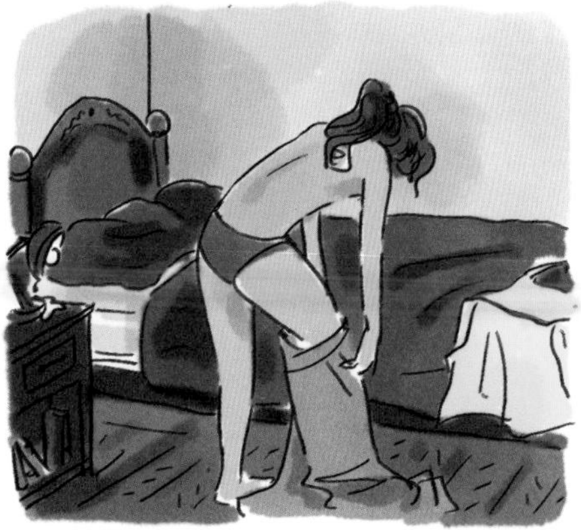

Or the day I got bullied during water polo.

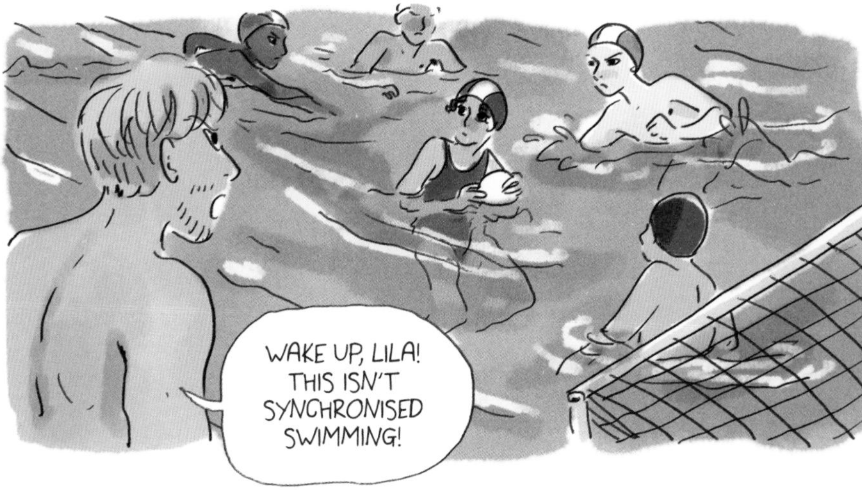
WAKE UP, LILA! THIS ISN'T SYNCHRONISED SWIMMING!

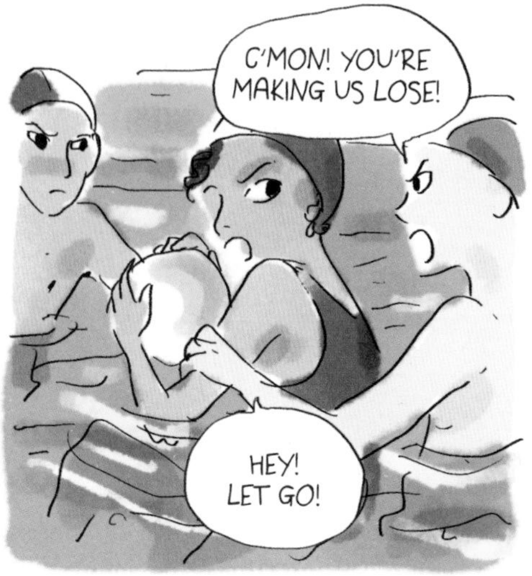
C'MON! YOU'RE MAKING US LOSE!
HEY! LET GO!

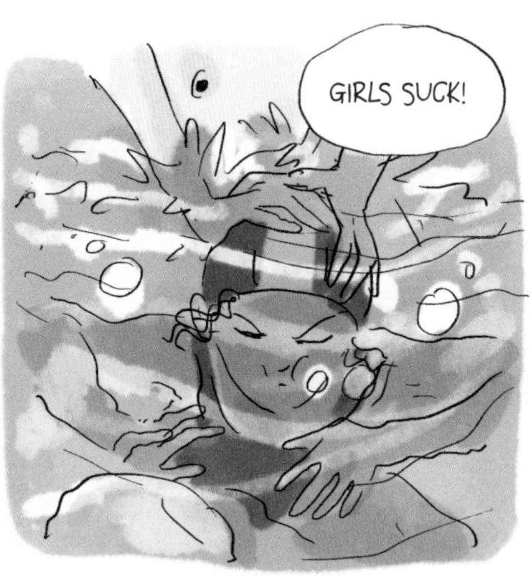
GIRLS SUCK!

Or the time my grandma bought me a Hello Kitty bag for Christmas.

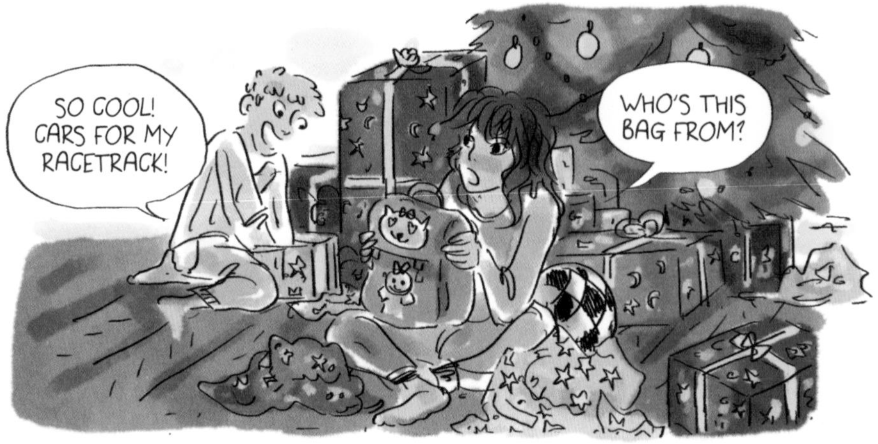
SO COOL! CARS FOR MY RACETRACK!
WHO'S THIS BAG FROM?

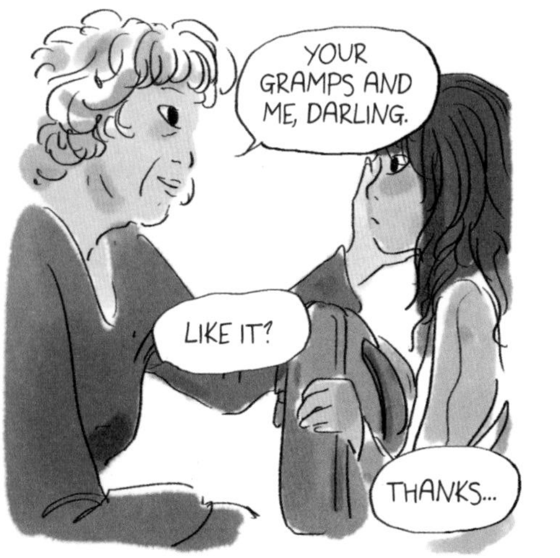
YOUR GRAMPS AND ME, DARLING.
LIKE IT?
THANKS...

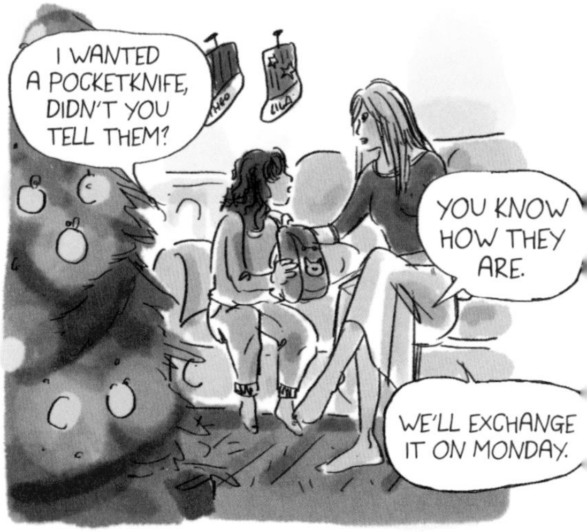
I WANTED A POCKETKNIFE, DIDN'T YOU TELL THEM?
YOU KNOW HOW THEY ARE.
WE'LL EXCHANGE IT ON MONDAY.

But I'd rather begin with the day when it all started to go wrong.
Said like that, it's kinda pessimistic. I'm not a pessimist.
Lemme start over...

The day I asked myself:

Is this some kind of joke?

I'll remember that summer for the rest of my life.

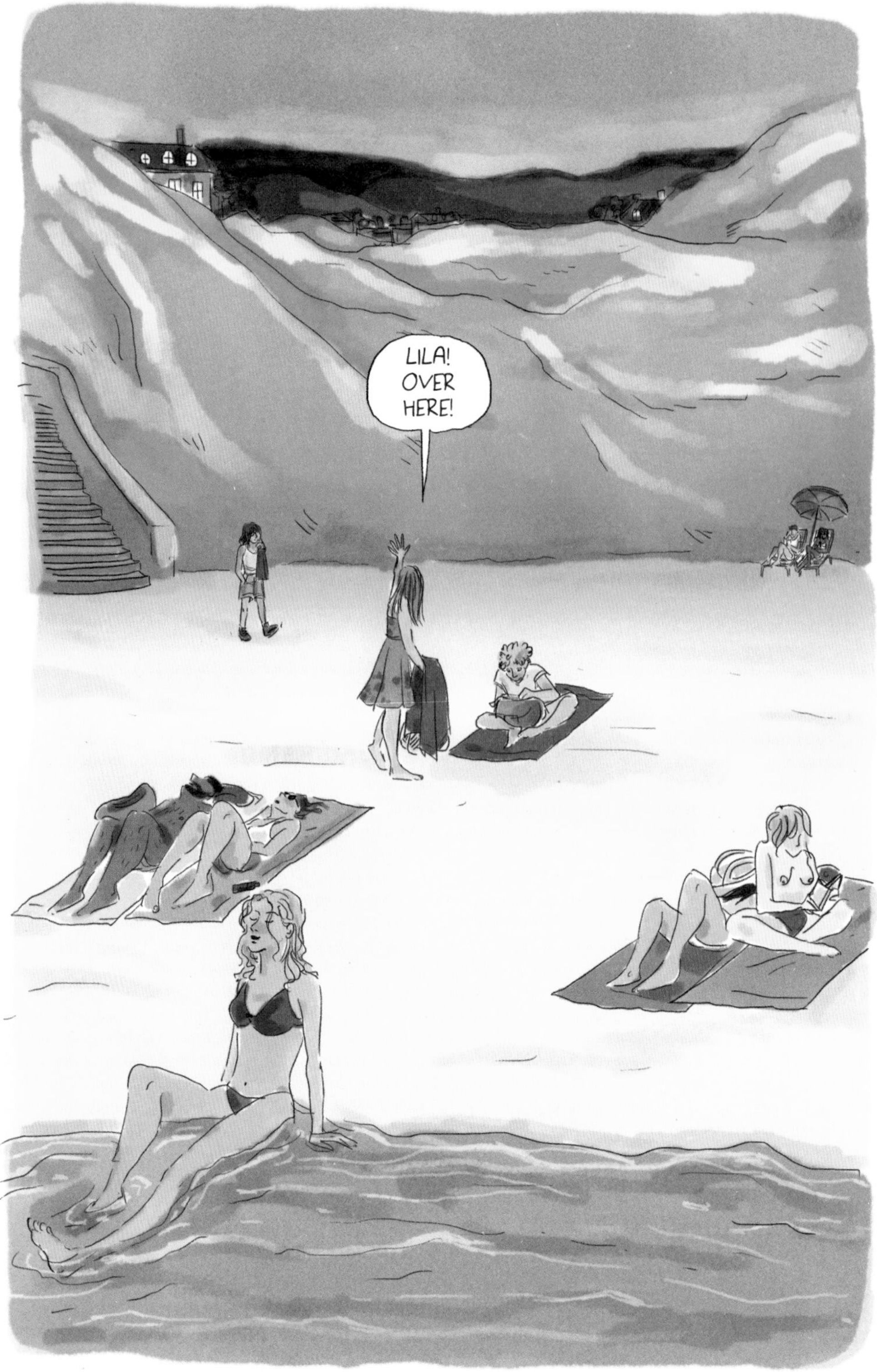
LILA! OVER HERE!

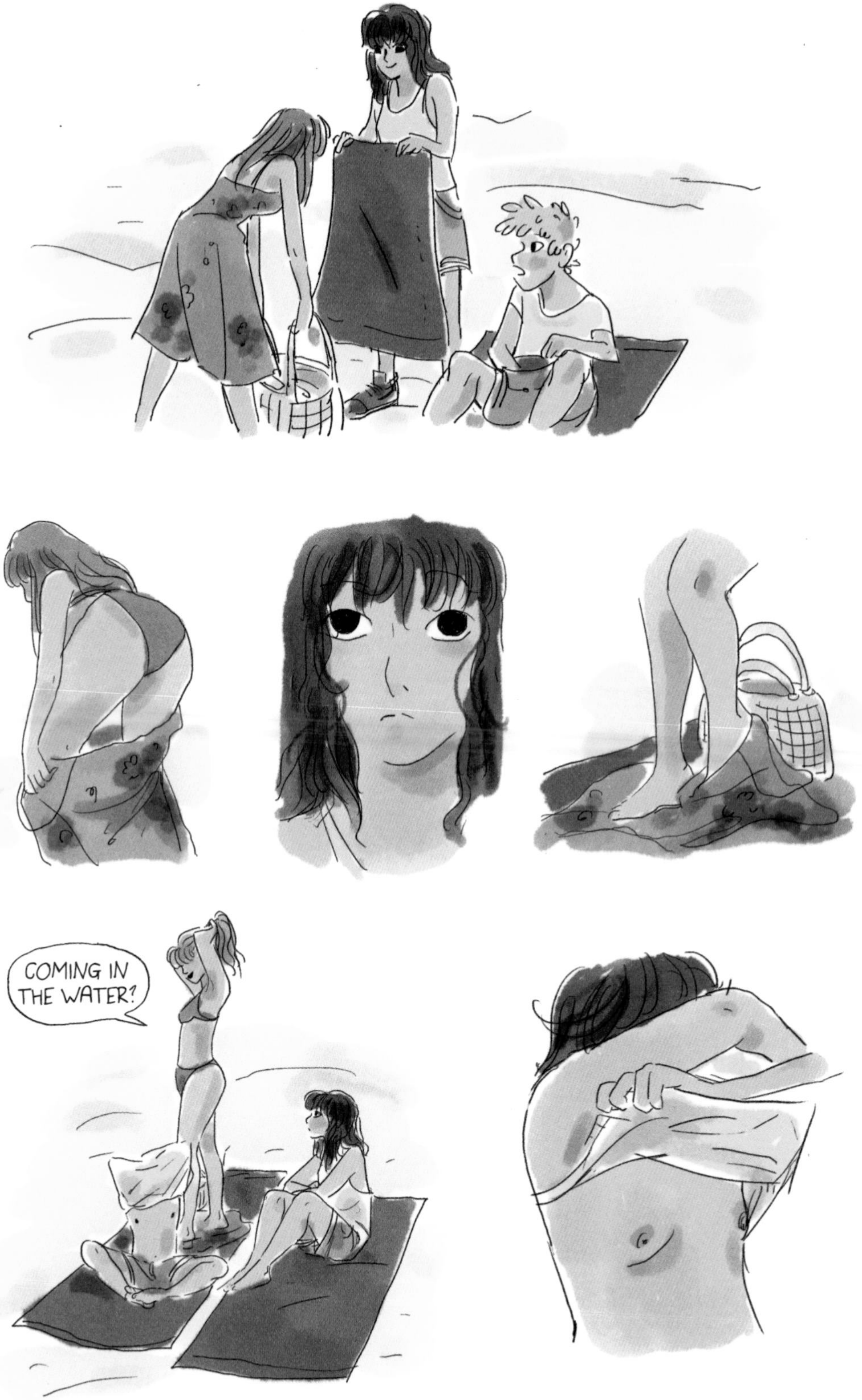
COMING IN THE WATER?

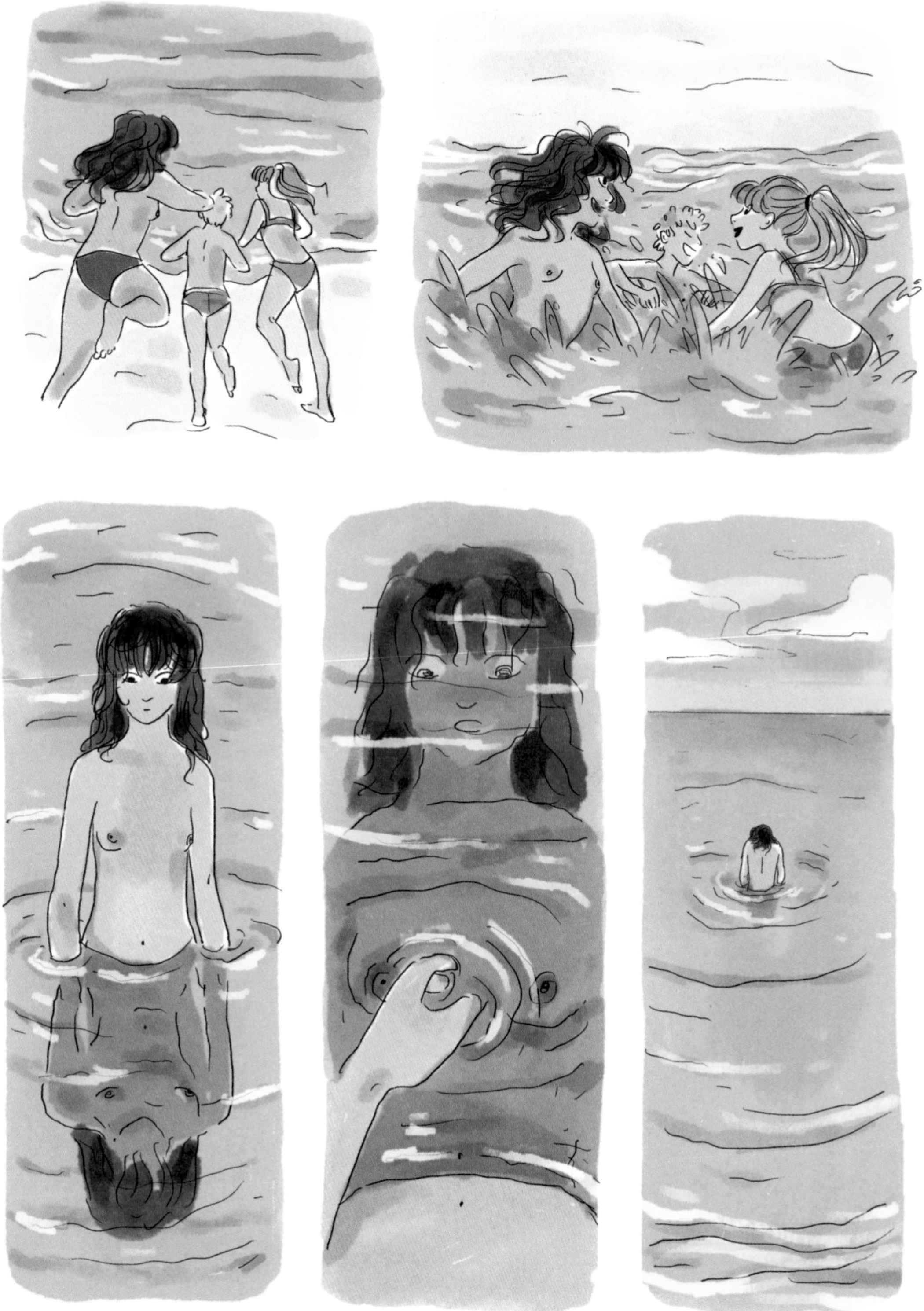

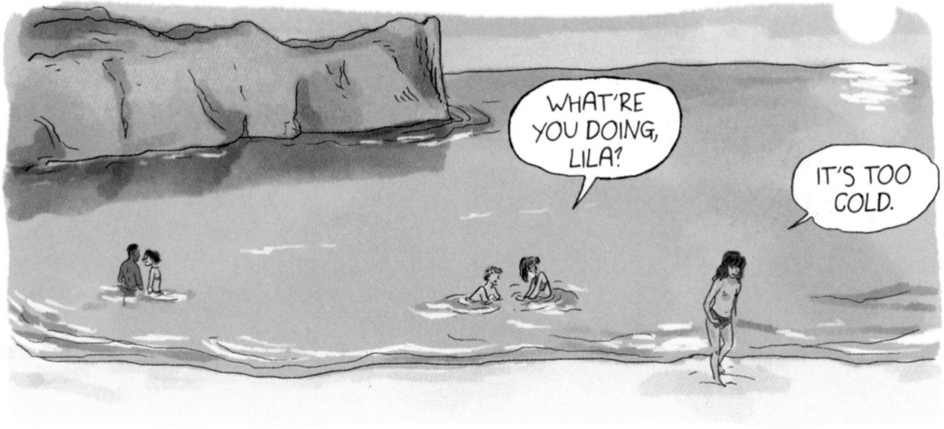
WHAT'RE YOU DOING, LILA?
IT'S TOO COLD.

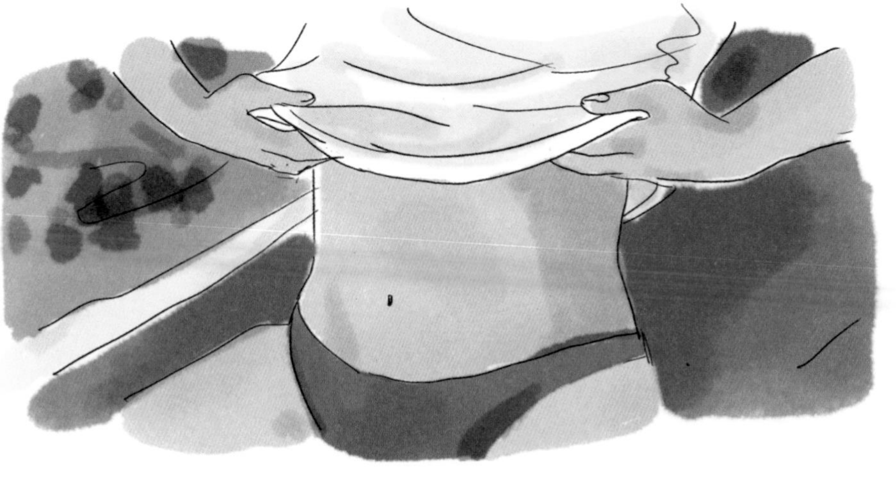

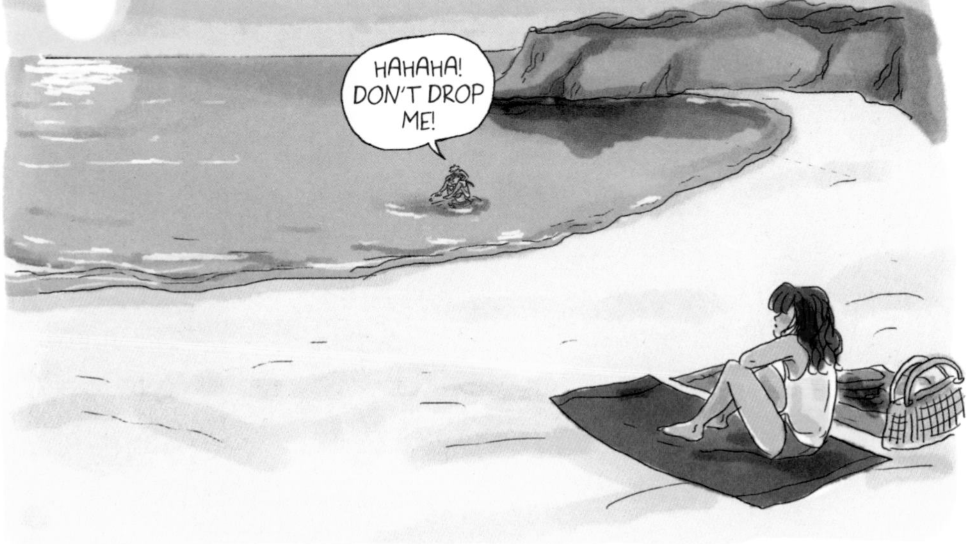
HAHAHA! DON'T DROP ME!

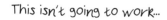

This isn't going to work...

LILA, OPEN UP!

LILA! I'M GONNA PISS MY PANTS!

YOU DISGUST ME.

LILAAAAA!!

TOOK LONG ENOUGH! GOT YOUR PERIOD OR SOMETHING?

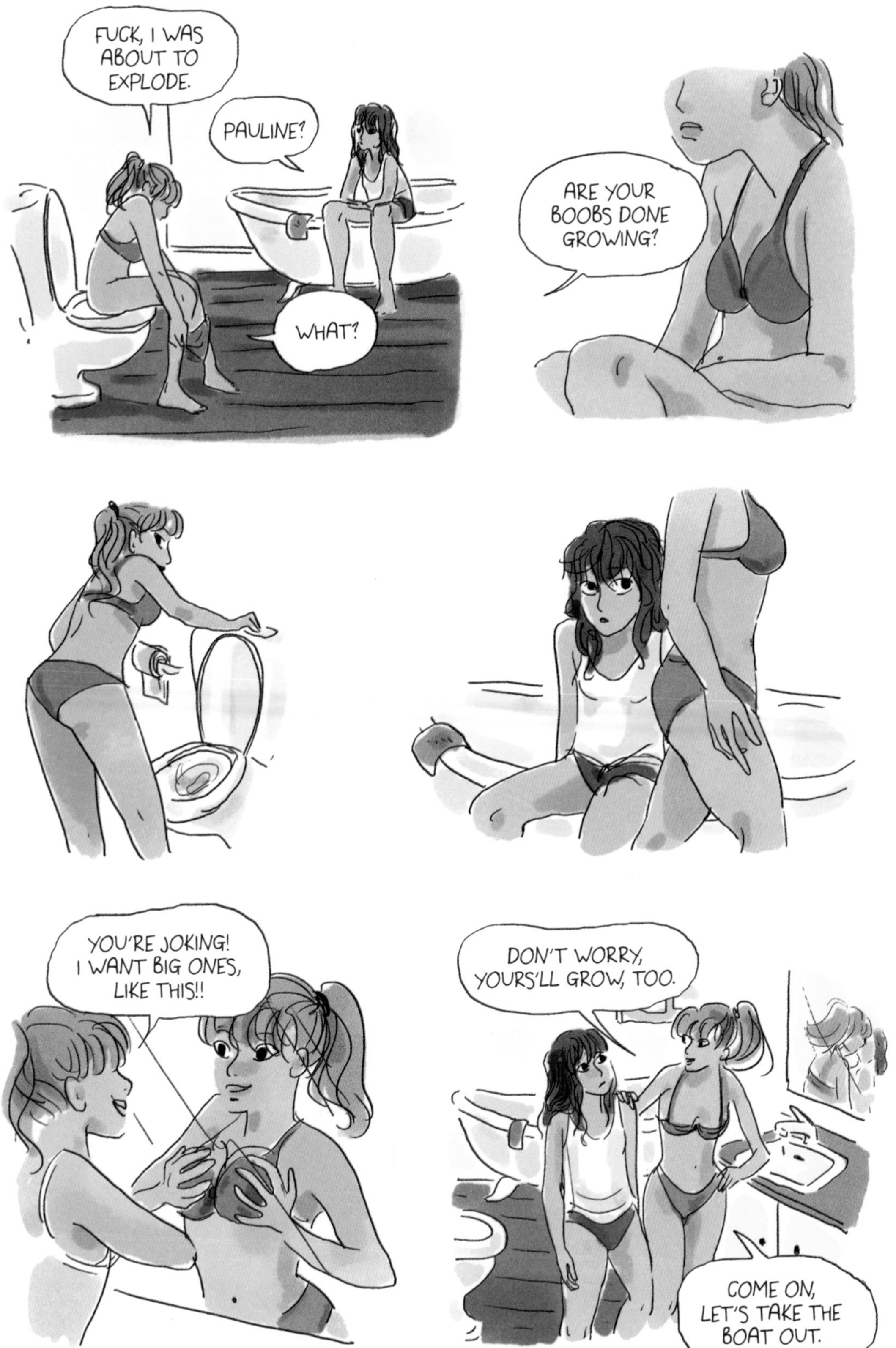
FUCK, I WAS ABOUT TO EXPLODE.
PAULINE?
WHAT?
ARE YOUR BOOBS DONE GROWING?
YOU'RE JOKING! I WANT BIG ONES, LIKE THIS!!
DON'T WORRY, YOURS'LL GROW, TOO.
COME ON, LET'S TAKE THE BOAT OUT.

I love Pauline. If she wasn't my cousin...

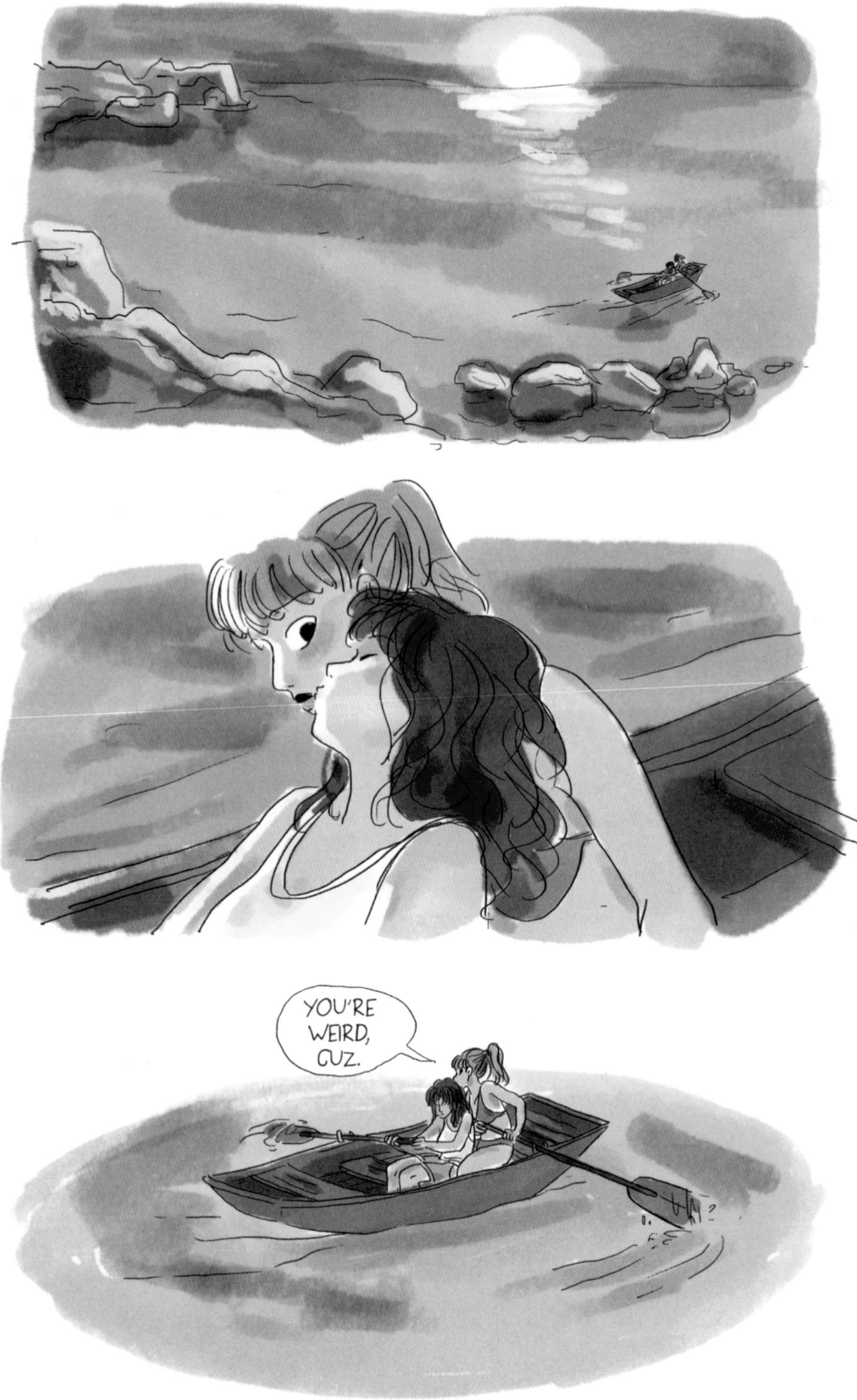
YOU'RE WEIRD, CUZ.

For once, I'm happy that the holidays are over.
I don't have to walk around naked any more.

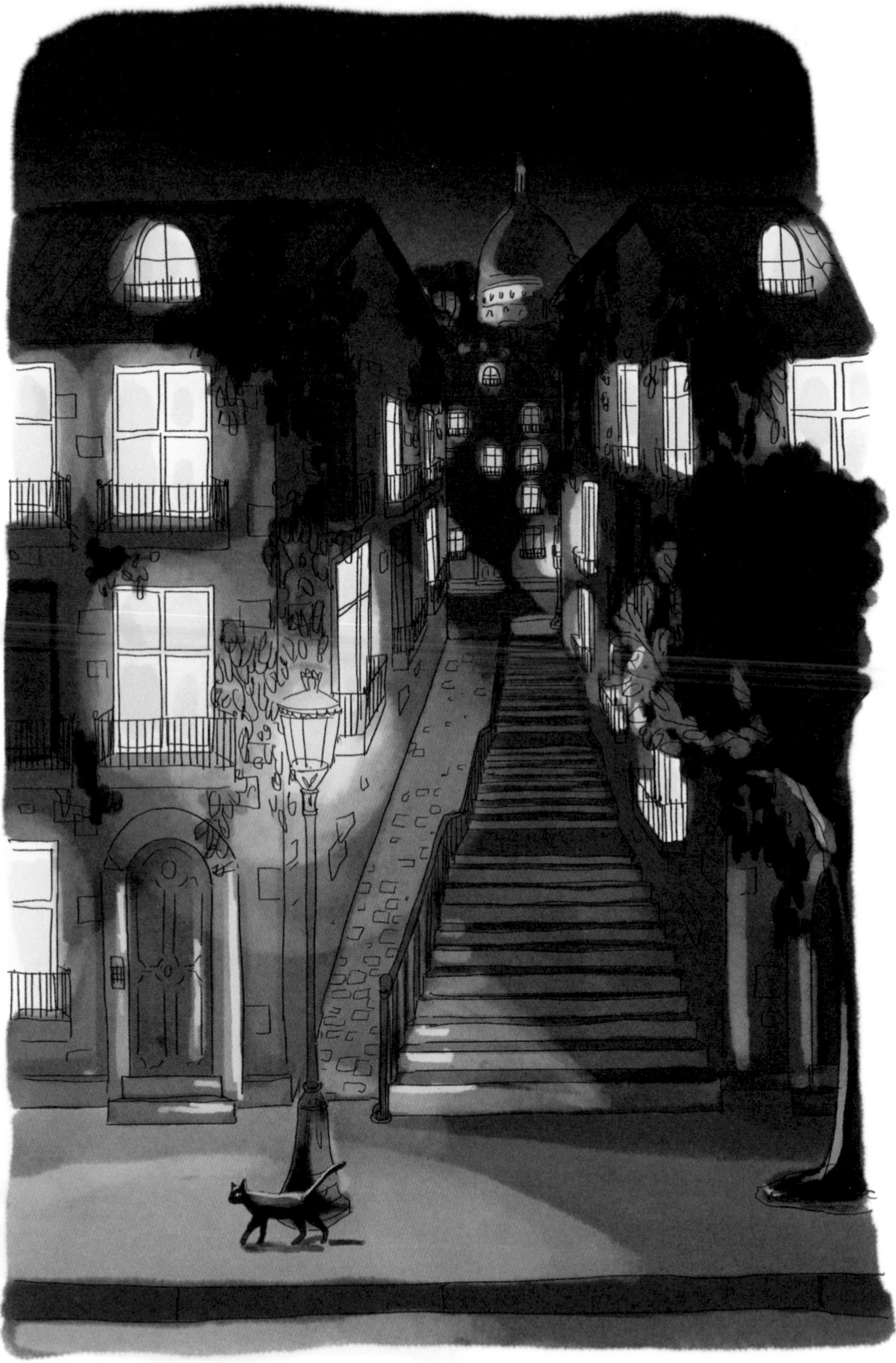

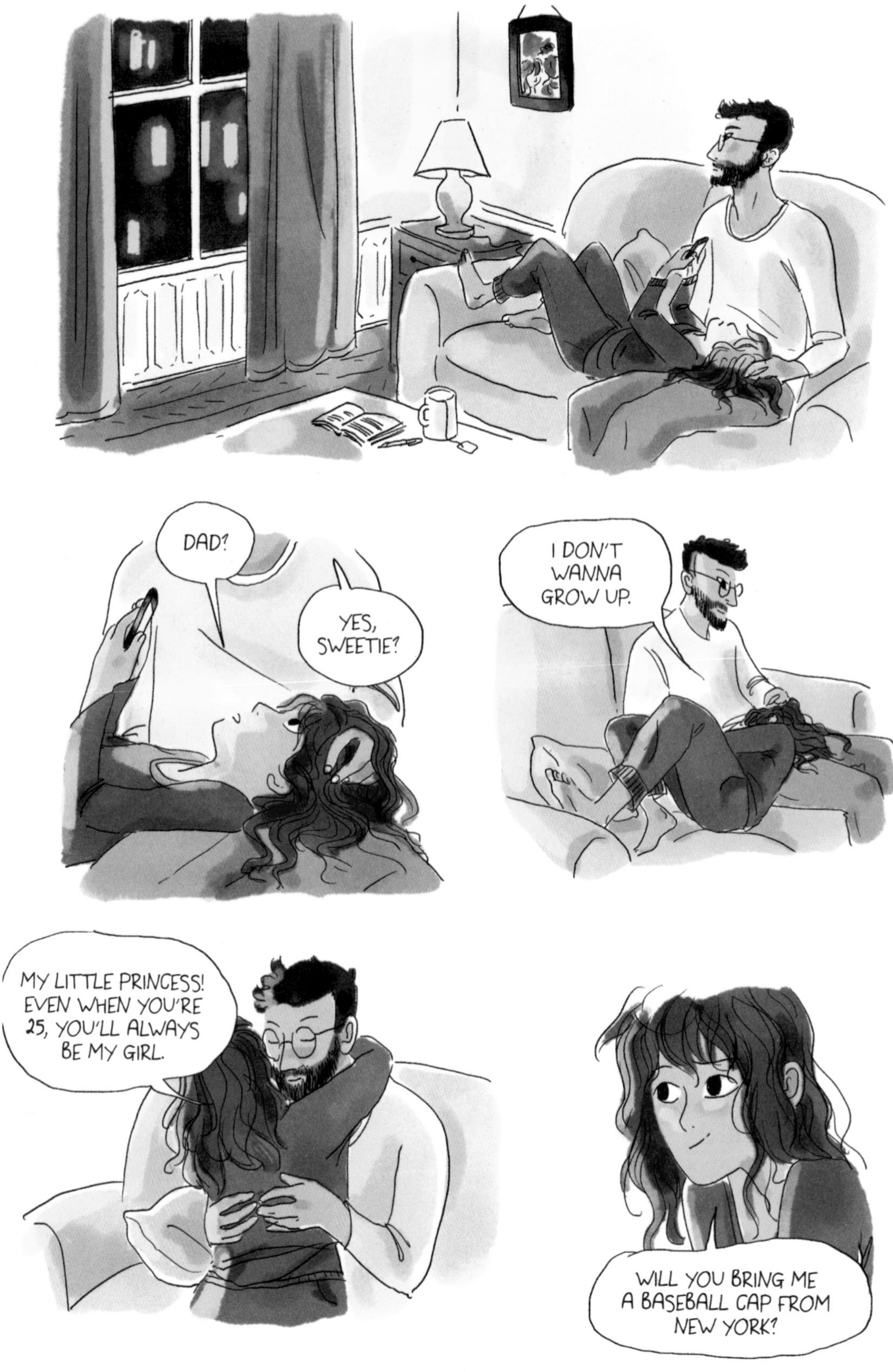
DAD?
YES, SWEETIE?
I DON'T WANNA GROW UP.
MY LITTLE PRINCESS! EVEN WHEN YOU'RE 25, YOU'LL ALWAYS BE MY GIRL.
WILL YOU BRING ME A BASEBALL CAP FROM NEW YORK?

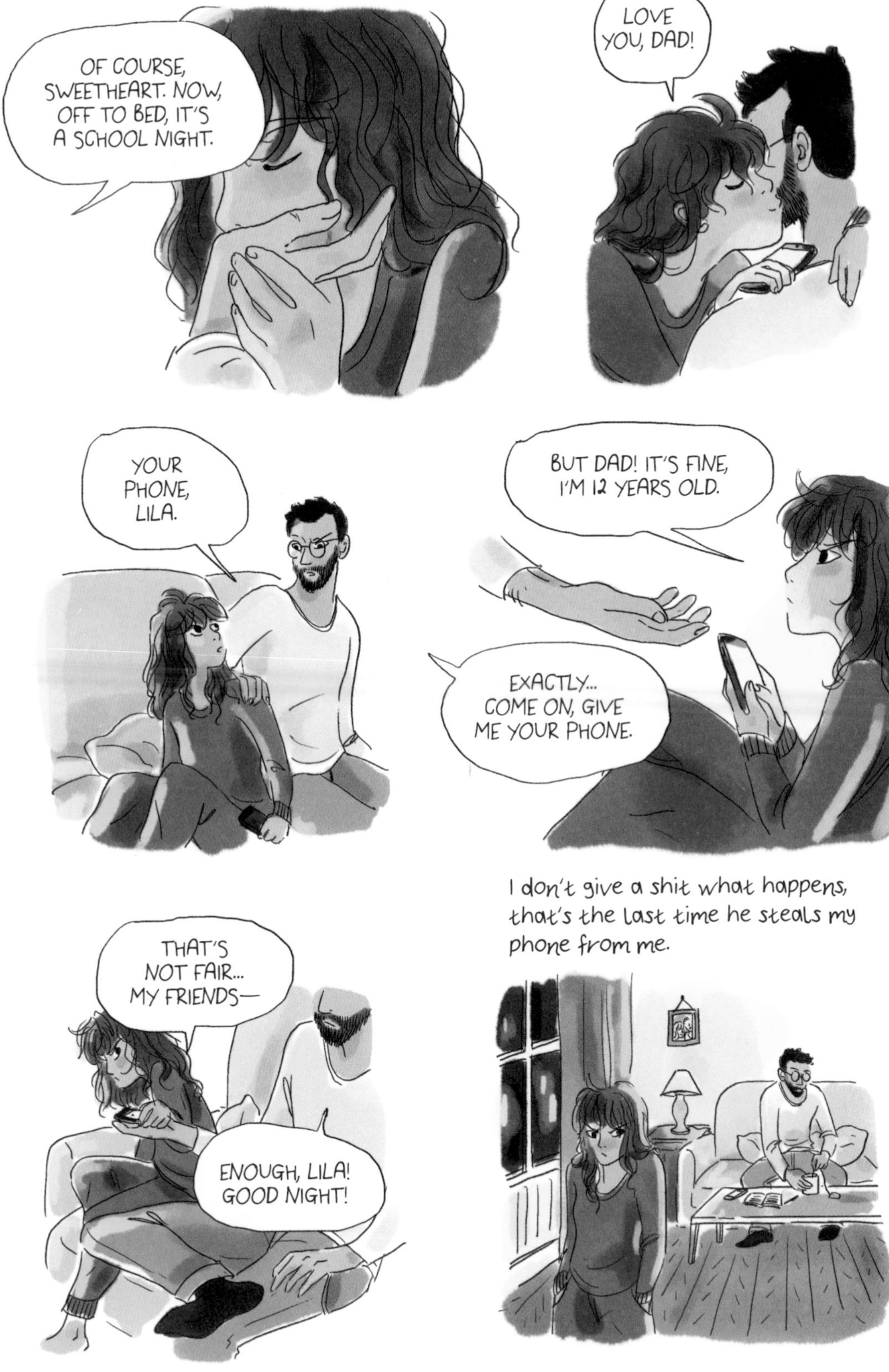
OF COURSE, SWEETHEART. NOW, OFF TO BED, IT'S A SCHOOL NIGHT.
LOVE YOU, DAD!
YOUR PHONE, LILA.
BUT DAD! IT'S FINE, I'M 12 YEARS OLD.
EXACTLY... COME ON, GIVE ME YOUR PHONE.
THAT'S NOT FAIR... MY FRIENDS—
ENOUGH, LILA! GOOD NIGHT!
I don't give a shit what happens, that's the last time he steals my phone from me.

My best mates. When we played football, I was the only girl. You always told me: "You're not like the others, Lila." I love you. Forever.

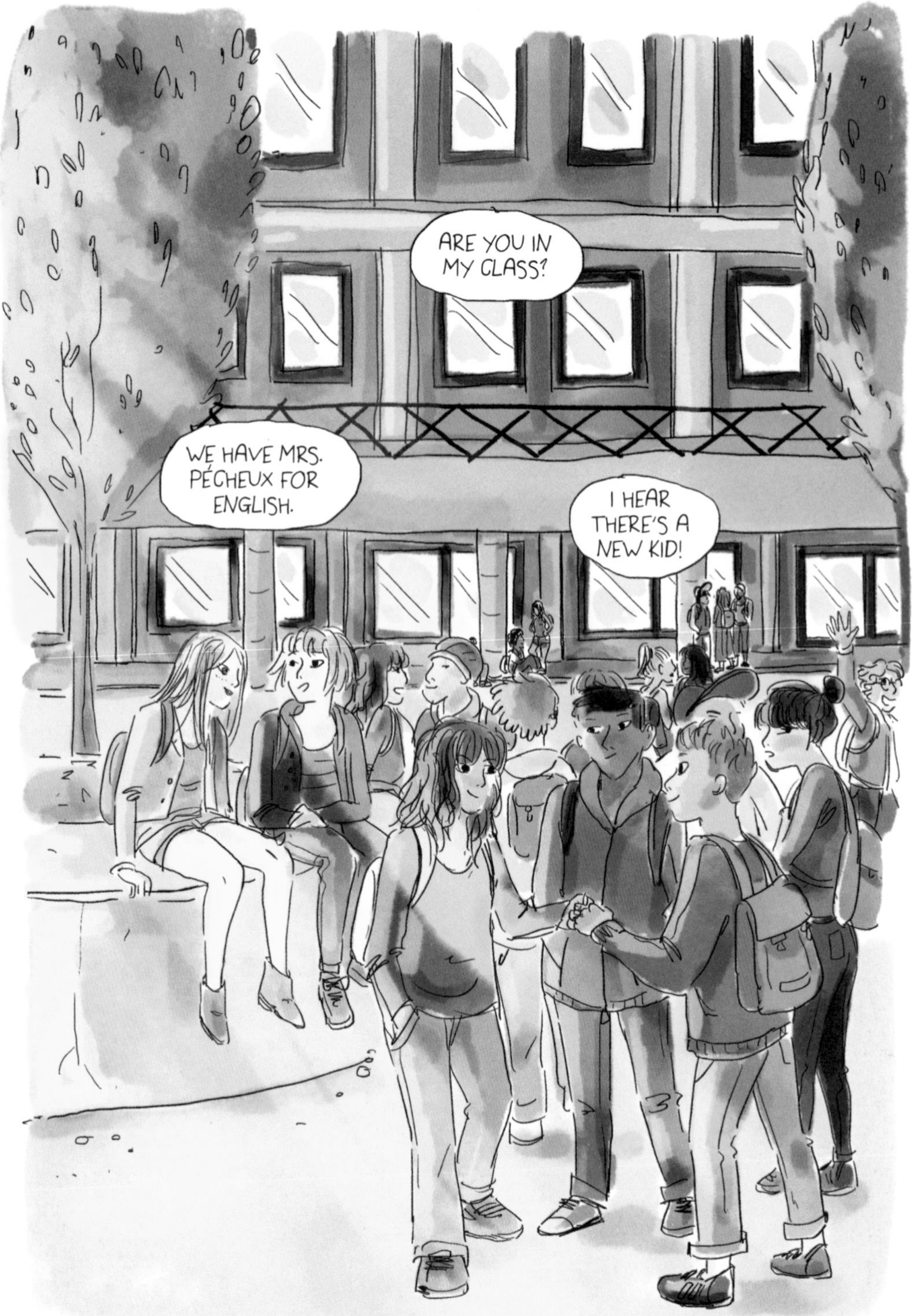
ARE YOU IN MY CLASS?
WE HAVE MRS. PÉCHEUX FOR ENGLISH.
I HEAR THERE'S A NEW KID!

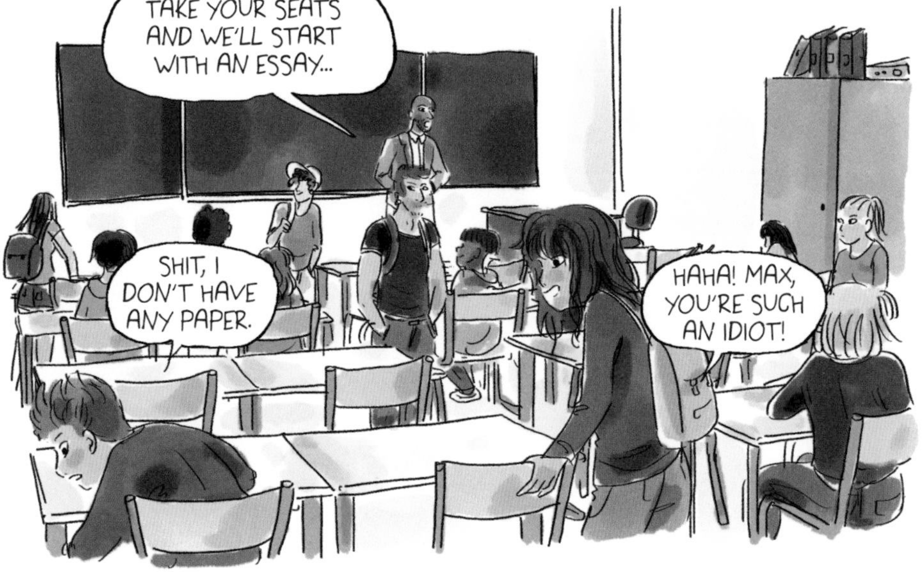
TAKE YOUR SEATS AND WE'LL START WITH AN ESSAY...
SHIT, I DON'T HAVE ANY PAPER.
HAHA! MAX, YOU'RE SUCH AN IDIOT!

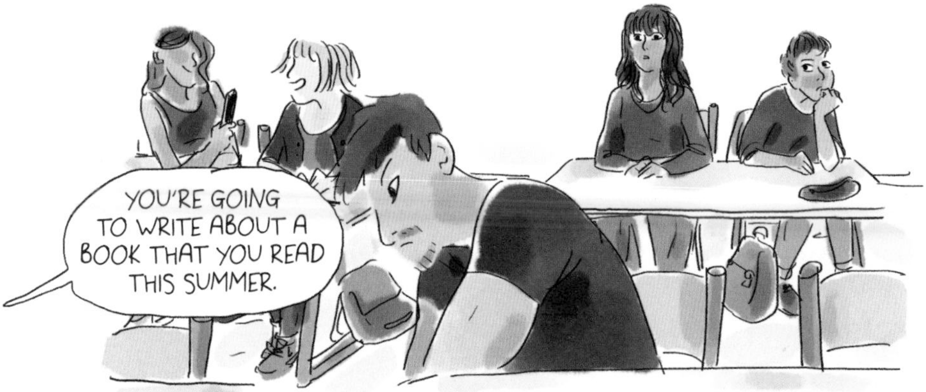
YOU'RE GOING TO WRITE ABOUT A BOOK THAT YOU READ THIS SUMMER.

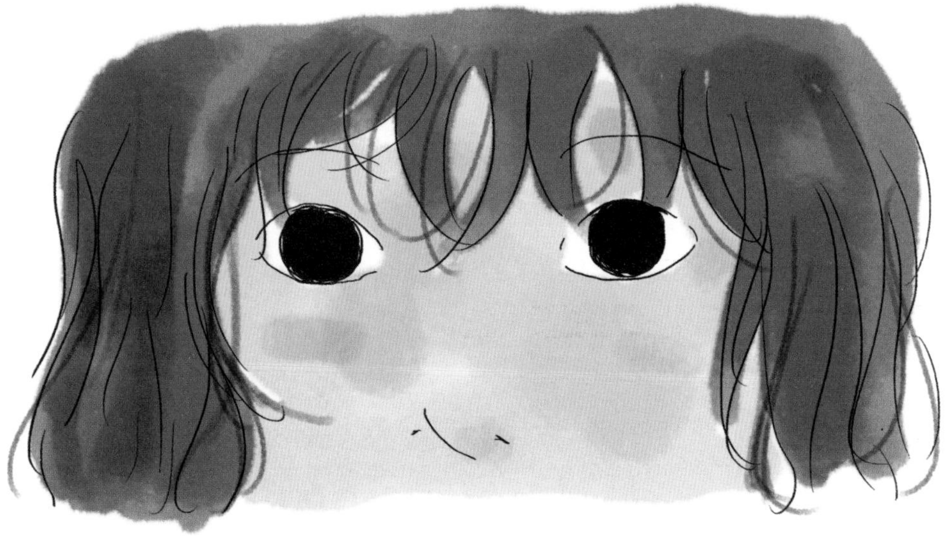

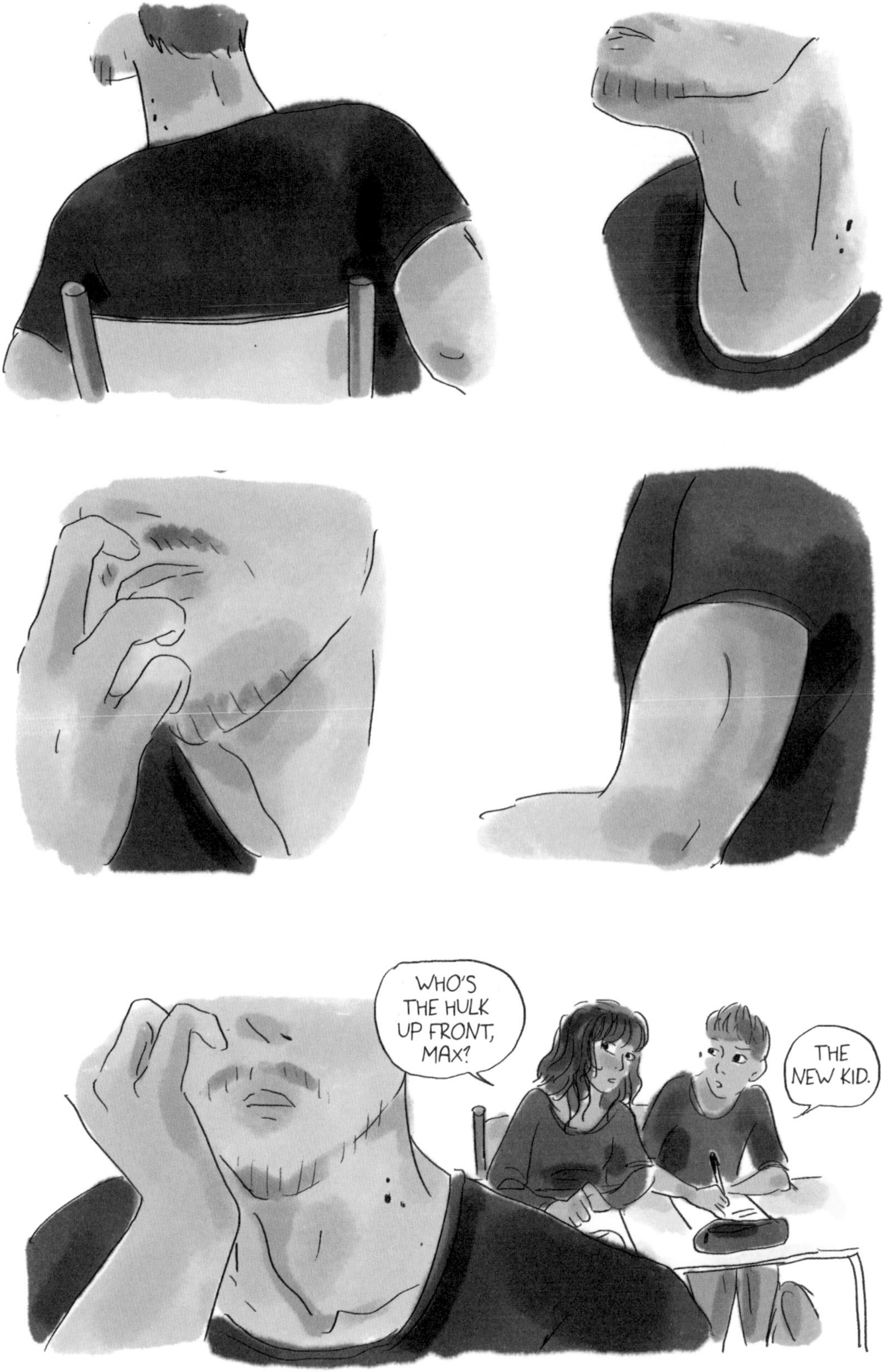
WHO'S THE HULK UP FRONT, MAX?
THE NEW KID.

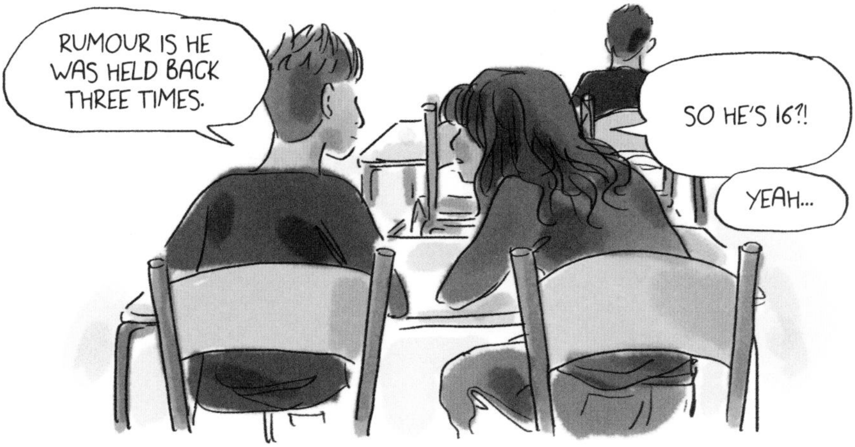
RUMOUR IS HE WAS HELD BACK THREE TIMES.
SO HE'S 16?!
YEAH...

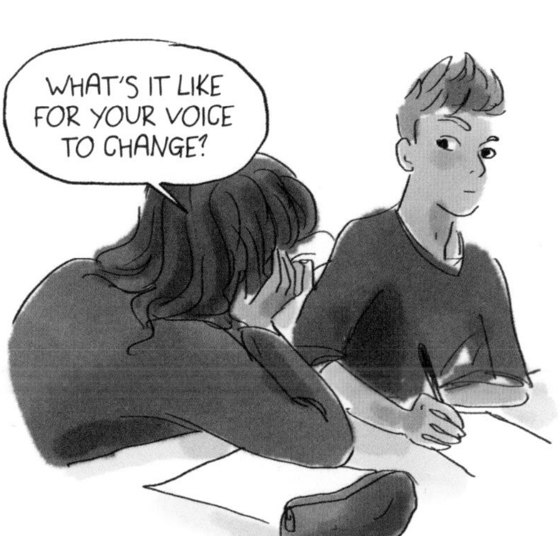
WHAT'S IT LIKE FOR YOUR VOICE TO CHANGE?

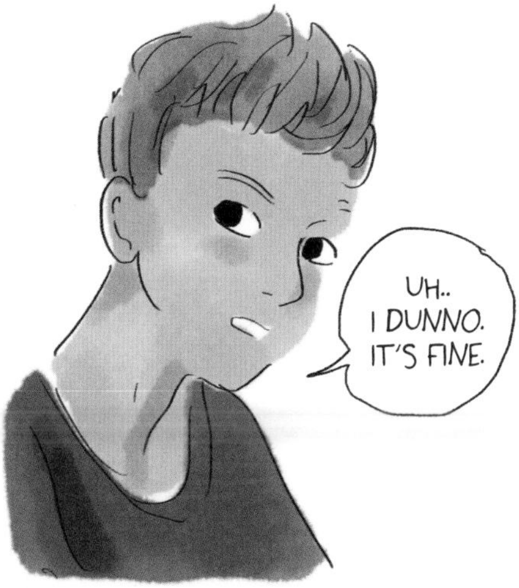
UH.. I DUNNO. IT'S FINE.

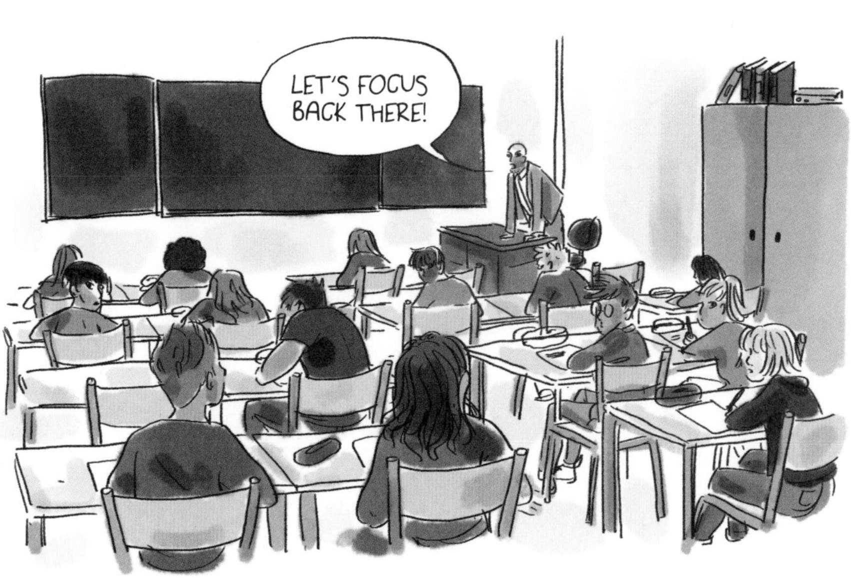
LET'S FOCUS BACK THERE!

Fights happen all the time at this point. I have a lump in the back of my throat, like a lychee that I can't swallow. It'll rot, so will I die?

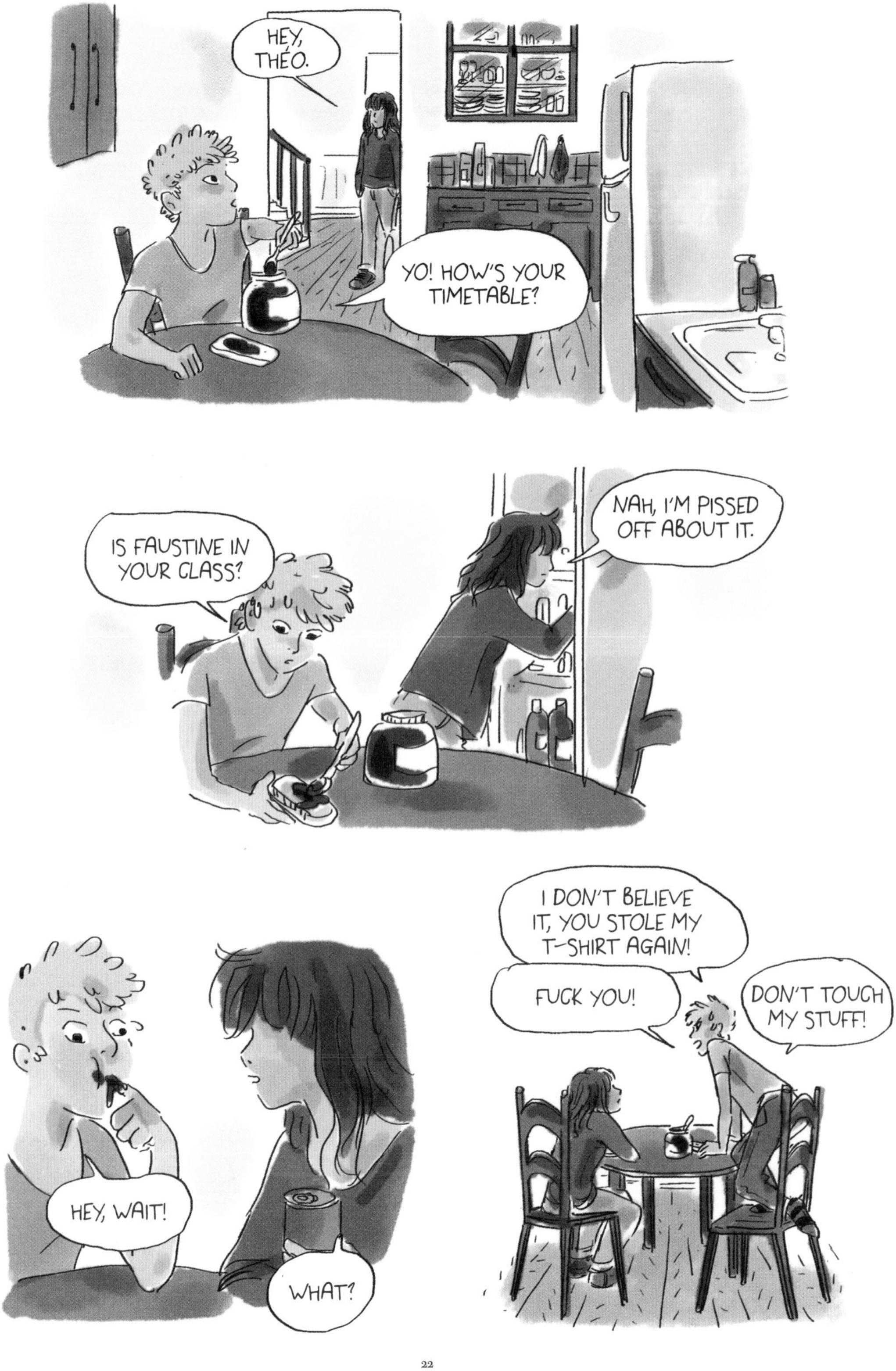

HEY, THÉO.
YO! HOW'S YOUR TIMETABLE?
IS FAUSTINE IN YOUR CLASS?
NAH, I'M PISSED OFF ABOUT IT.
HEY, WAIT!
WHAT?
I DON'T BELIEVE IT, YOU STOLE MY T-SHIRT AGAIN!
FUCK YOU!
DON'T TOUCH MY STUFF!

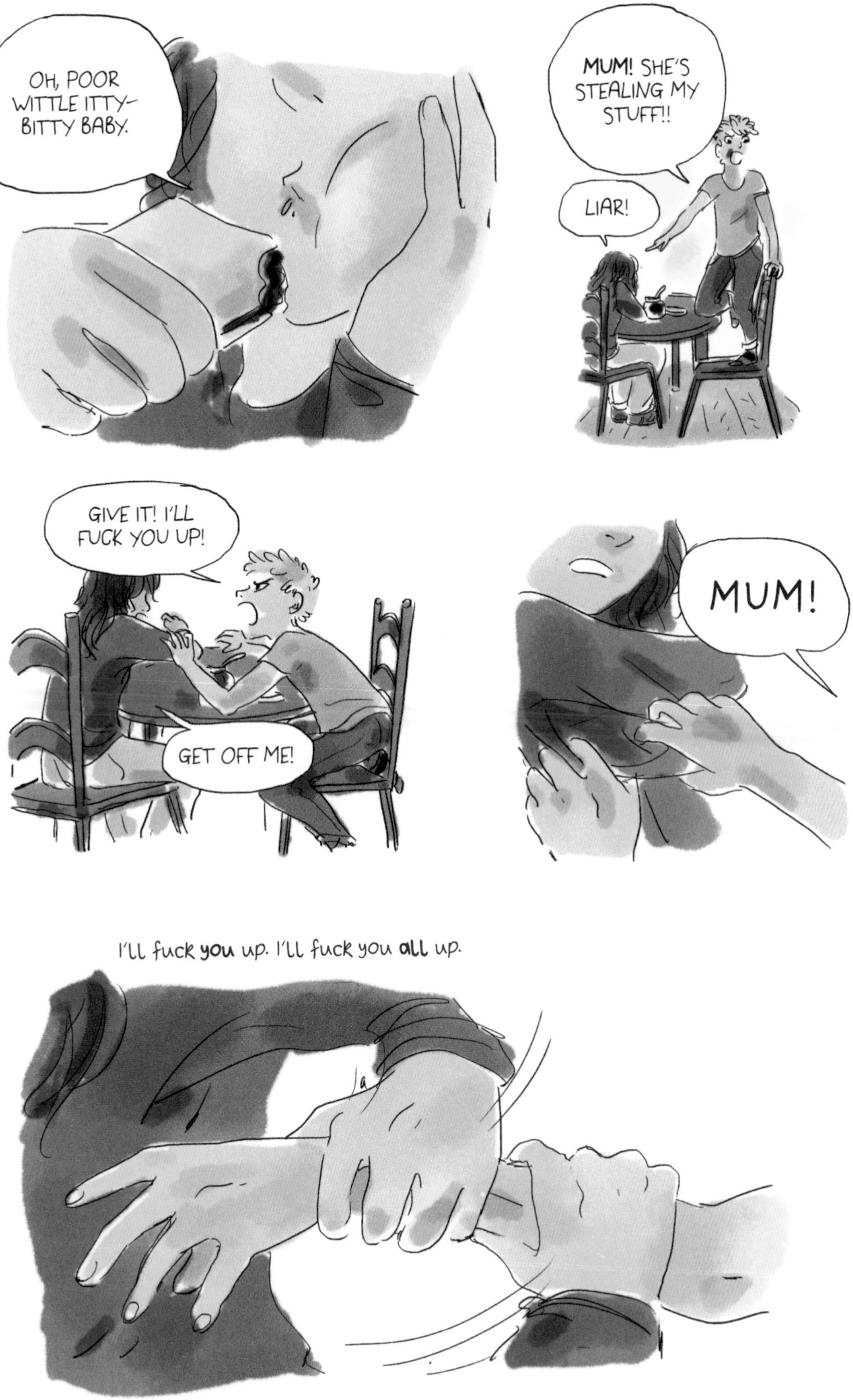
OH, POOR WITTLE ITTY-BITTY BABY.
MUM! SHE'S STEALING MY STUFF!!
LIAR!
GIVE IT! I'LL FUCK YOU UP!
GET OFF ME!
MUM!
I'll fuck you up. I'll fuck you all up.

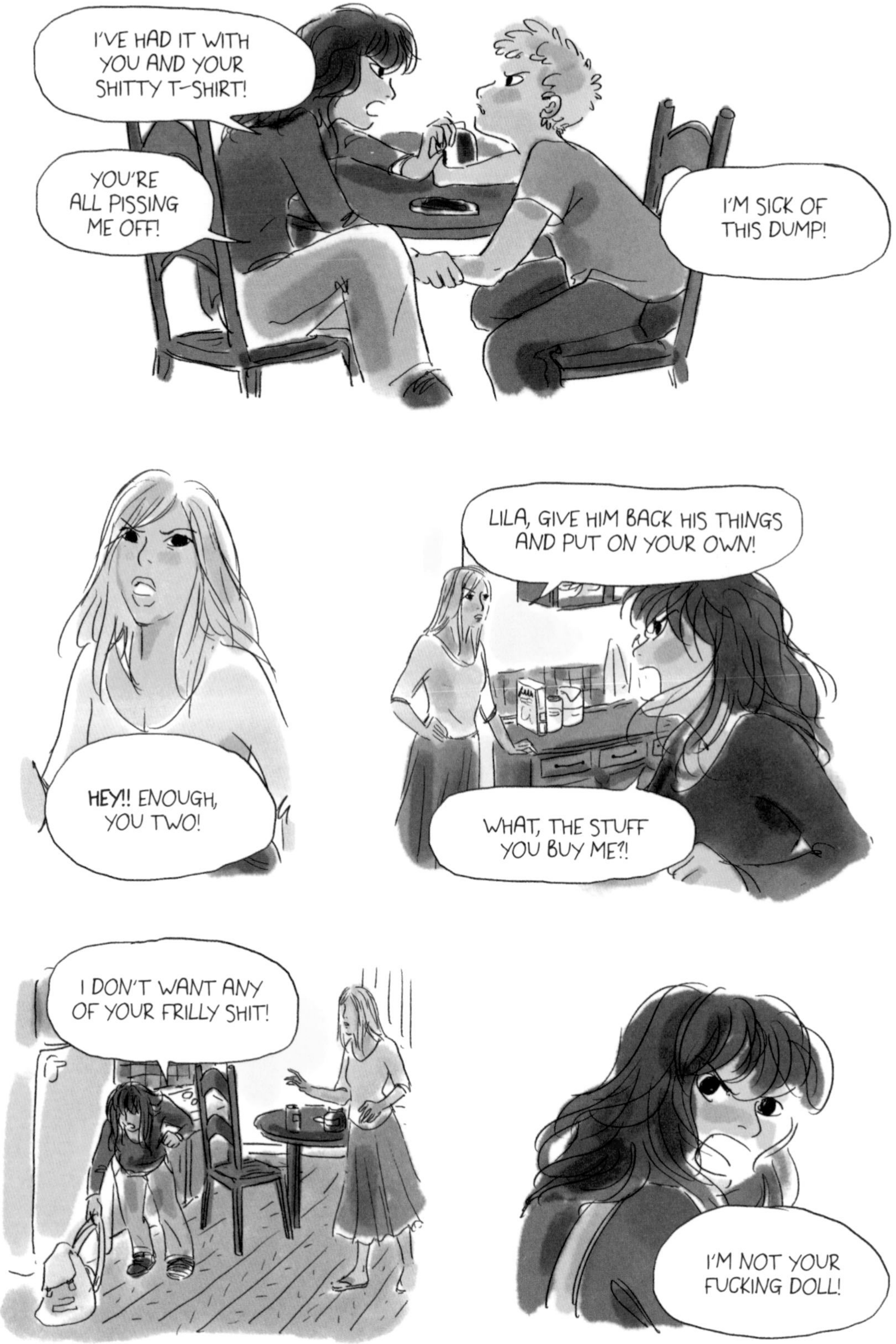
I'VE HAD IT WITH YOU AND YOUR SHITTY T-SHIRT!
YOU'RE ALL PISSING ME OFF!
I'M SICK OF THIS DUMP!
HEY!! ENOUGH, YOU TWO!
LILA, GIVE HIM BACK HIS THINGS AND PUT ON YOUR OWN!
WHAT, THE STUFF YOU BUY ME?!
I DON'T WANT ANY OF YOUR FRILLY SHIT!
I'M NOT YOUR FUCKING DOLL!

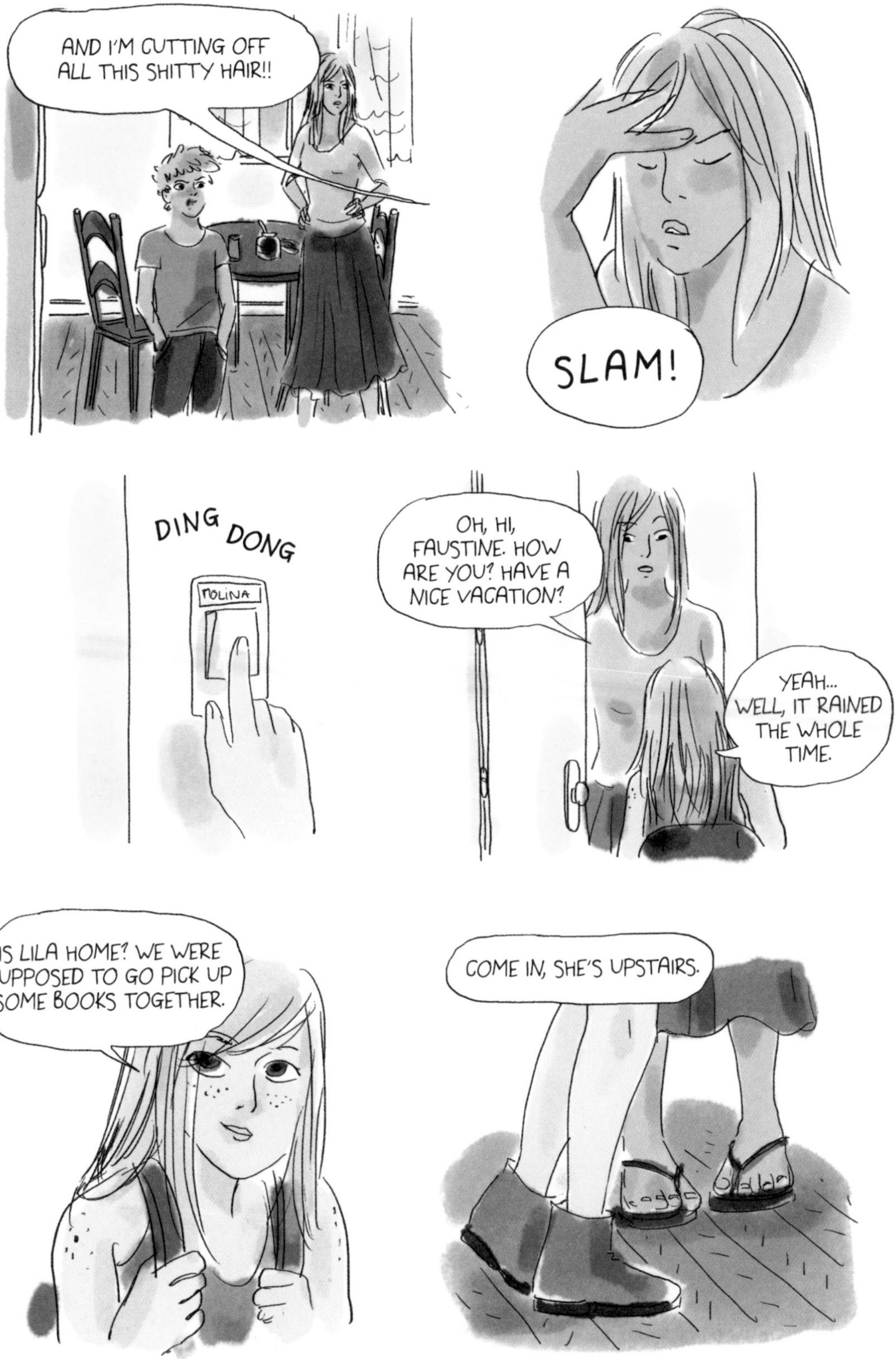
AND I'M CUTTING OFF ALL THIS SHITTY HAIR!!
SLAM!
DING DONG
MOLINA
OH, HI, FAUSTINE. HOW ARE YOU? HAVE A NICE VACATION?
YEAH... WELL, IT RAINED THE WHOLE TIME.
IS LILA HOME? WE WERE SUPPOSED TO GO PICK UP SOME BOOKS TOGETHER.
COME IN, SHE'S UPSTAIRS.

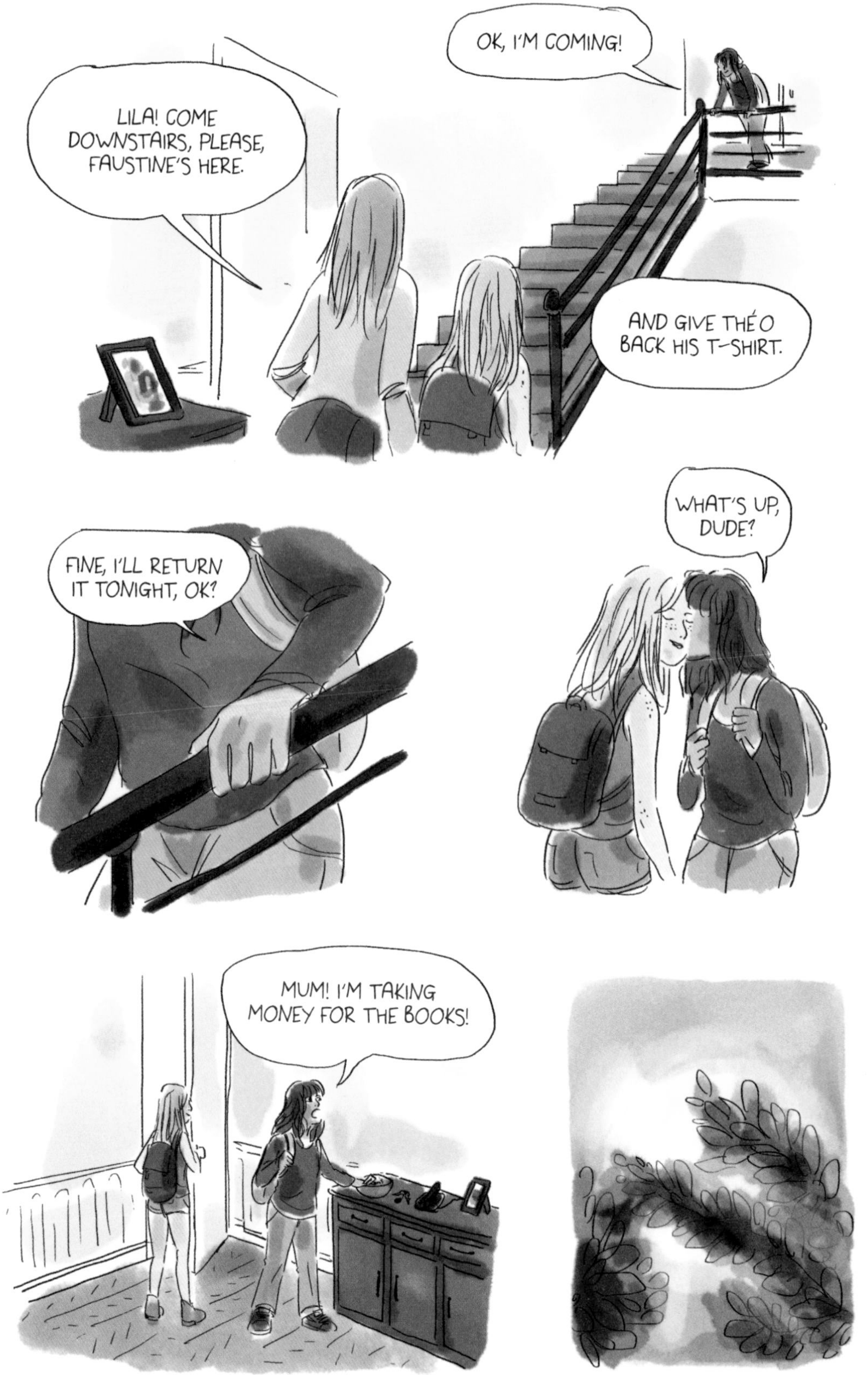

LILA! COME DOWNSTAIRS, PLEASE, FAUSTINE'S HERE.
OK, I'M COMING!
AND GIVE THÉO BACK HIS T-SHIRT.
FINE, I'LL RETURN IT TONIGHT, OK?
WHAT'S UP, DUDE?
MUM! I'M TAKING MONEY FOR THE BOOKS!

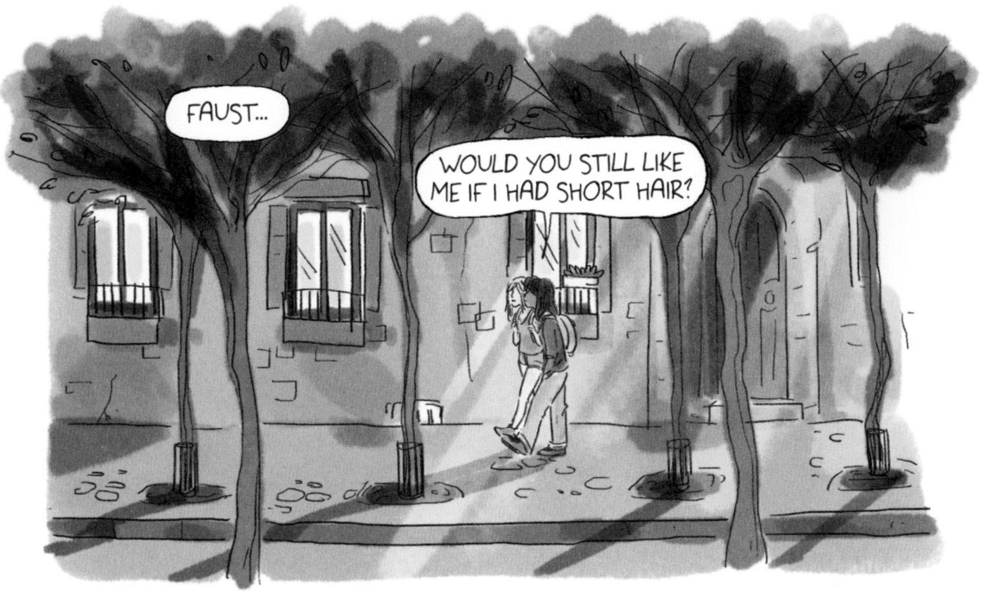
FAUST...
WOULD YOU STILL LIKE ME IF I HAD SHORT HAIR?

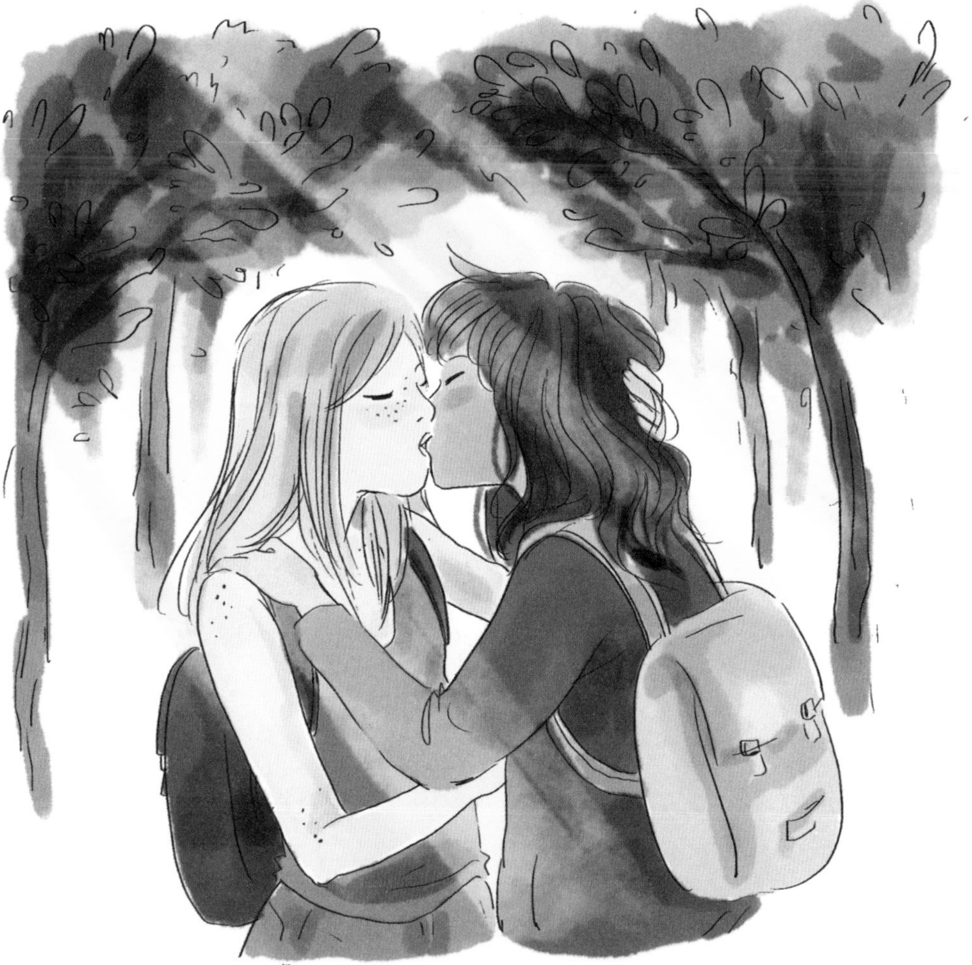

As a kid, I never cried, except when I wanted a toy at a store.

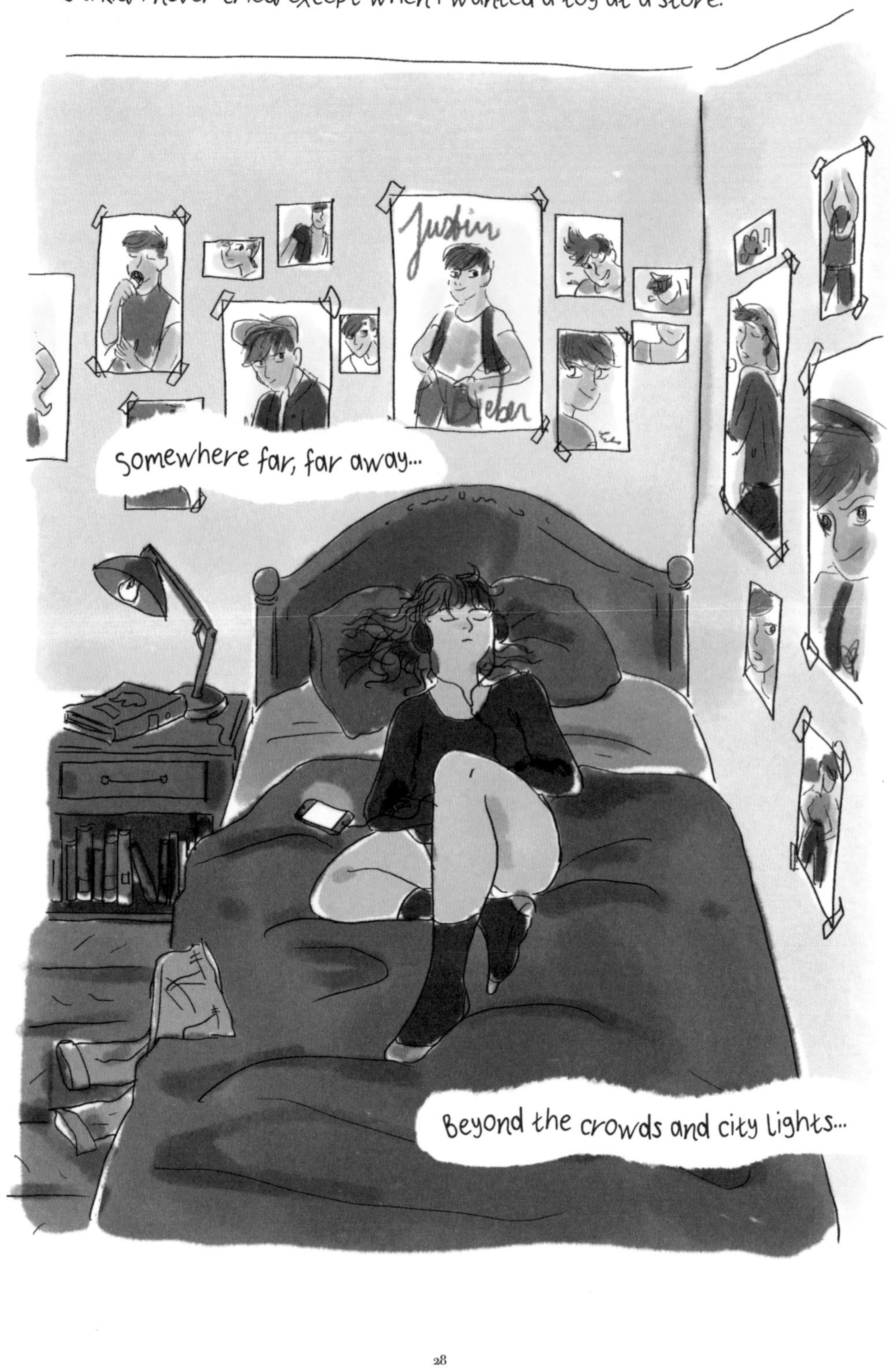
Justin
Somewhere far, far away...
Beyond the crowds and city lights...

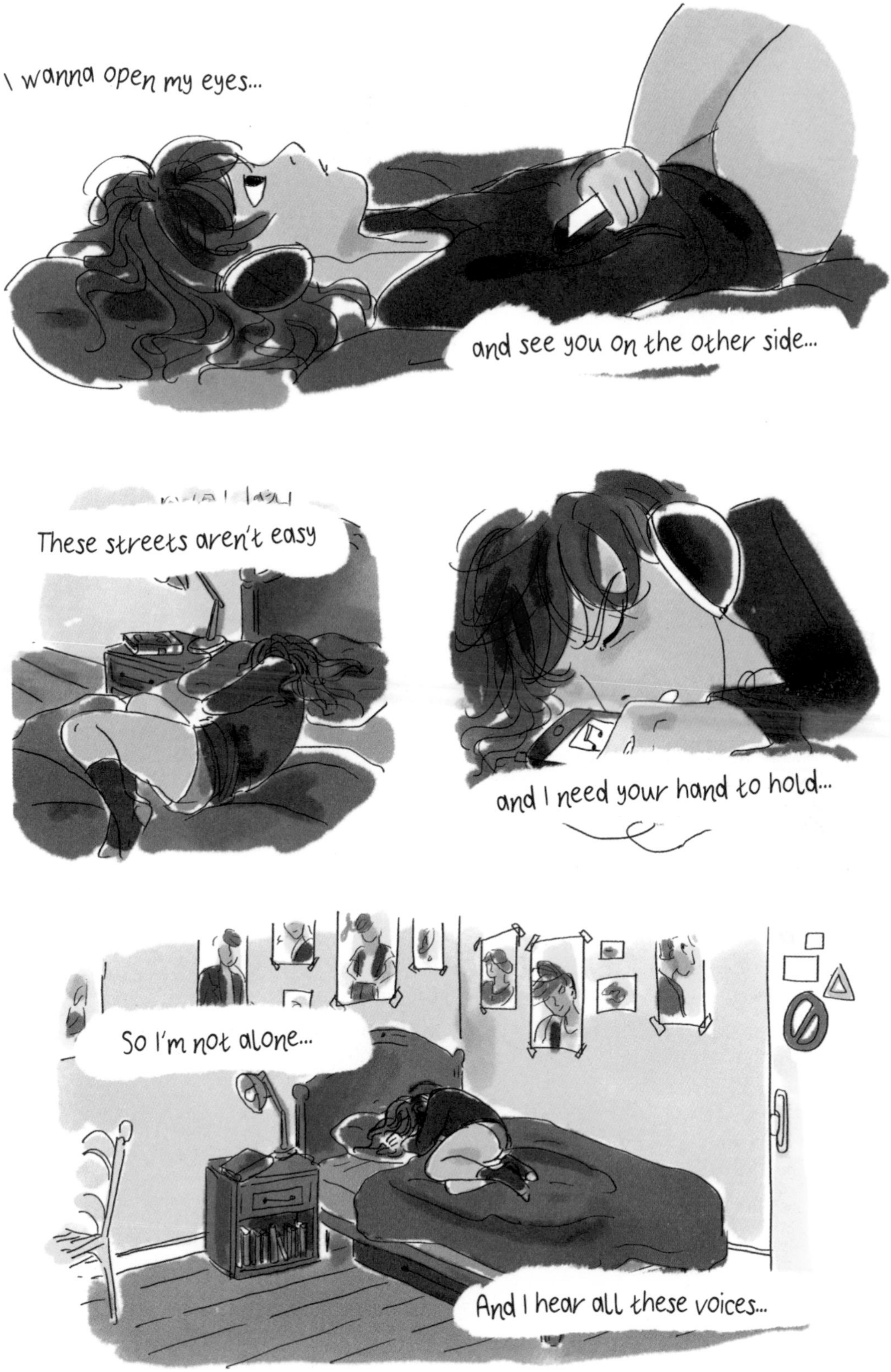

I wanna open my eyes...
and see you on the other side...
These streets aren't easy
and I need your hand to hold...
So I'm not alone...
And I hear all these voices...

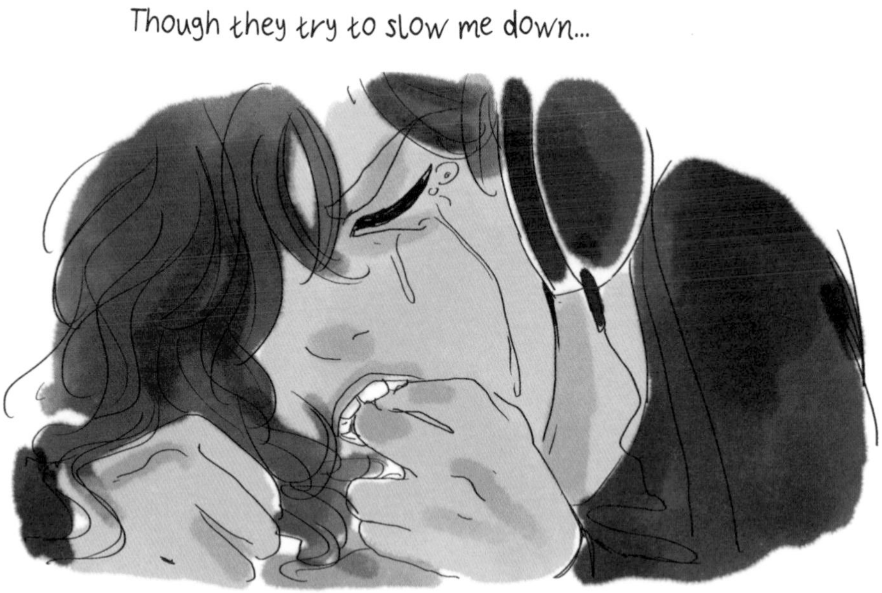
Though they try to slow me down...

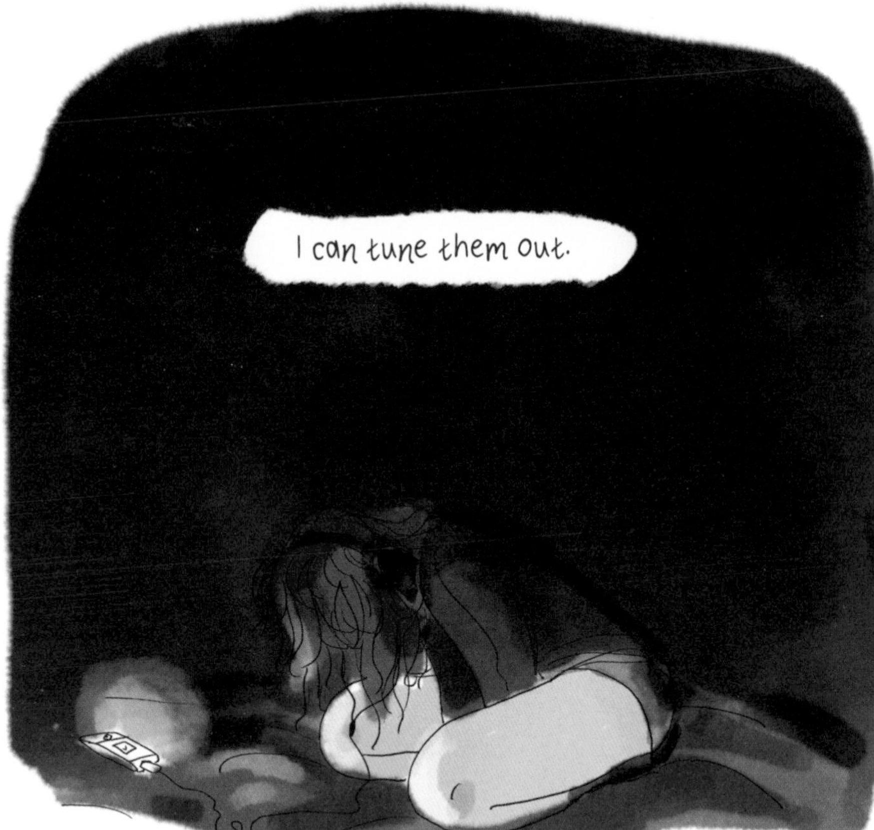
I can tune them out.

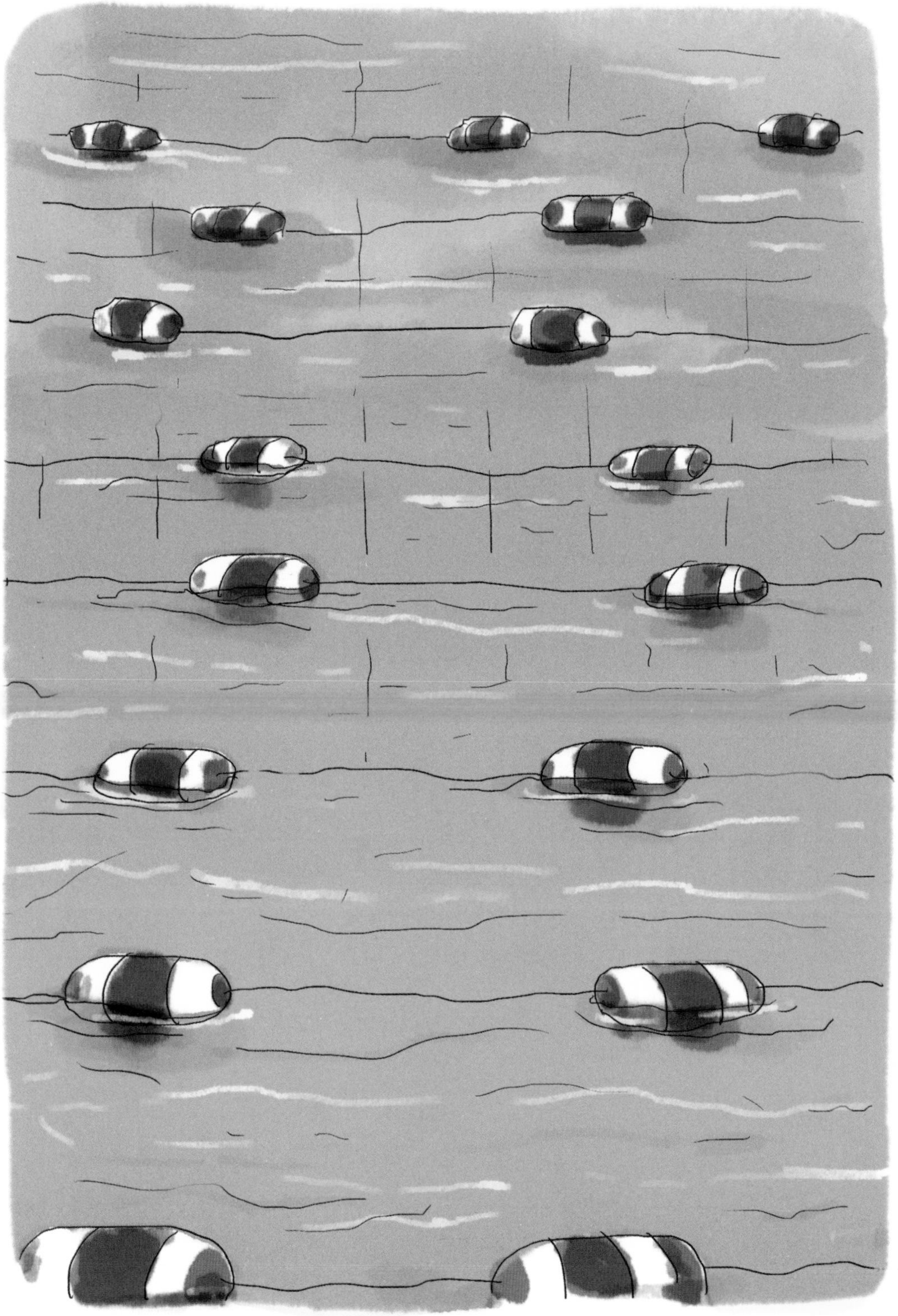

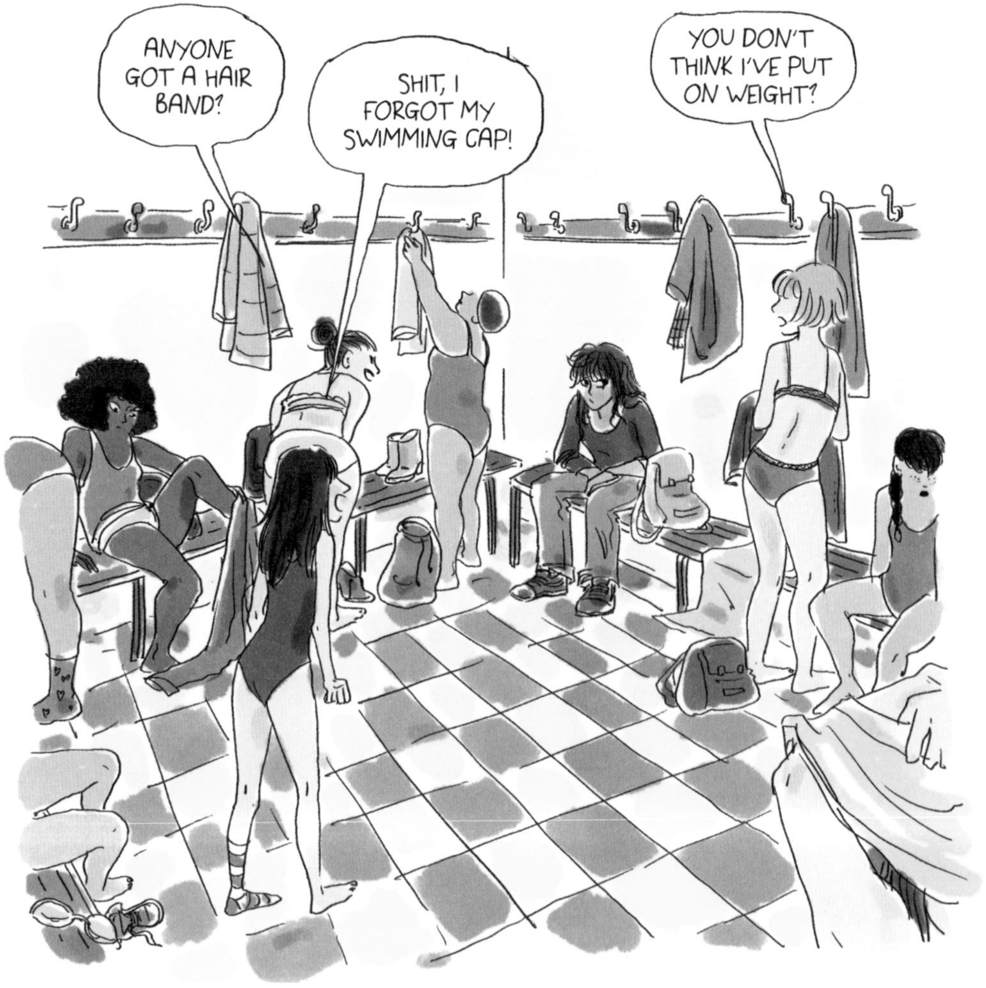
ANYONE GOT A HAIR BAND?
SHIT, I FORGOT MY SWIMMING CAP!
YOU DON'T THINK I'VE PUT ON WEIGHT?

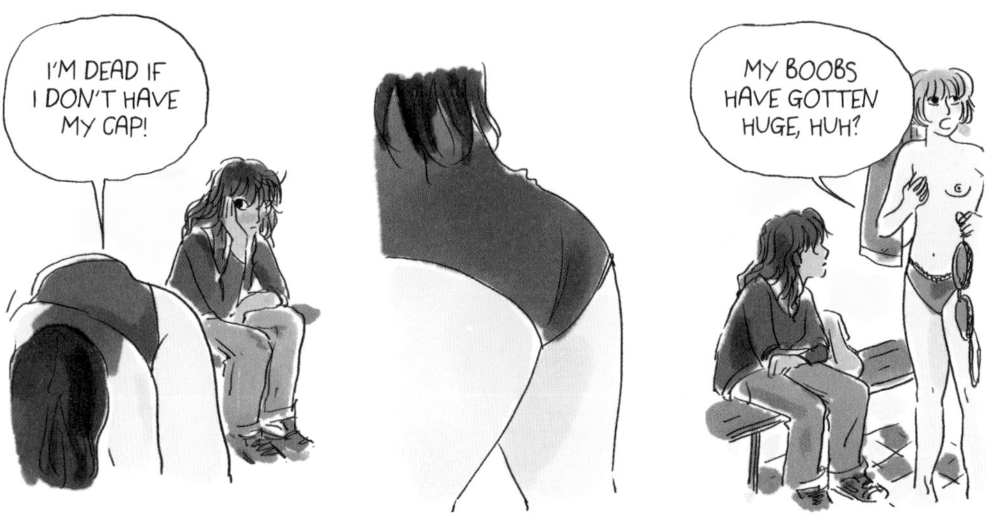
I'M DEAD IF I DON'T HAVE MY CAP!
MY BOOBS HAVE GOTTEN HUGE, HUH?

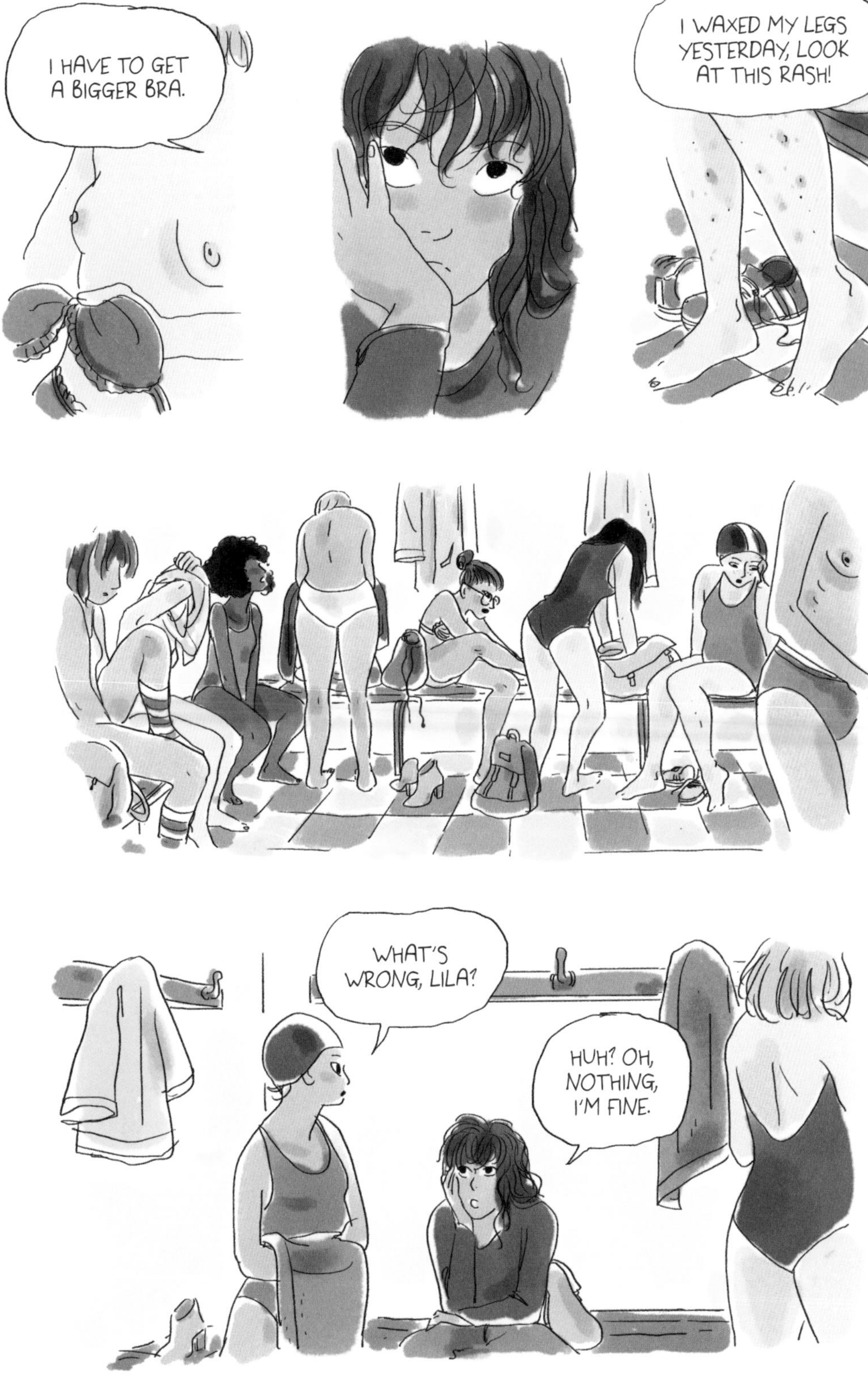
I HAVE TO GET A BIGGER BRA.
I WAXED MY LEGS YESTERDAY, LOOK AT THIS RASH!
WHAT'S WRONG, LILA?
HUH? OH, NOTHING, I'M FINE.

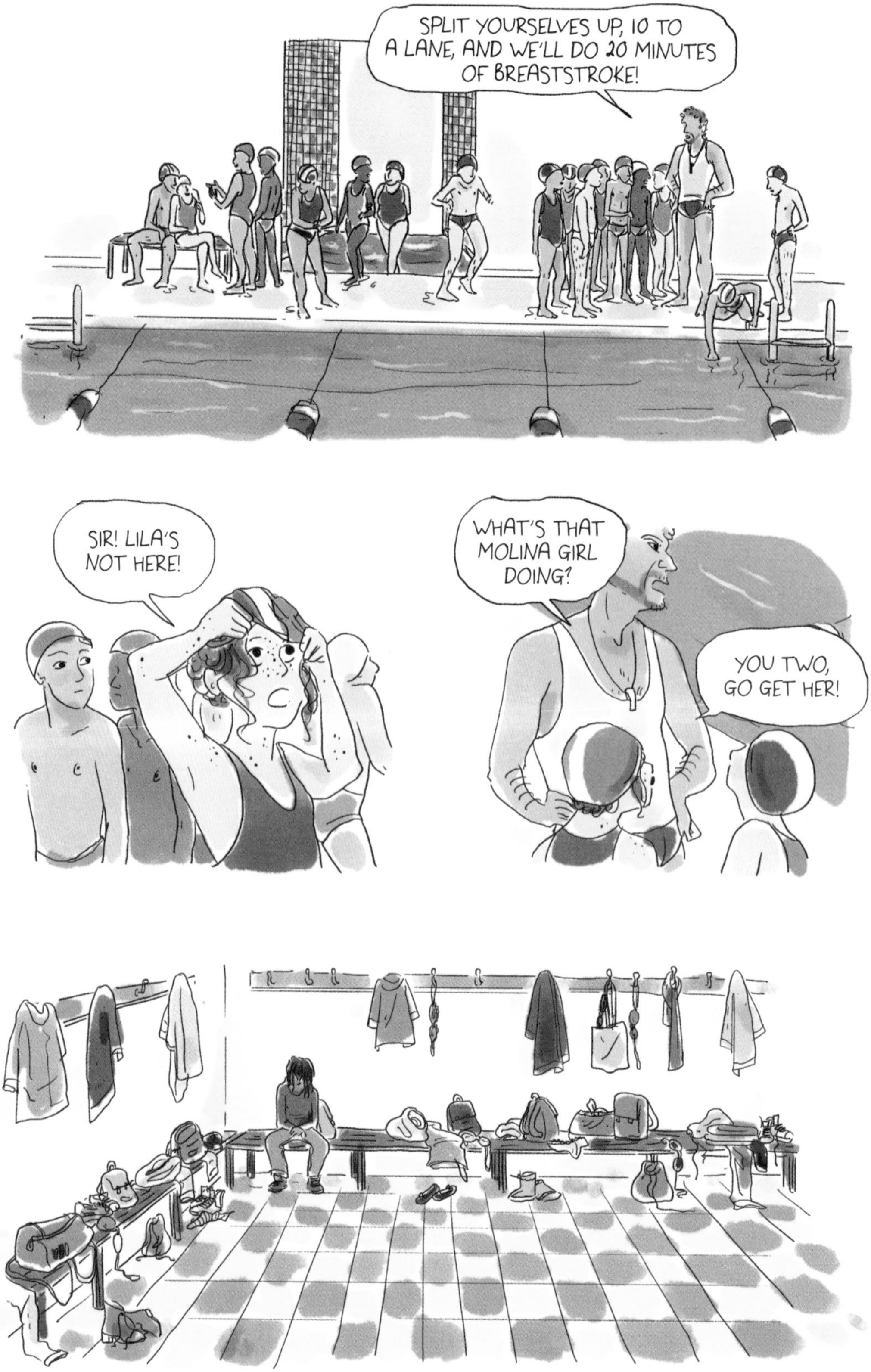
SPLIT YOURSELVES UP, 10 TO A LANE, AND WE'LL DO 20 MINUTES OF BREASTSTROKE!
SIR! LILA'S NOT HERE!
WHAT'S THAT MOLINA GIRL DOING?
YOU TWO, GO GET HER!

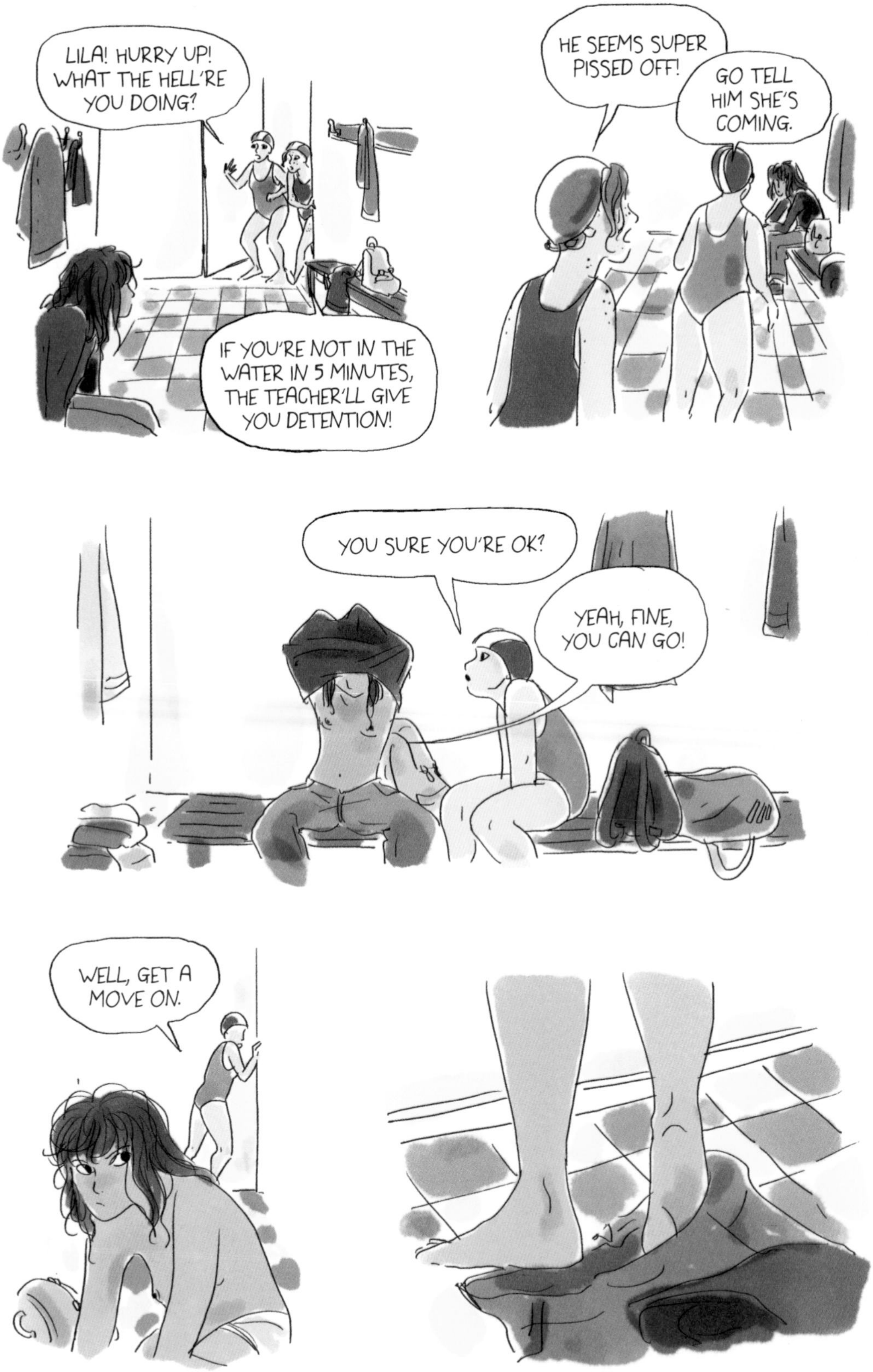
LILA! HURRY UP! WHAT THE HELL'RE YOU DOING?
IF YOU'RE NOT IN THE WATER IN 5 MINUTES, THE TEACHER'LL GIVE YOU DETENTION!
HE SEEMS SUPER PISSED OFF!
GO TELL HIM SHE'S COMING.
YOU SURE YOU'RE OK?
YEAH, FINE, YOU CAN GO!
WELL, GET A MOVE ON.

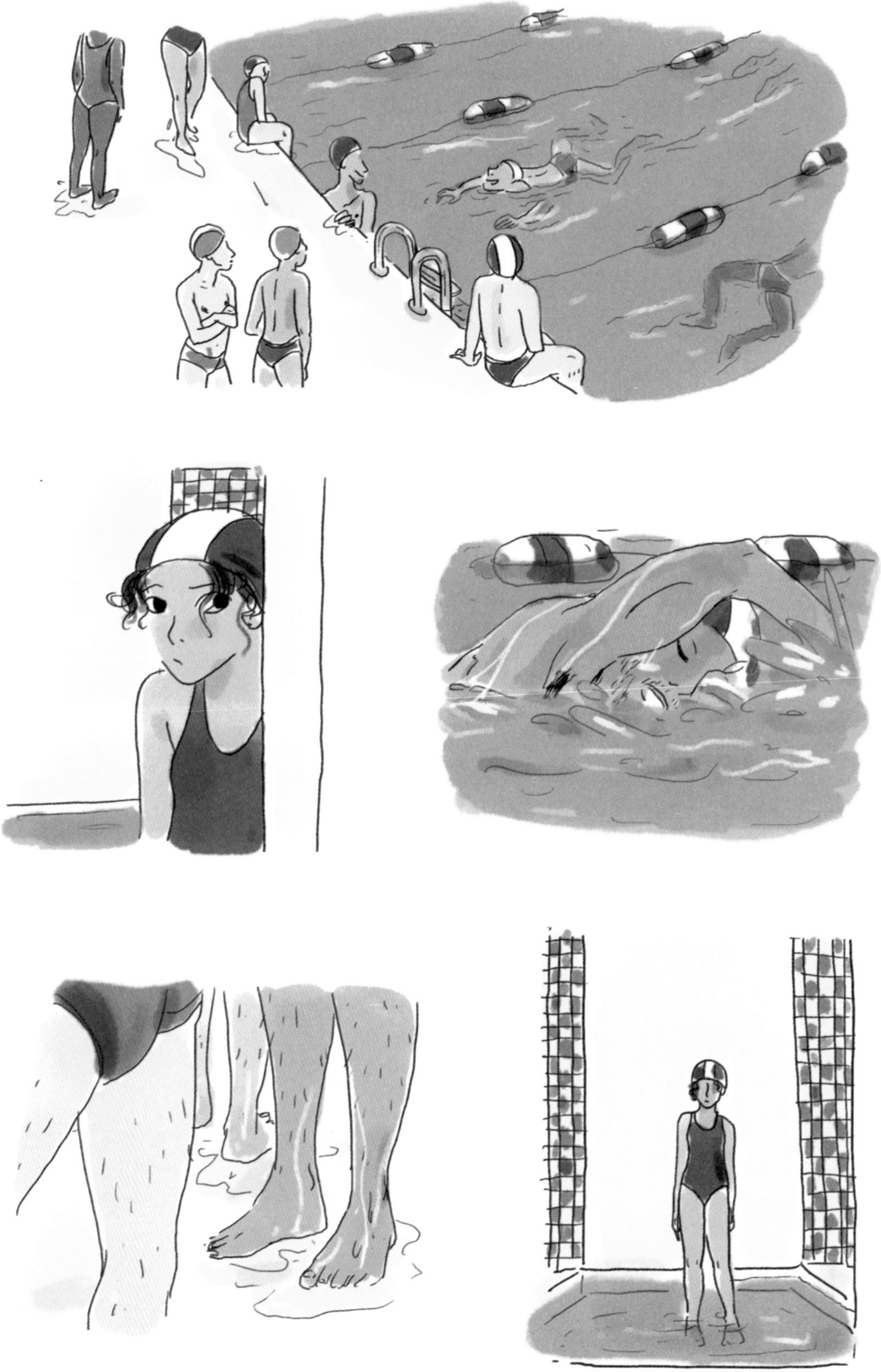

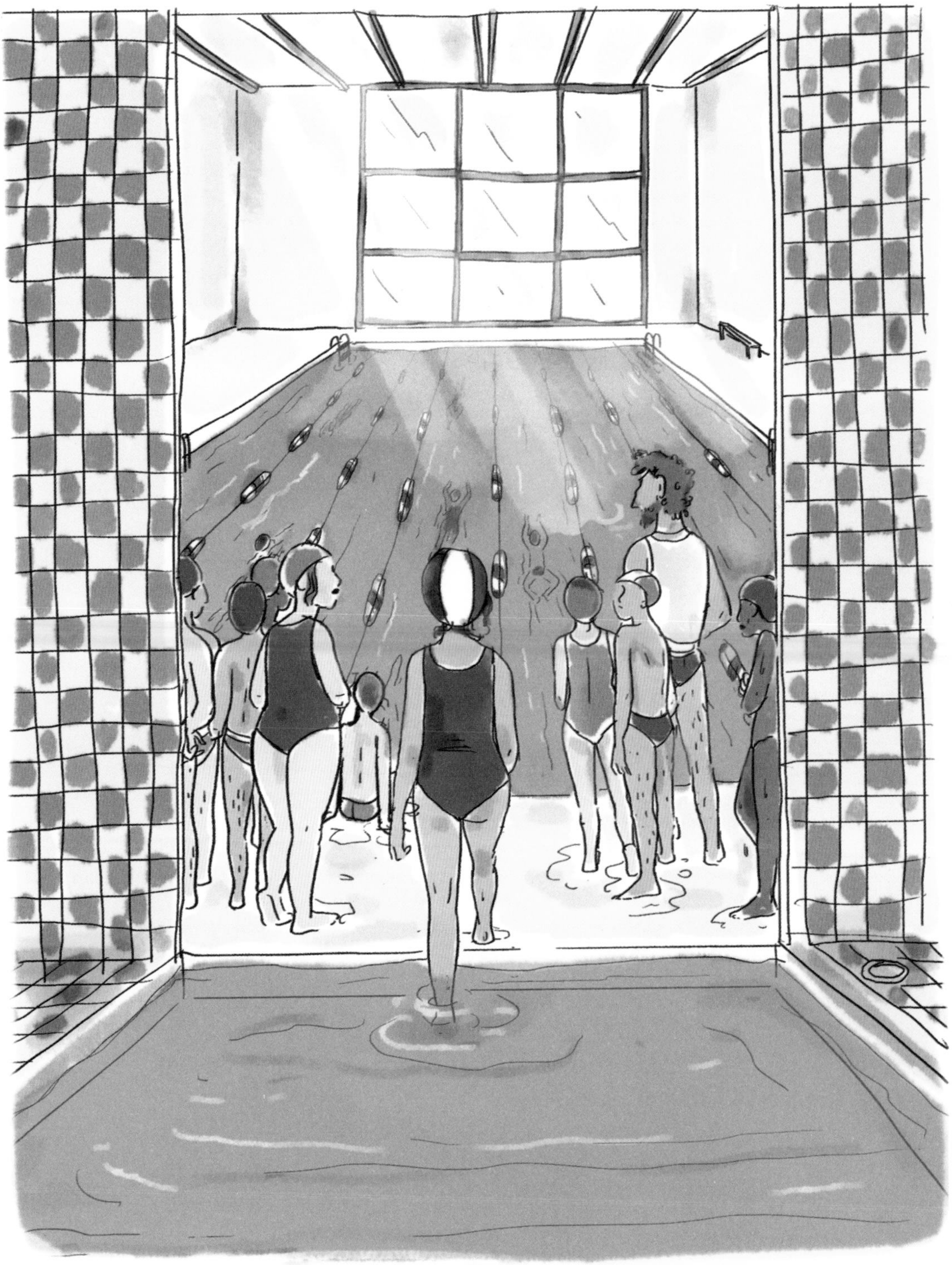

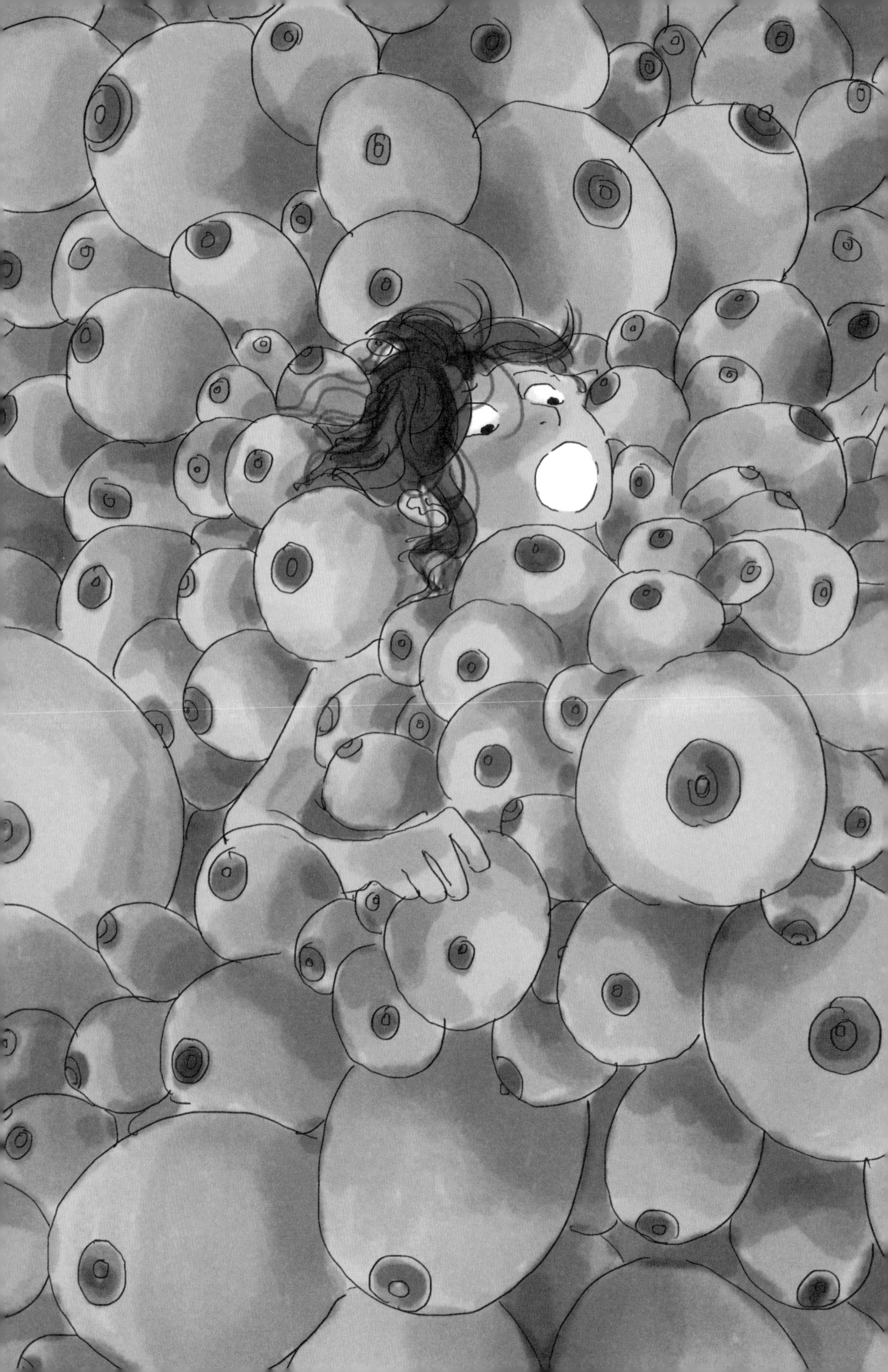

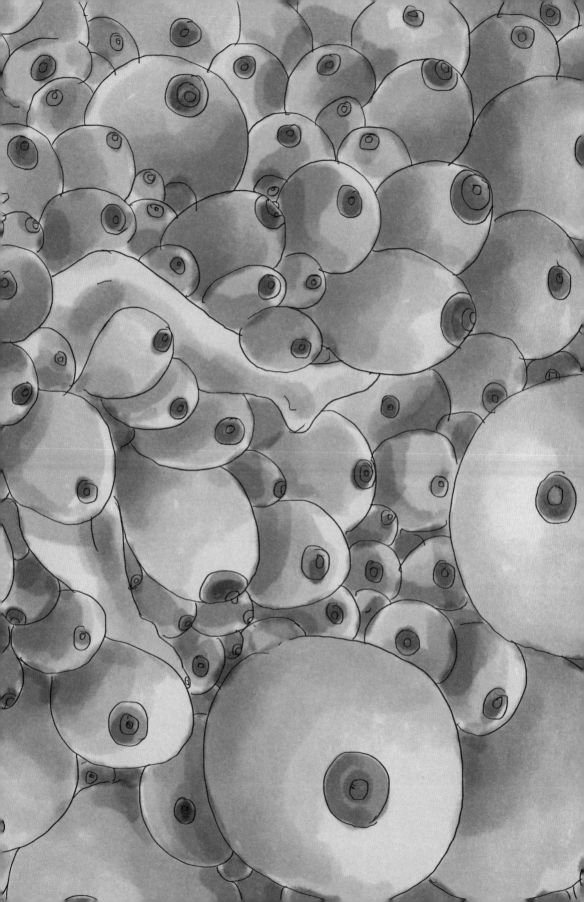

I get my period. It sickens me.

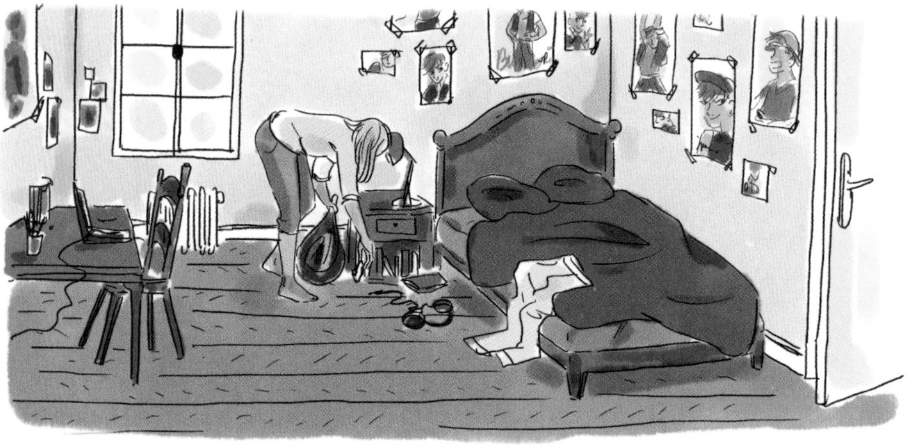

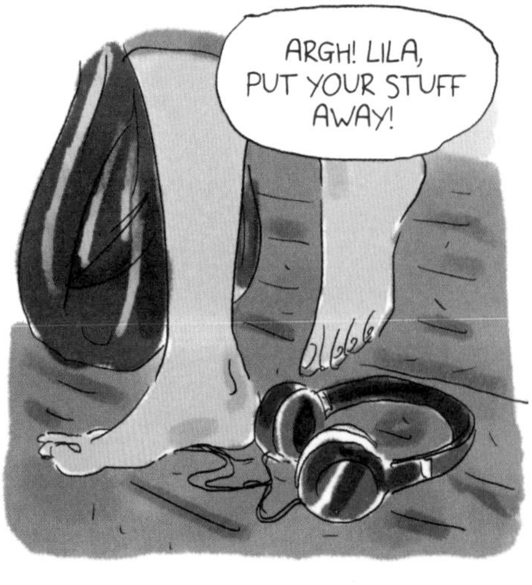
ARGH! LILA, PUT YOUR STUFF AWAY!

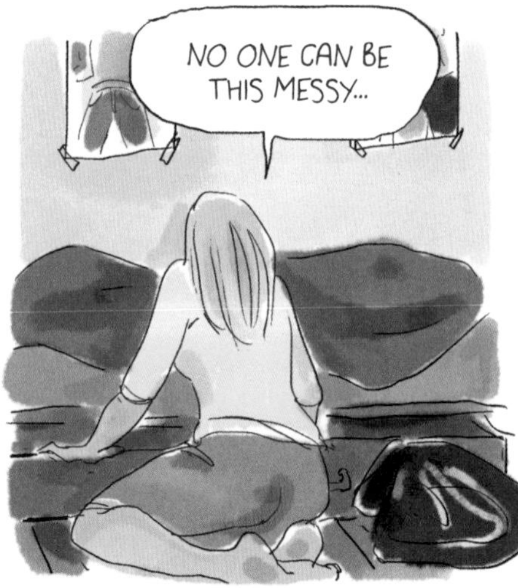
NO ONE CAN BE THIS MESSY...

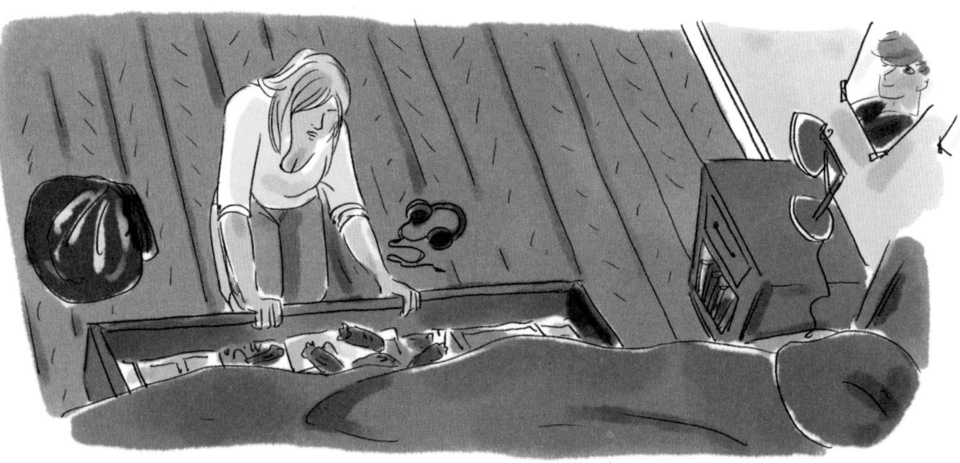

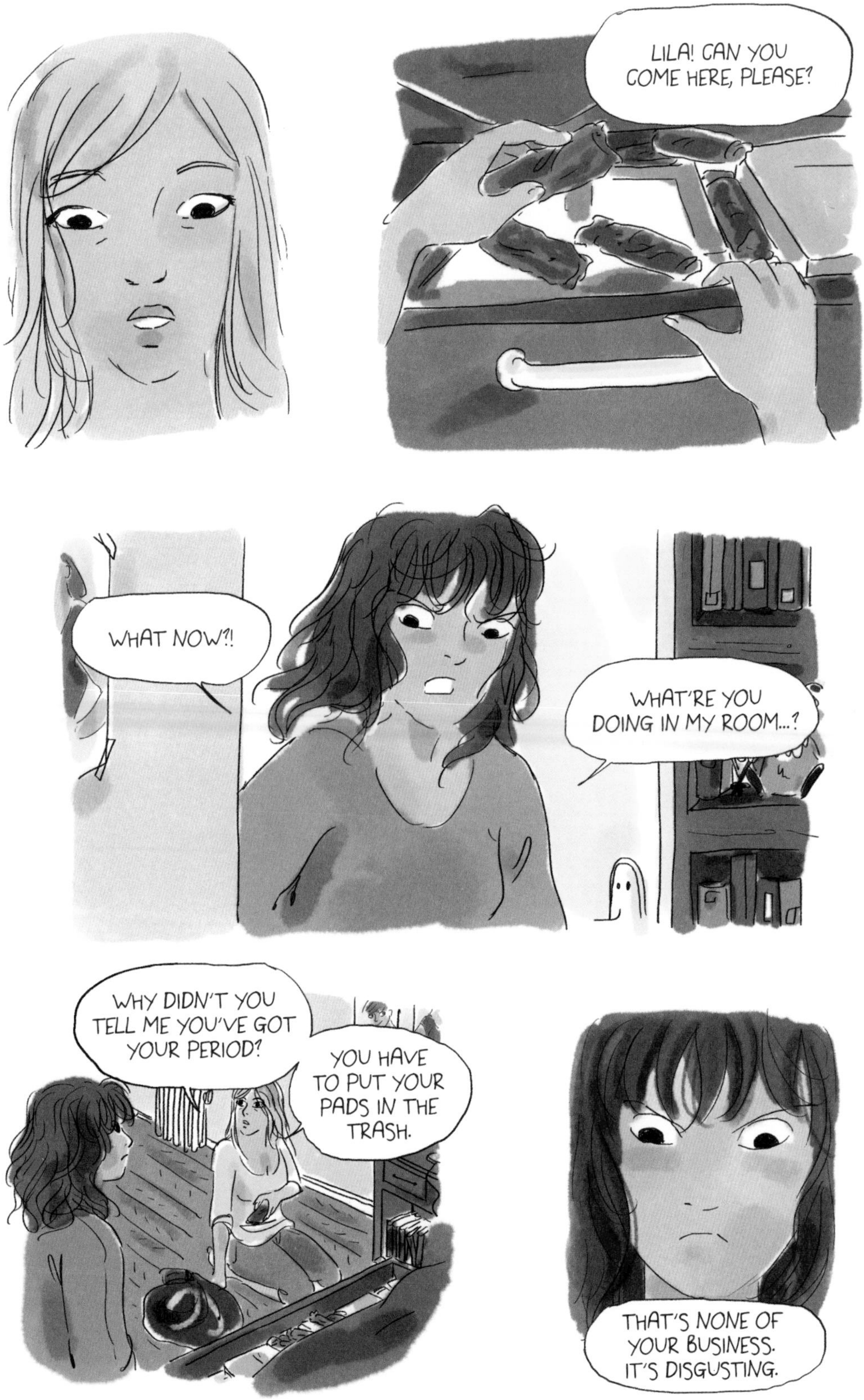
LILA! CAN YOU COME HERE, PLEASE?
WHAT NOW?!
WHAT'RE YOU DOING IN MY ROOM...?
WHY DIDN'T YOU TELL ME YOU'VE GOT YOUR PERIOD?
YOU HAVE TO PUT YOUR PADS IN THE TRASH.
THAT'S NONE OF YOUR BUSINESS. IT'S DISGUSTING.

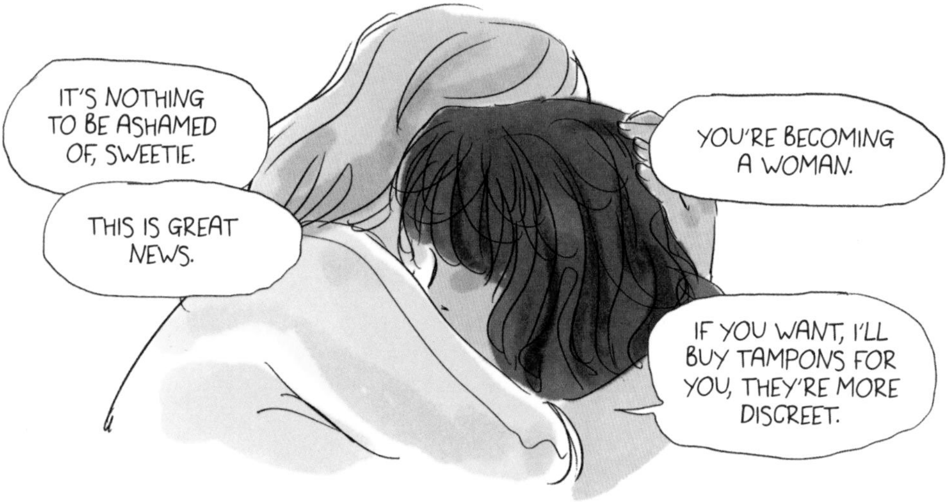
IT'S NOTHING TO BE ASHAMED OF, SWEETIE.
THIS IS GREAT NEWS.
YOU'RE BECOMING A WOMAN.
IF YOU WANT, I'LL BUY TAMPONS FOR YOU, THEY'RE MORE DISCREET.

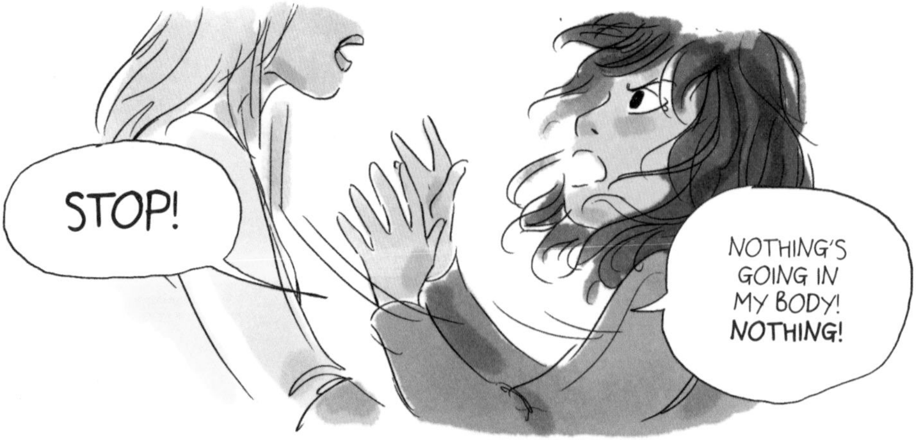
STOP!
NOTHING'S GOING IN MY BODY! **NOTHING!**

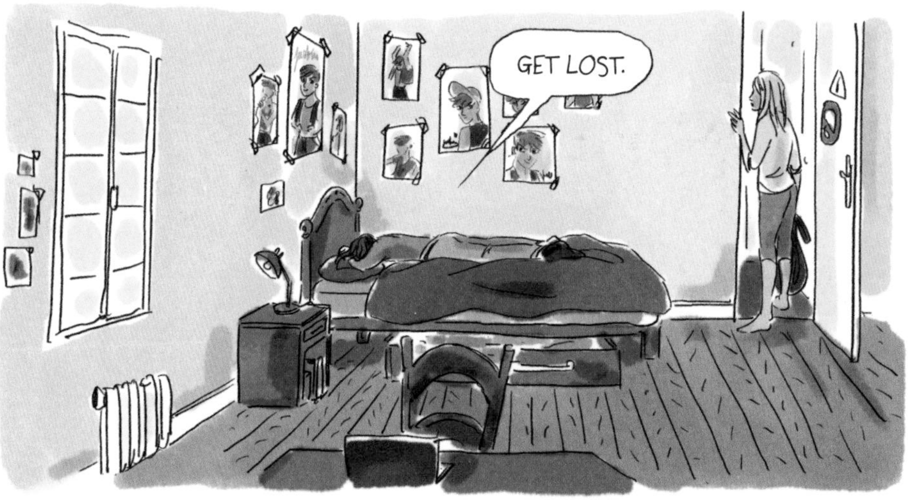
GET LOST.

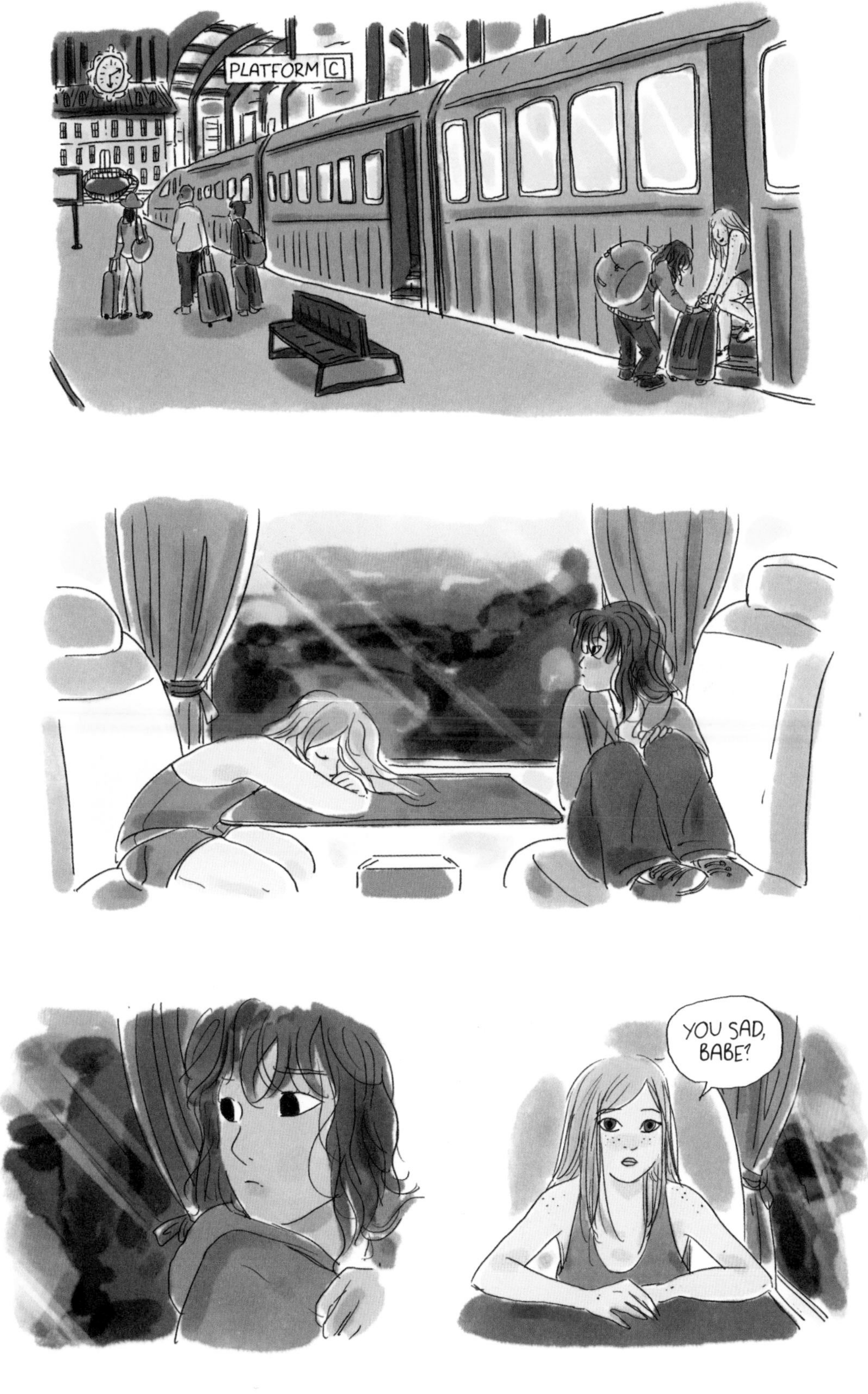
PLATFORM C
YOU SAD, BABE?

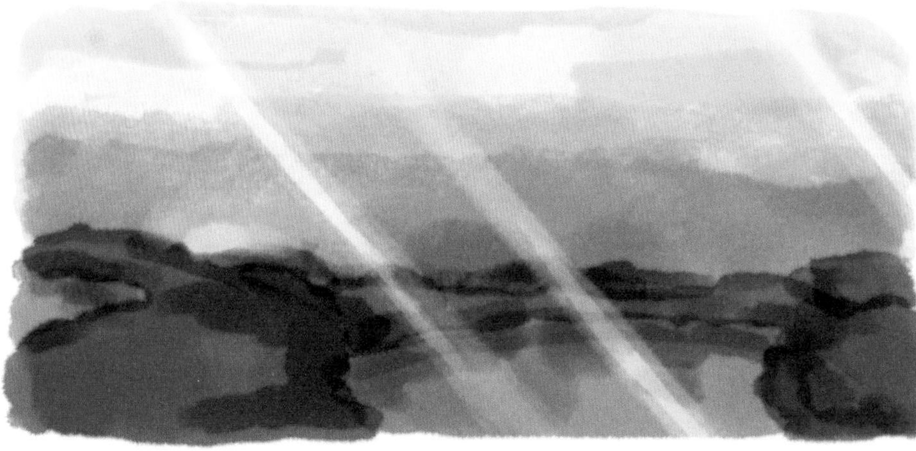

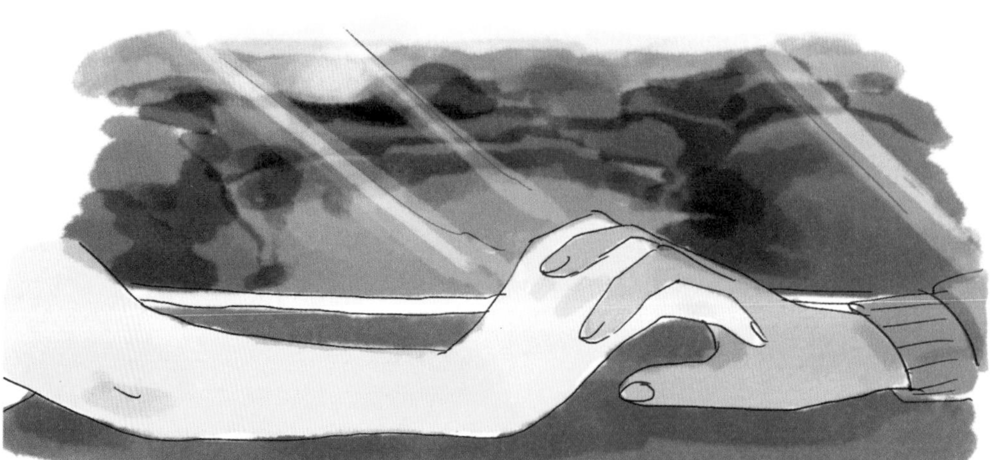

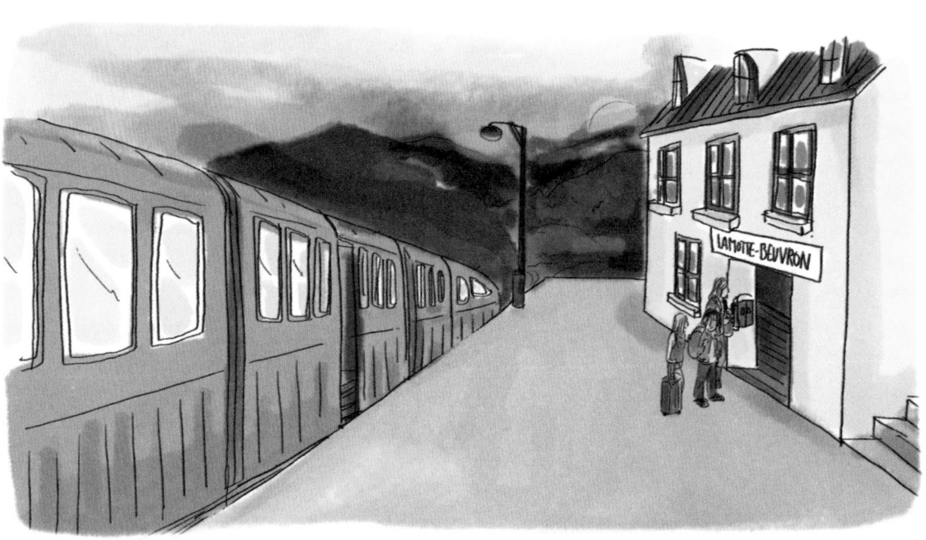
LAMOTTE-BEUVRON

I'm attracted to girls. I like their butts, their boobs, their hair. Girls are beautiful, especially Faustine.

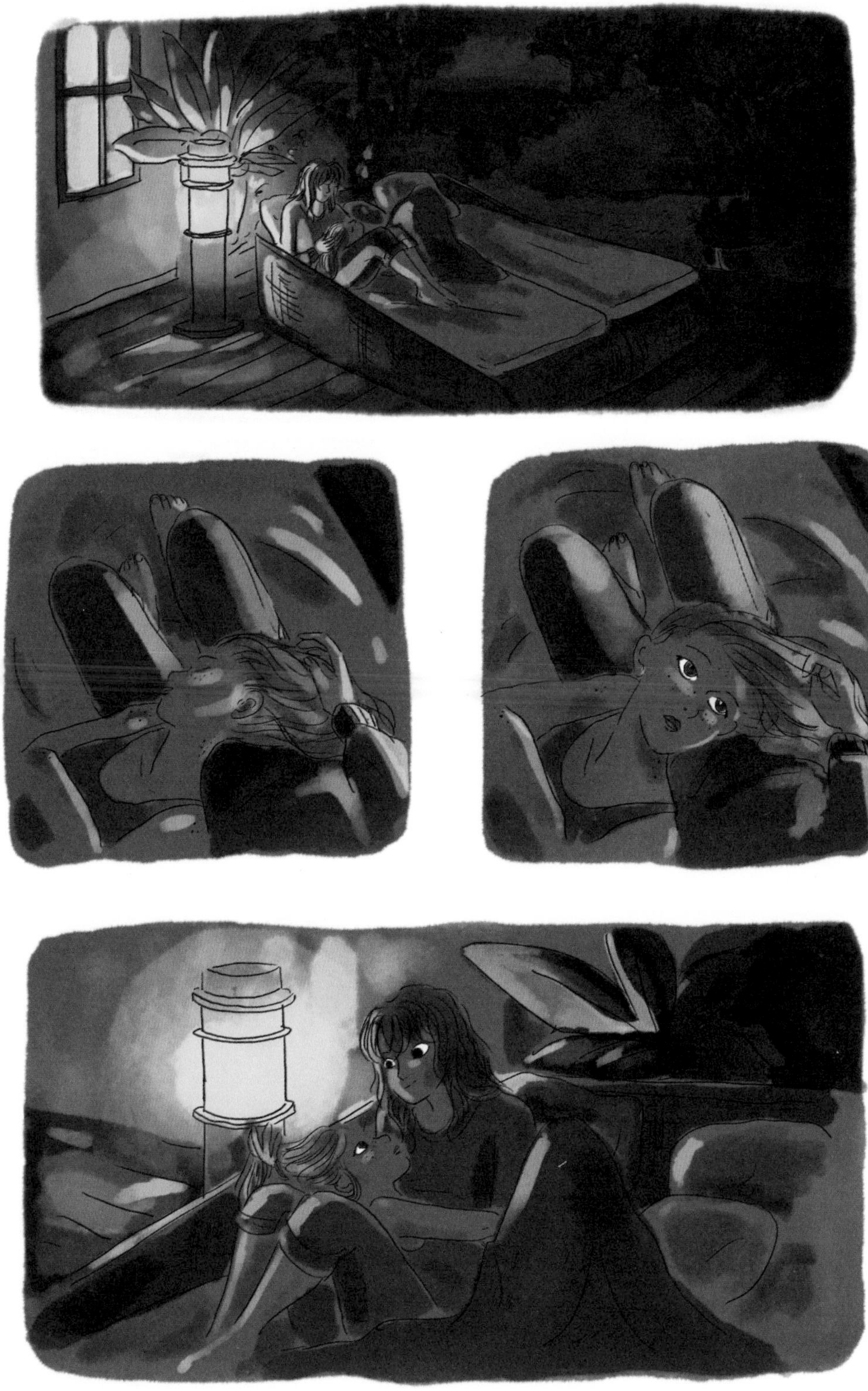

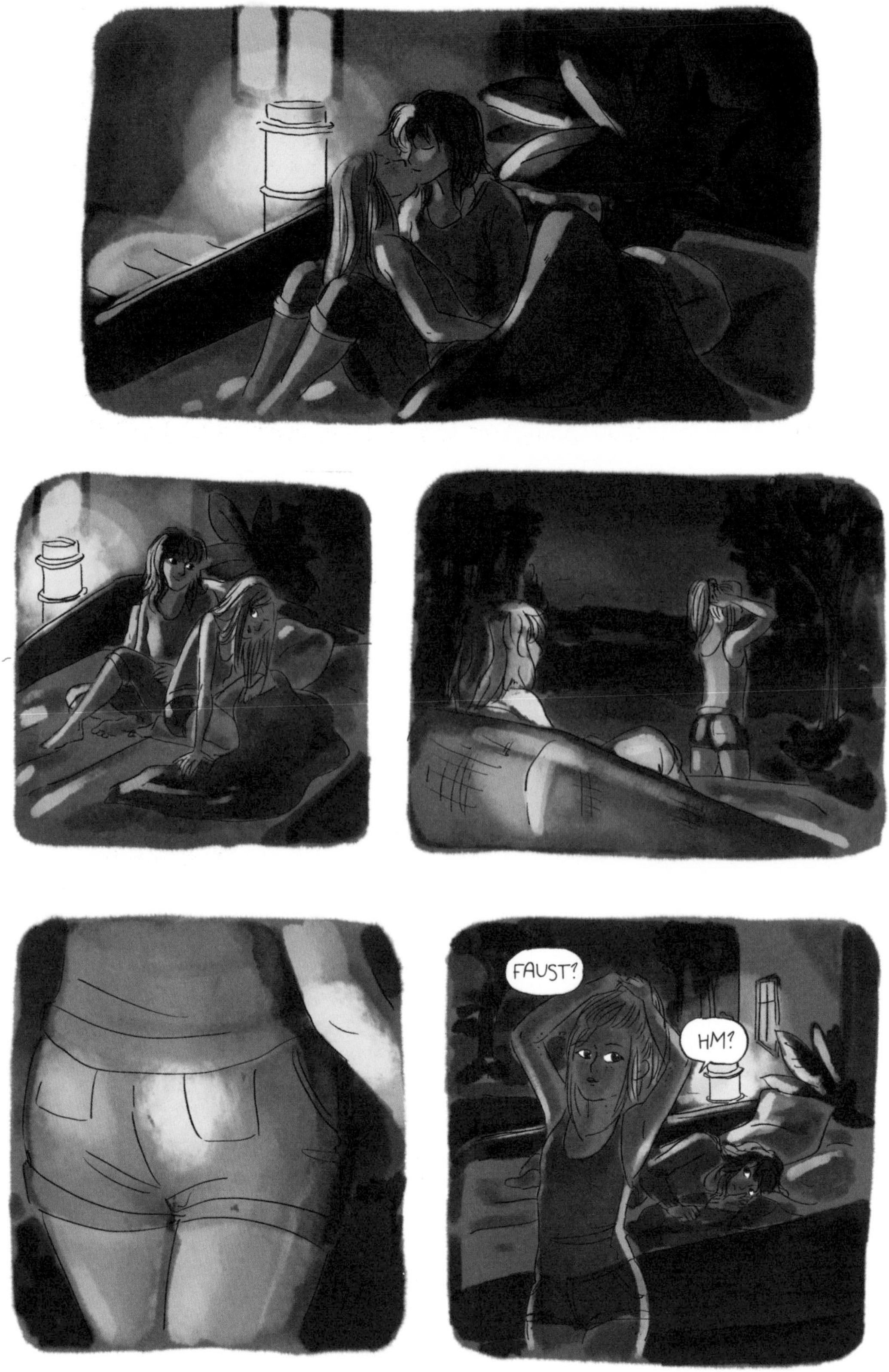
FAUST?
HM?

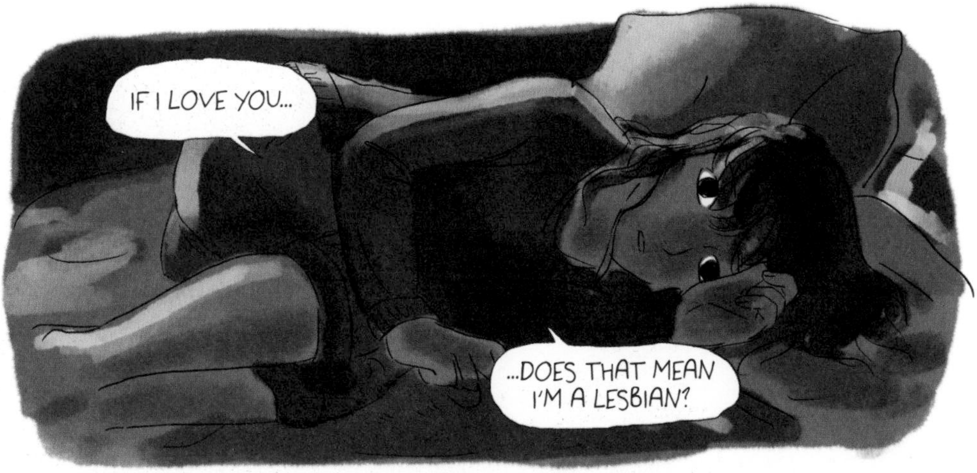
IF I LOVE YOU...
...DOES THAT MEAN I'M A LESBIAN?

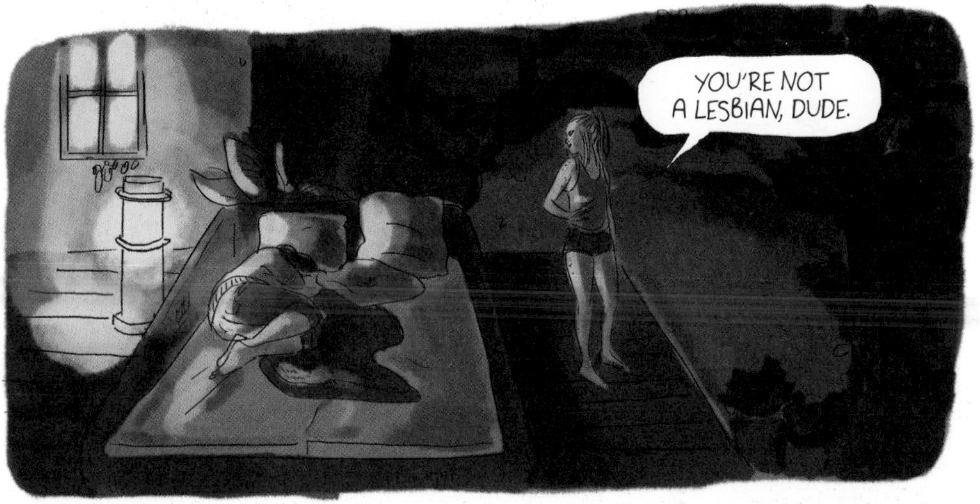
YOU'RE NOT A LESBIAN, DUDE.

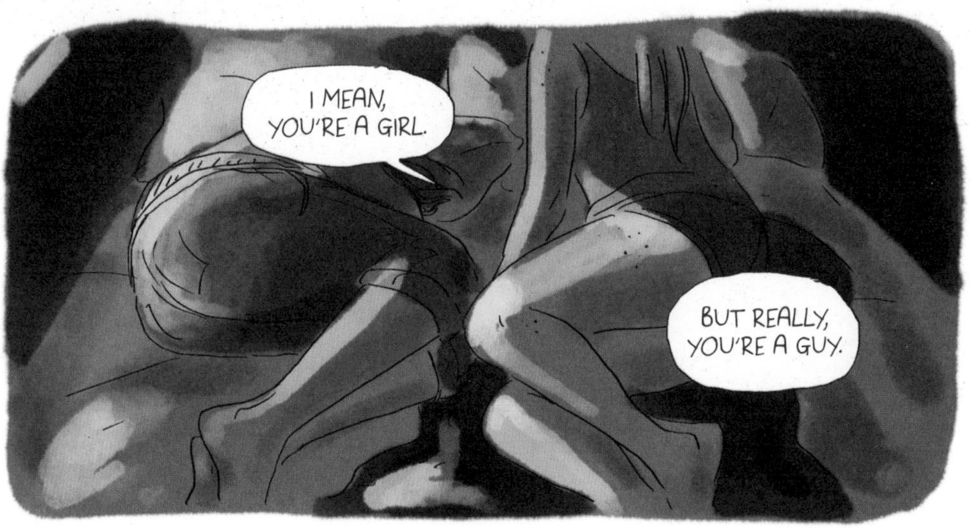
I MEAN, YOU'RE A GIRL.
BUT REALLY, YOU'RE A GUY.

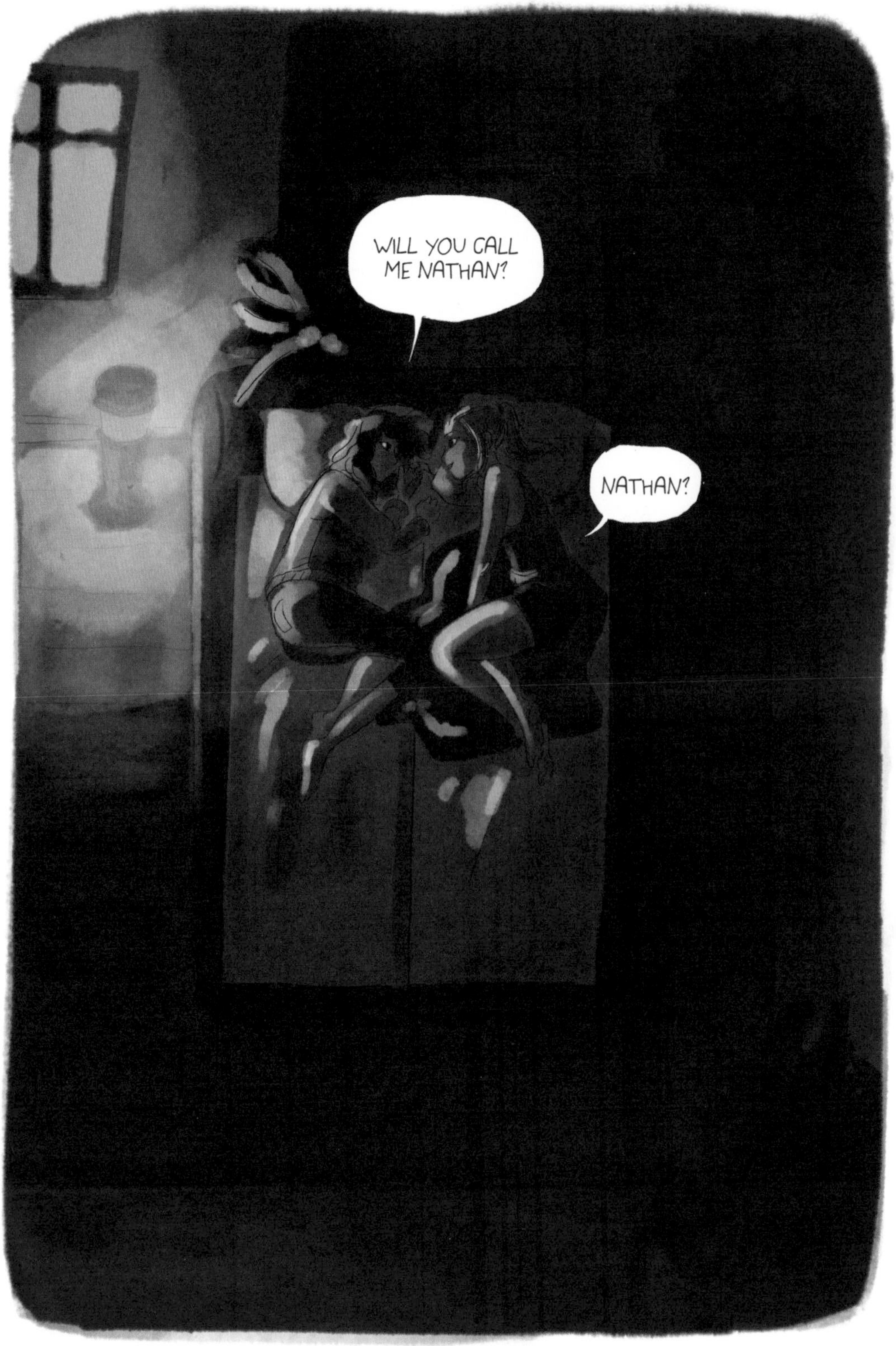
WILL YOU CALL ME NATHAN?
NATHAN?

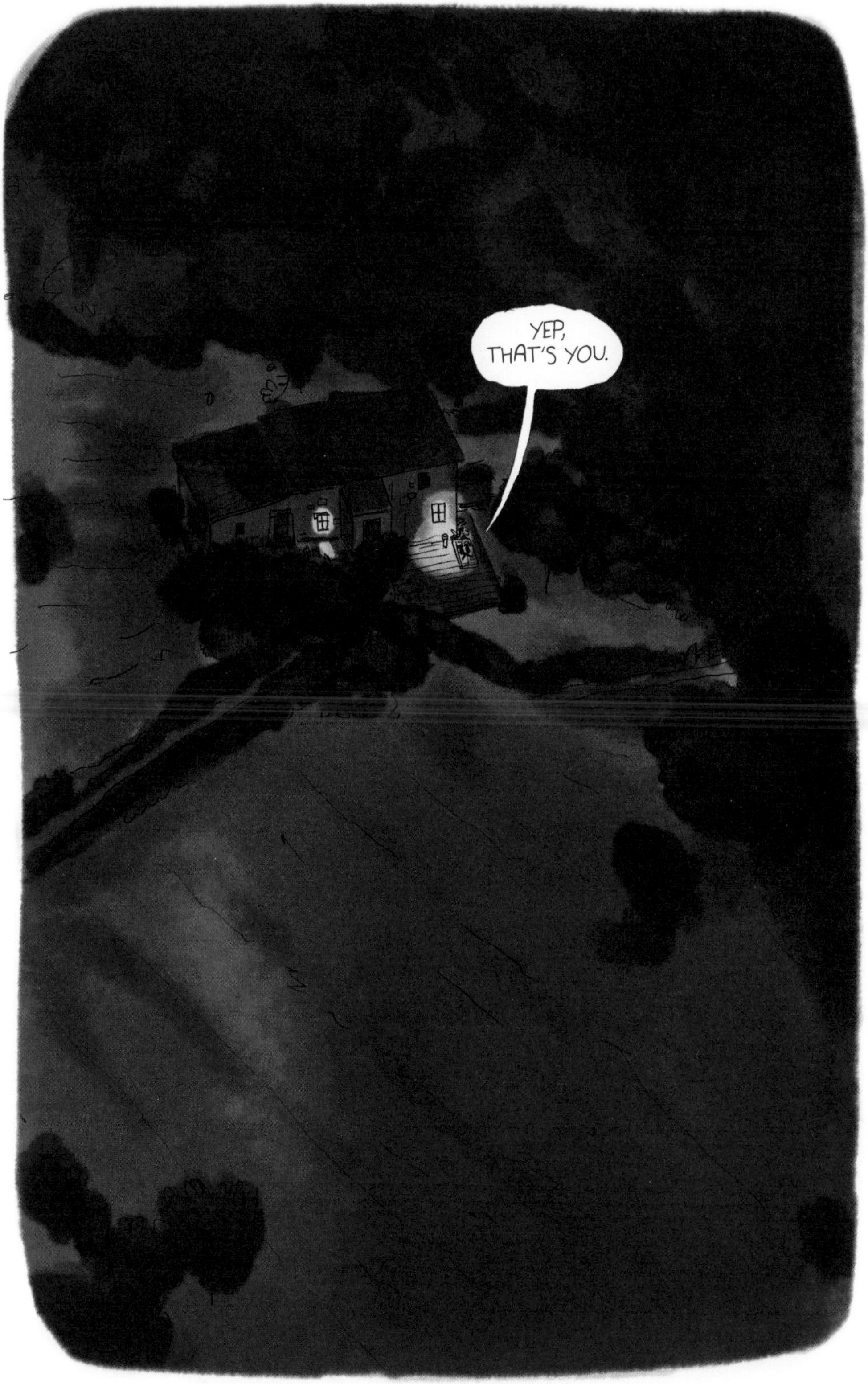
YEP, THAT'S YOU.

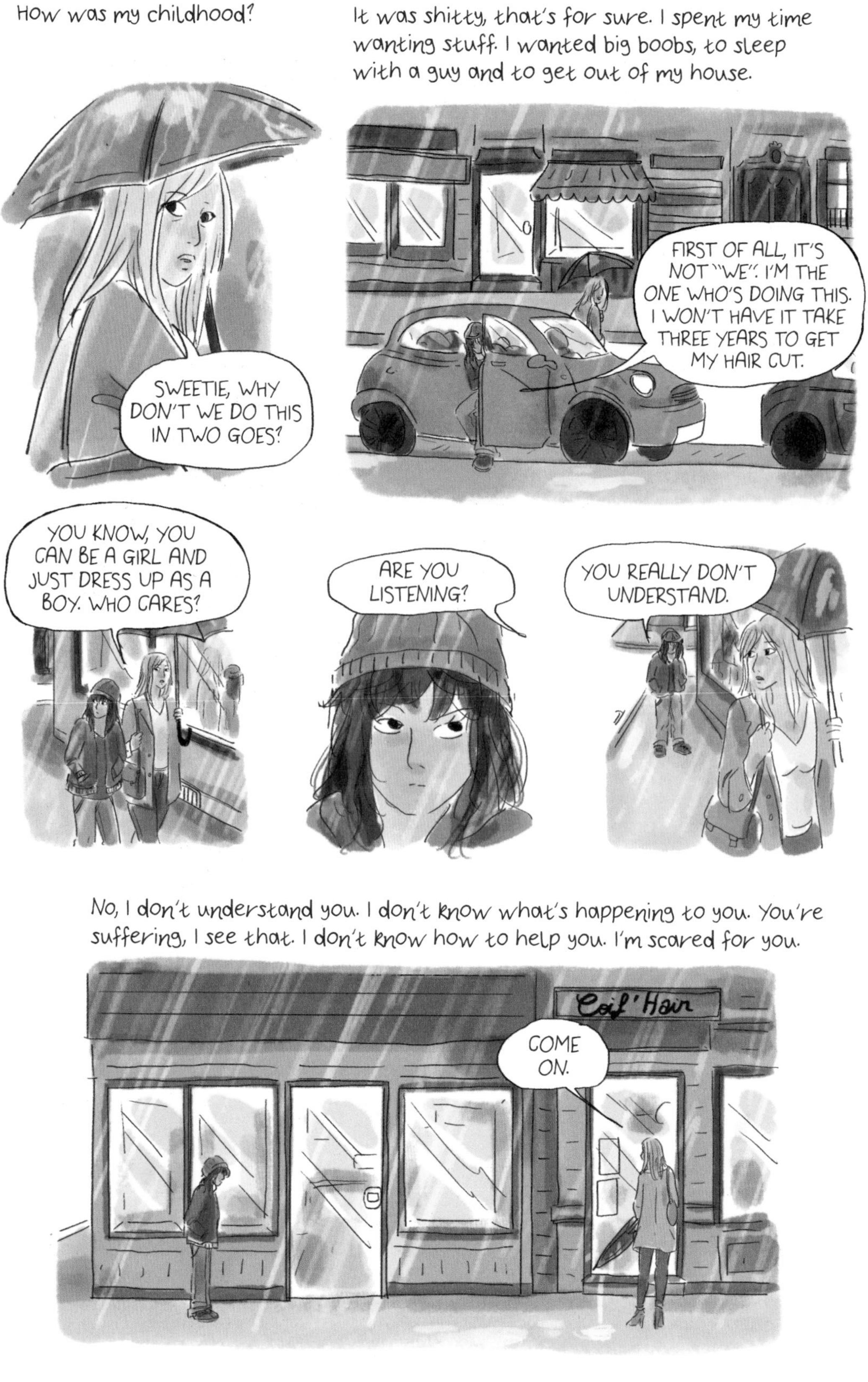
How was my childhood?
It was shitty, that's for sure. I spent my time wanting stuff. I wanted big boobs, to sleep with a guy and to get out of my house.
SWEETIE, WHY DON'T WE DO THIS IN TWO GOES?
FIRST OF ALL, IT'S NOT "WE". I'M THE ONE WHO'S DOING THIS. I WON'T HAVE IT TAKE THREE YEARS TO GET MY HAIR CUT.
YOU KNOW, YOU CAN BE A GIRL AND JUST DRESS UP AS A BOY. WHO CARES?
ARE YOU LISTENING?
YOU REALLY DON'T UNDERSTAND.
No, I don't understand you. I don't know what's happening to you. You're suffering, I see that. I don't know how to help you. I'm scared for you.
Coif'Hair
COME ON.

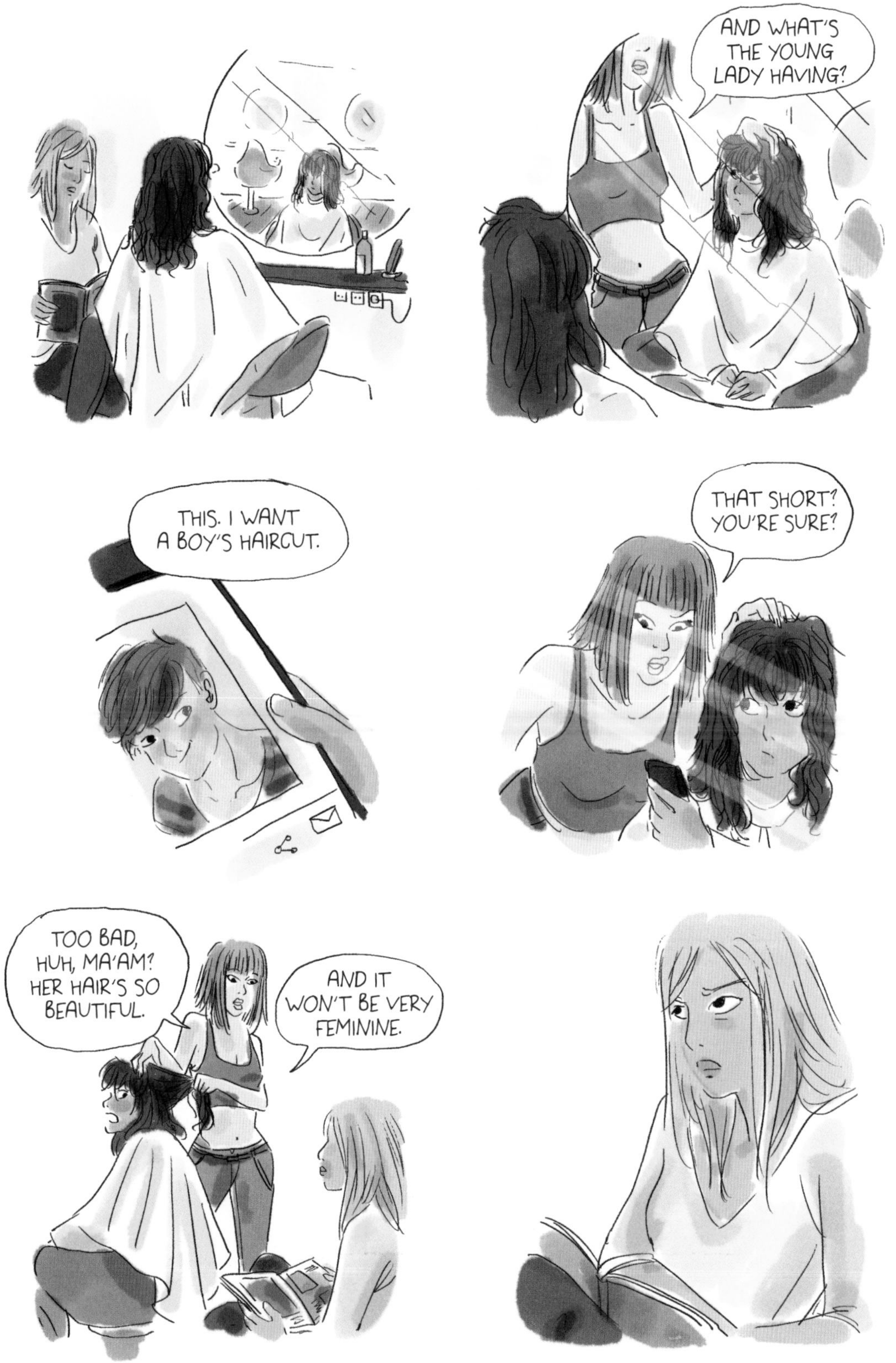
AND WHAT'S THE YOUNG LADY HAVING?
THIS. I WANT A BOY'S HAIRCUT.
THAT SHORT? YOU'RE SURE?
TOO BAD, HUH, MA'AM? HER HAIR'S SO BEAUTIFUL.
AND IT WON'T BE VERY FEMININE.

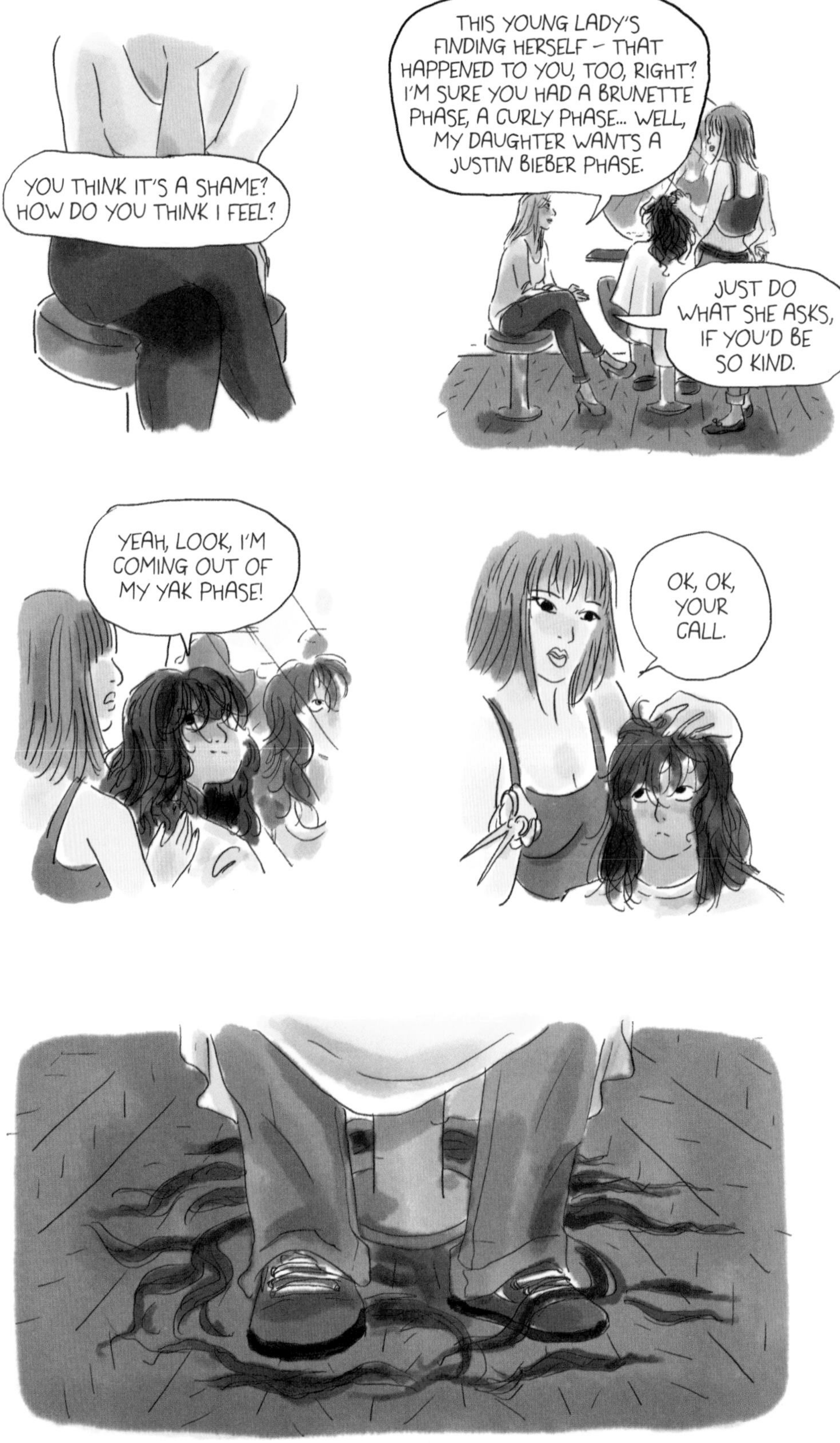
YOU THINK IT'S A SHAME? HOW DO YOU THINK I FEEL?
THIS YOUNG LADY'S FINDING HERSELF – THAT HAPPENED TO YOU, TOO, RIGHT? I'M SURE YOU HAD A BRUNETTE PHASE, A CURLY PHASE... WELL, MY DAUGHTER WANTS A JUSTIN BIEBER PHASE.
JUST DO WHAT SHE ASKS, IF YOU'D BE SO KIND.
YEAH, LOOK, I'M COMING OUT OF MY YAK PHASE!
OK, OK, YOUR CALL.

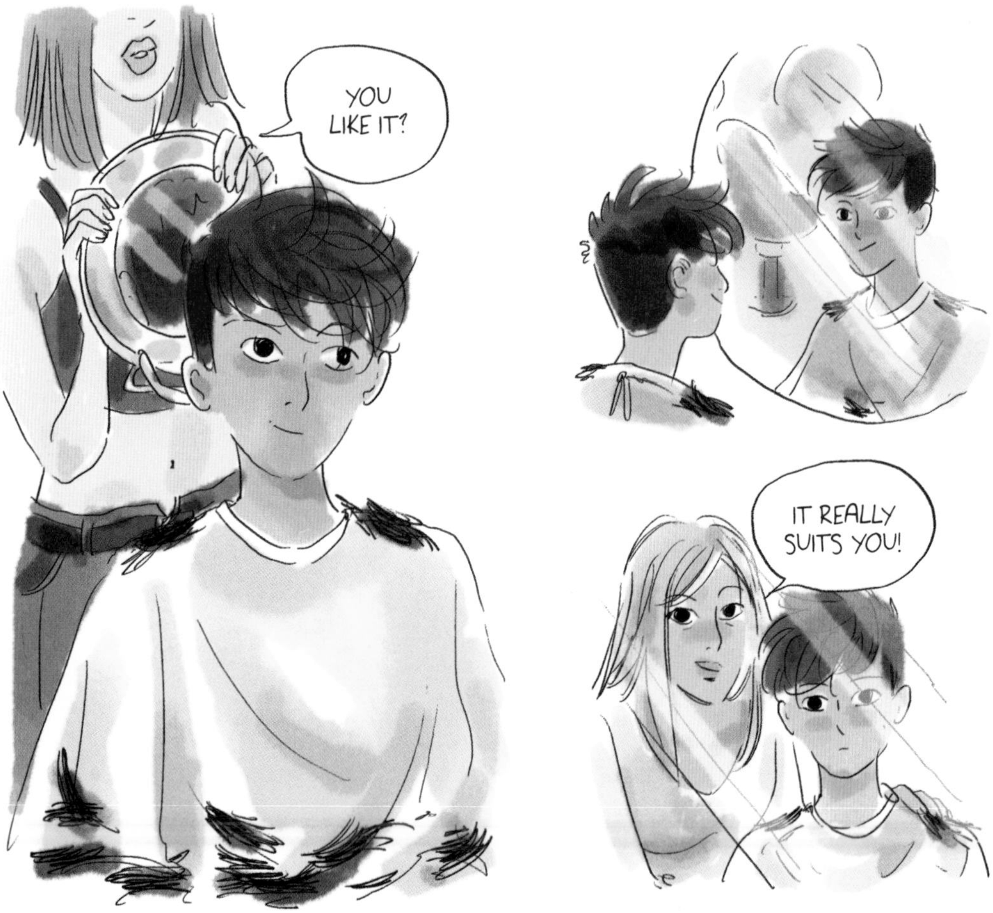
YOU LIKE IT?
IT REALLY SUITS YOU!

My sweet little girl. In six months, you're going to tell me that you're a lesbian. I never dreamed that would happen.

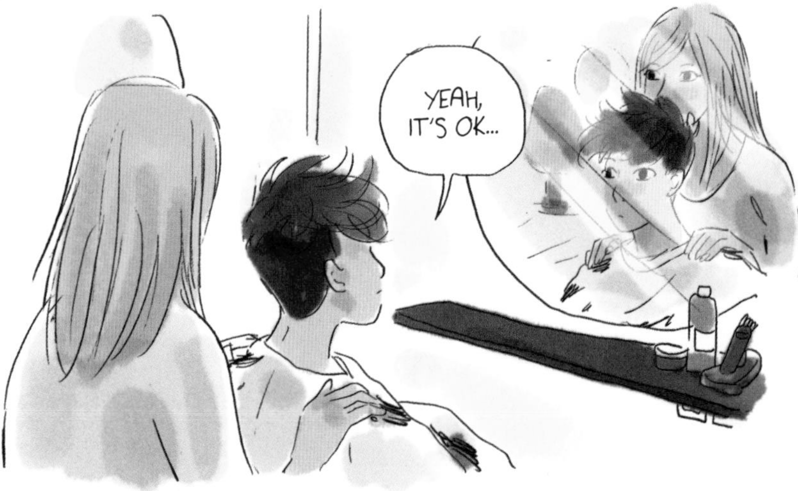
YEAH, IT'S OK...

Well... It's not that bad, you could have joined the jihad.

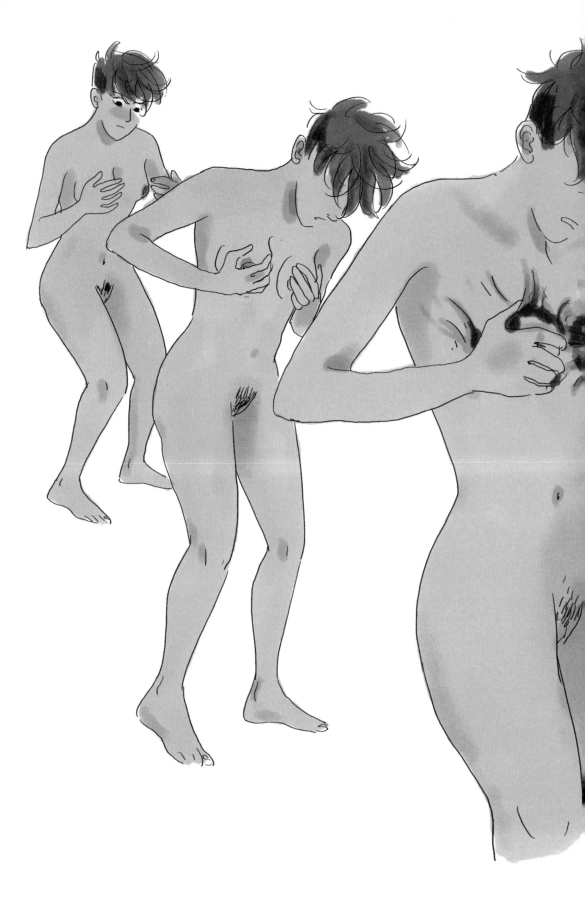

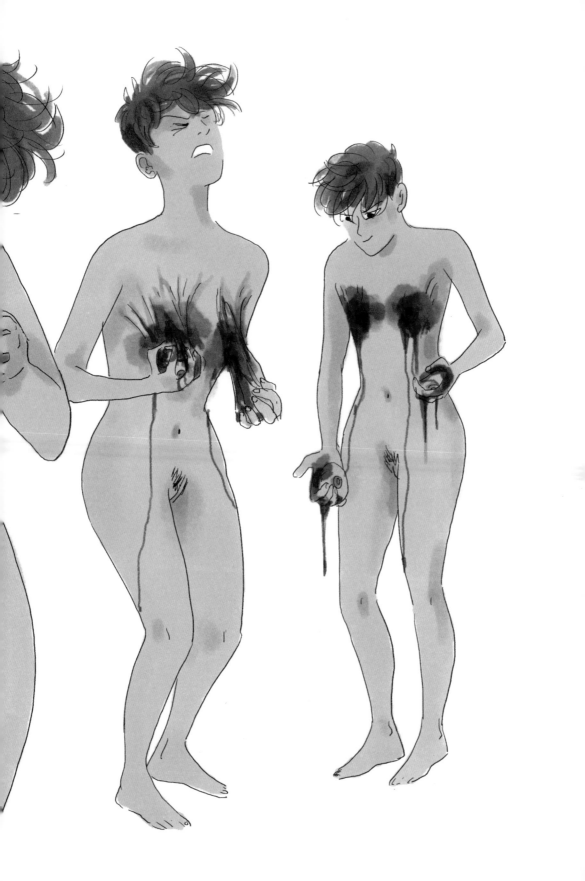

At school, the younger kids adopt me as the shrink on duty.
But this shrink doesn't even understand their own life.

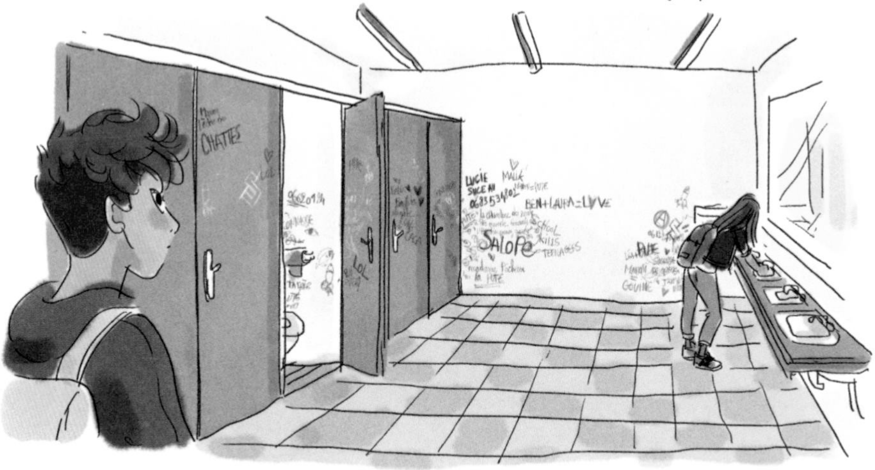

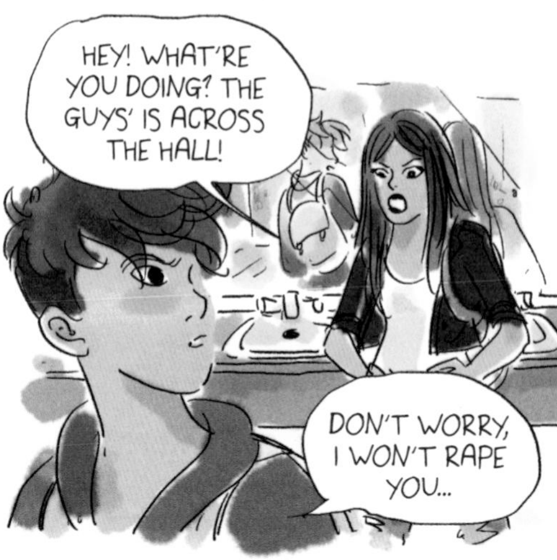
HEY! WHAT'RE YOU DOING? THE GUYS' IS ACROSS THE HALL!
DON'T WORRY, I WON'T RAPE YOU...

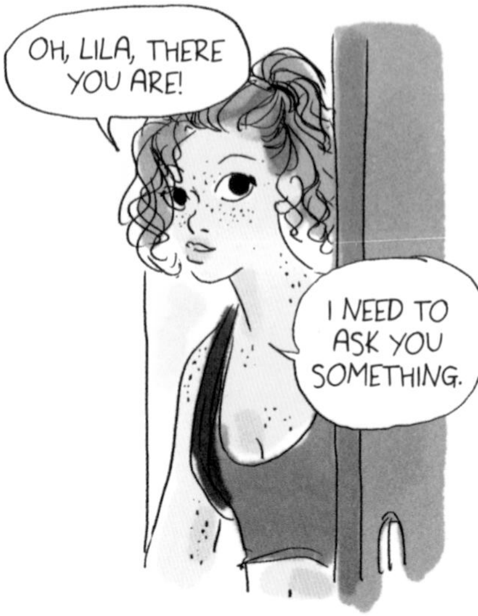
OH, LILA, THERE YOU ARE!
I NEED TO ASK YOU SOMETHING.

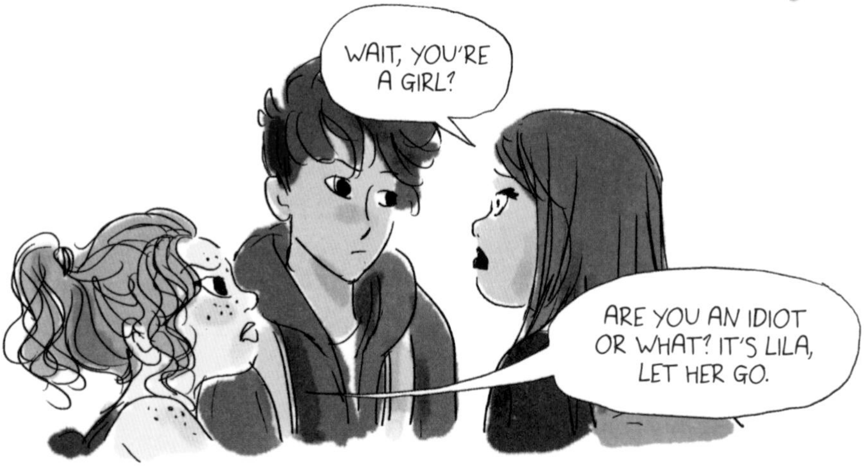
WAIT, YOU'RE A GIRL?
ARE YOU AN IDIOT OR WHAT? IT'S LILA, LET HER GO.

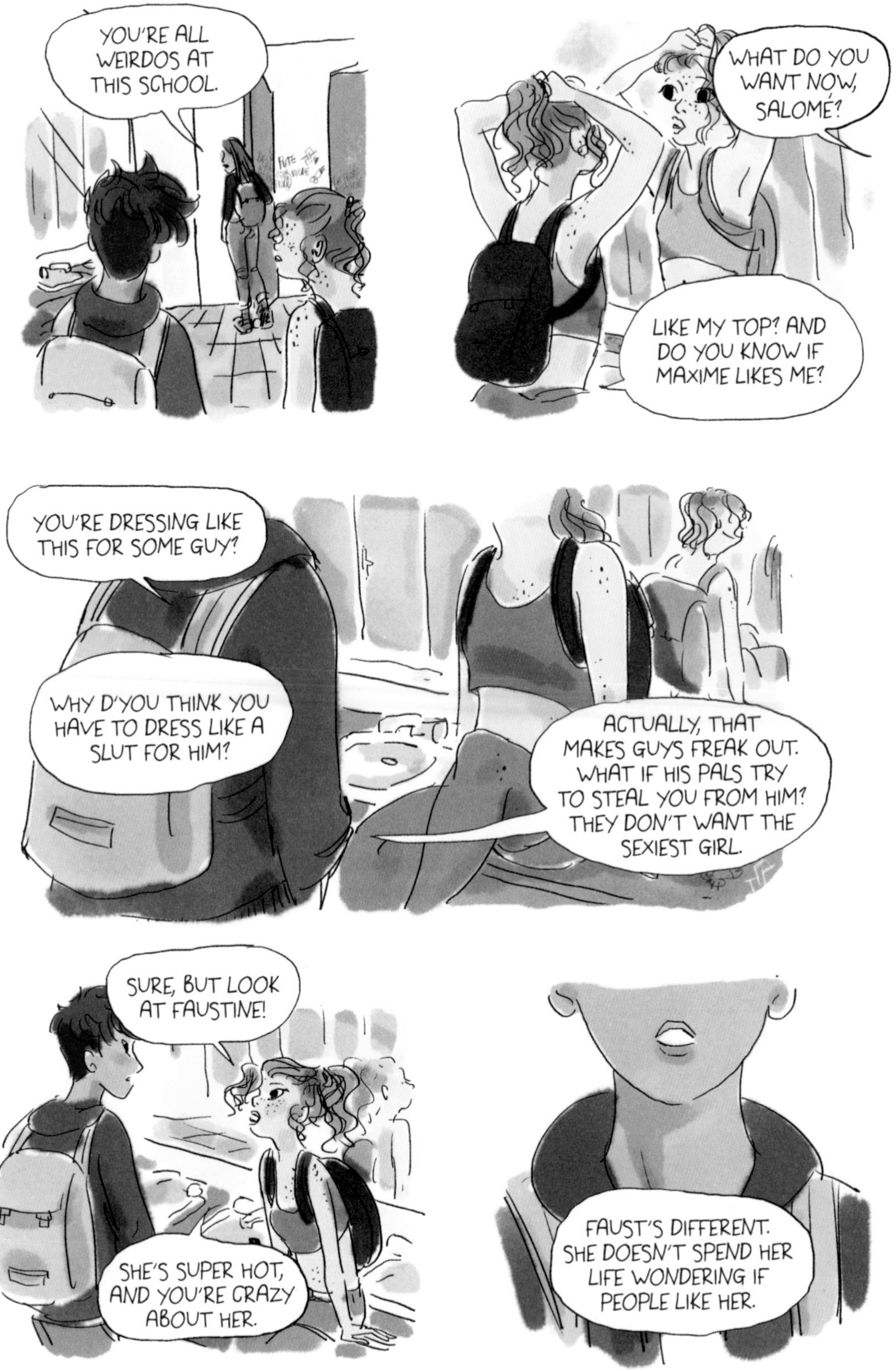

YOU'RE ALL WEIRDOS AT THIS SCHOOL.
WHAT DO YOU WANT NOW, SALOMÉ?
LIKE MY TOP? AND DO YOU KNOW IF MAXIME LIKES ME?
YOU'RE DRESSING LIKE THIS FOR SOME GUY?
WHY D'YOU THINK YOU HAVE TO DRESS LIKE A SLUT FOR HIM?
ACTUALLY, THAT MAKES GUYS FREAK OUT. WHAT IF HIS PALS TRY TO STEAL YOU FROM HIM? THEY DON'T WANT THE SEXIEST GIRL.
SURE, BUT LOOK AT FAUSTINE!
SHE'S SUPER HOT, AND YOU'RE CRAZY ABOUT HER.
FAUST'S DIFFERENT. SHE DOESN'T SPEND HER LIFE WONDERING IF PEOPLE LIKE HER.

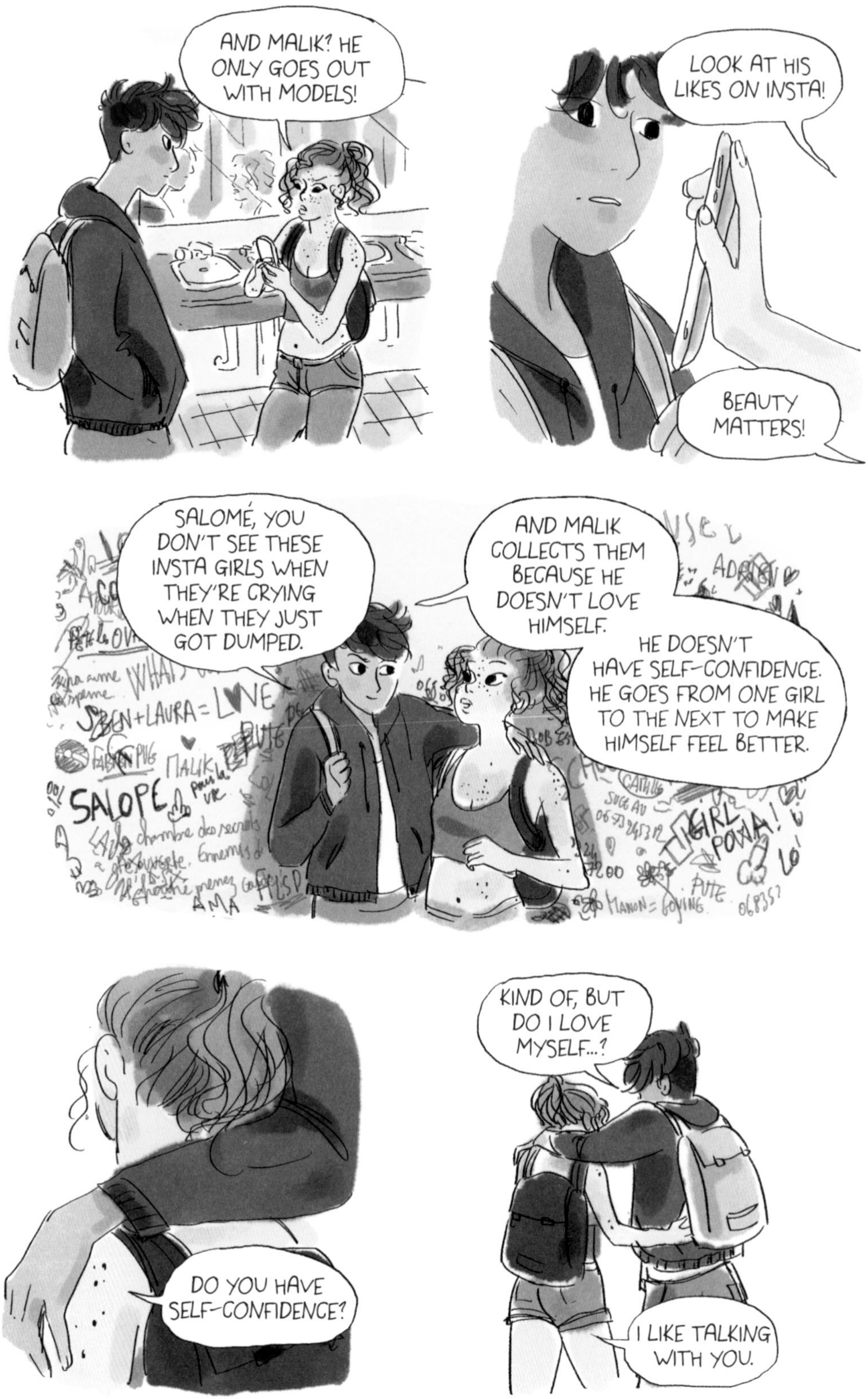
AND MALIK? HE ONLY GOES OUT WITH MODELS!
LOOK AT HIS LIKES ON INSTA!
BEAUTY MATTERS!
SALOMÉ, YOU DON'T SEE THESE INSTA GIRLS WHEN THEY'RE CRYING WHEN THEY JUST GOT DUMPED.
AND MALIK COLLECTS THEM BECAUSE HE DOESN'T LOVE HIMSELF.
HE DOESN'T HAVE SELF-CONFIDENCE. HE GOES FROM ONE GIRL TO THE NEXT TO MAKE HIMSELF FEEL BETTER.
DO YOU HAVE SELF-CONFIDENCE?
KIND OF, BUT DO I LOVE MYSELF...?
I LIKE TALKING WITH YOU.

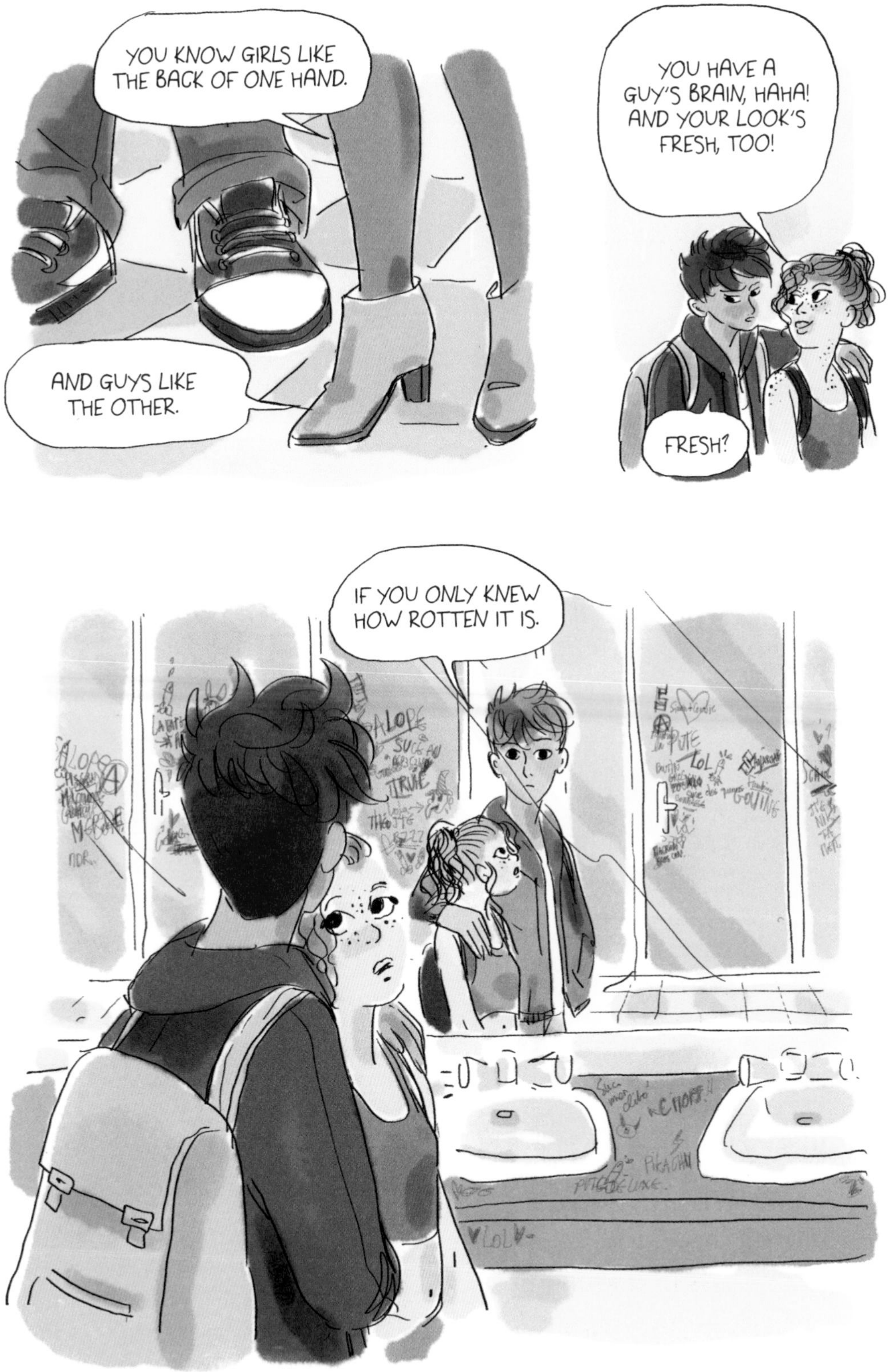
YOU KNOW GIRLS LIKE THE BACK OF ONE HAND.
AND GUYS LIKE THE OTHER.
YOU HAVE A GUY'S BRAIN, HAHA! AND YOUR LOOK'S FRESH, TOO!
FRESH?
IF YOU ONLY KNEW HOW ROTTEN IT IS.

I hate myself.

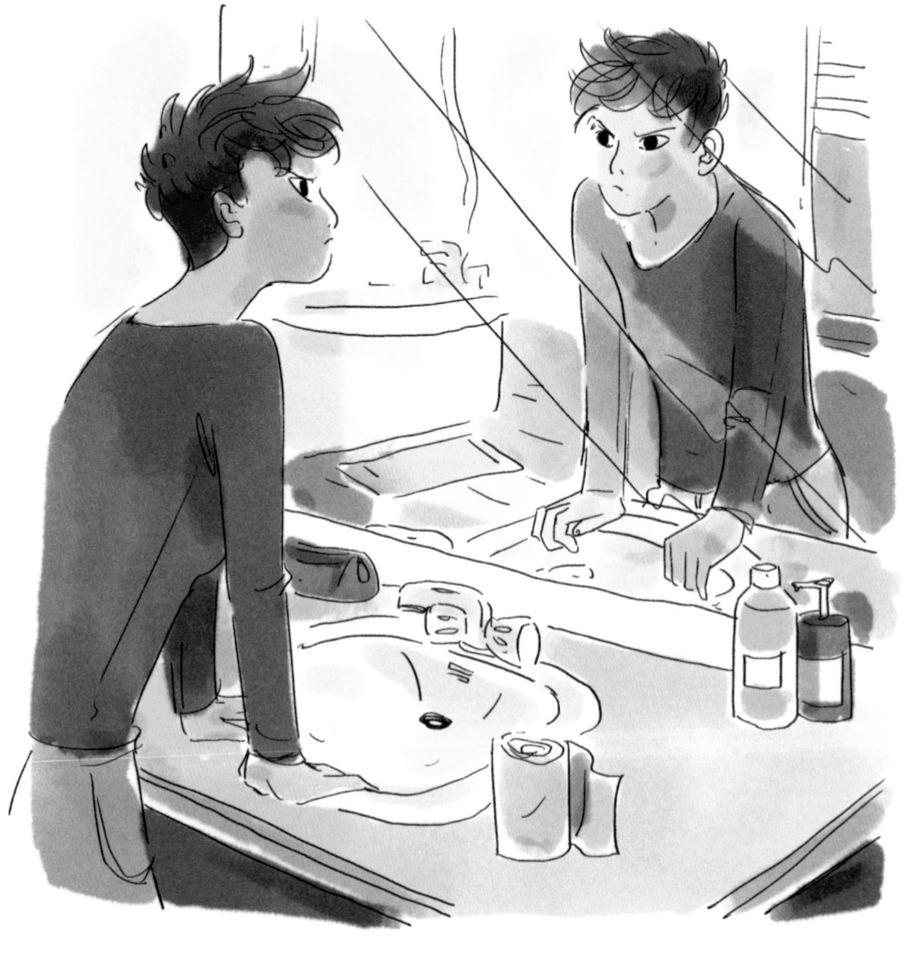

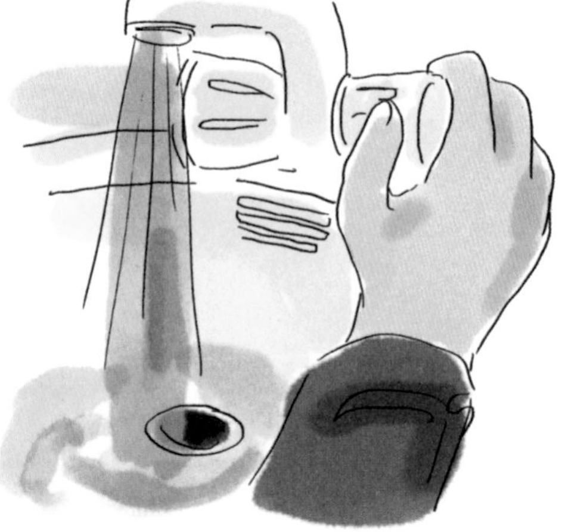

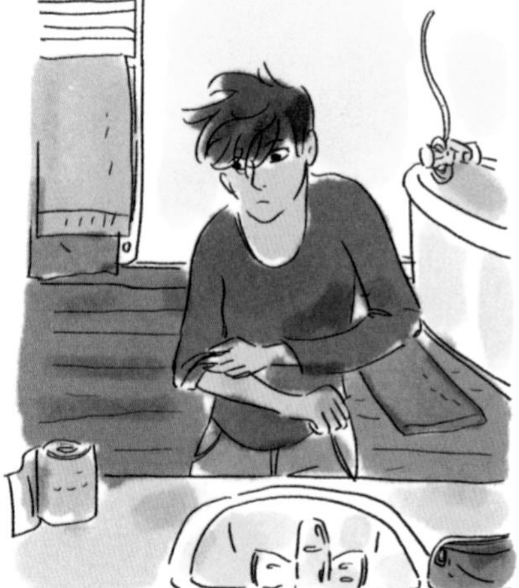

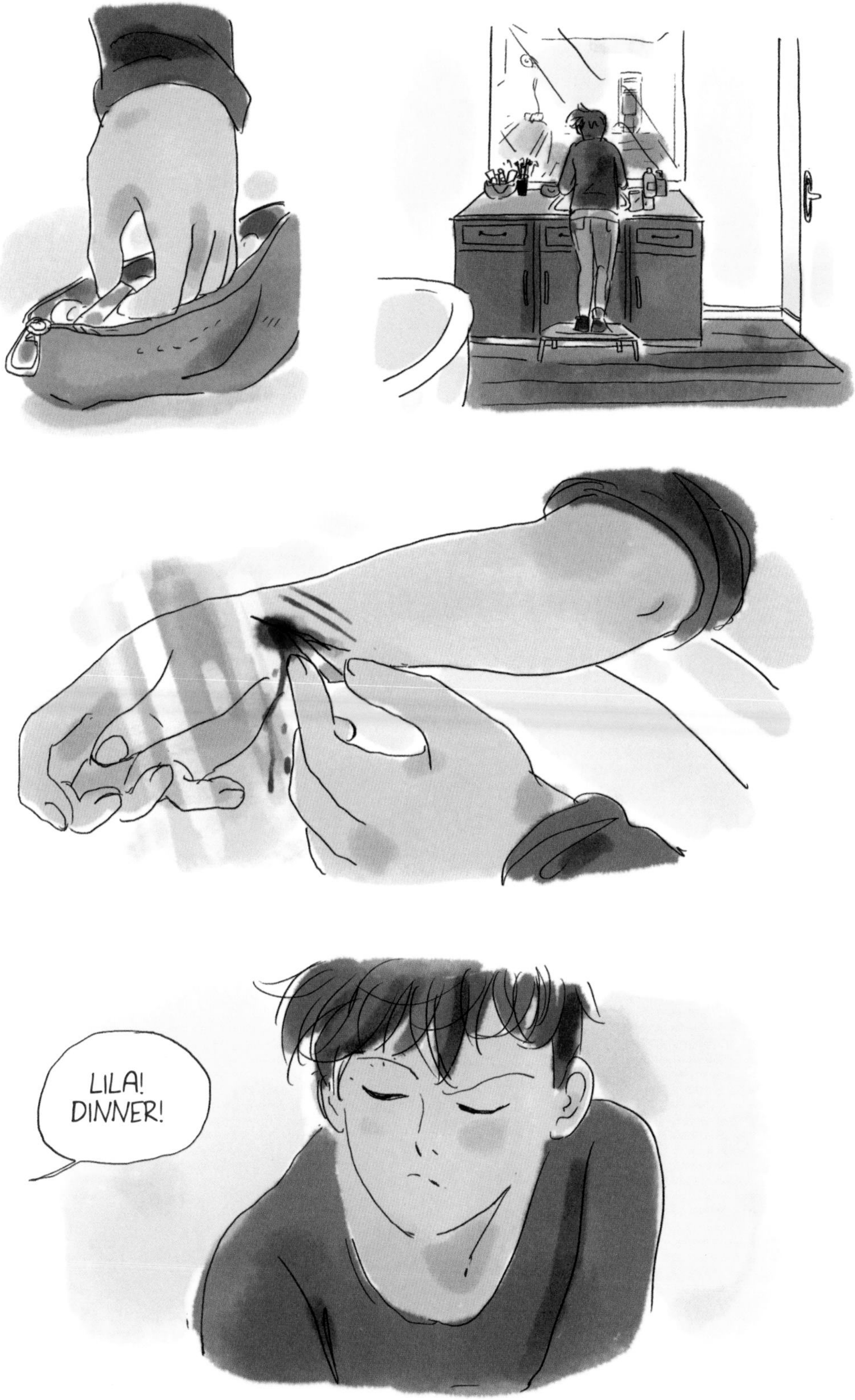
LILA!
DINNER!

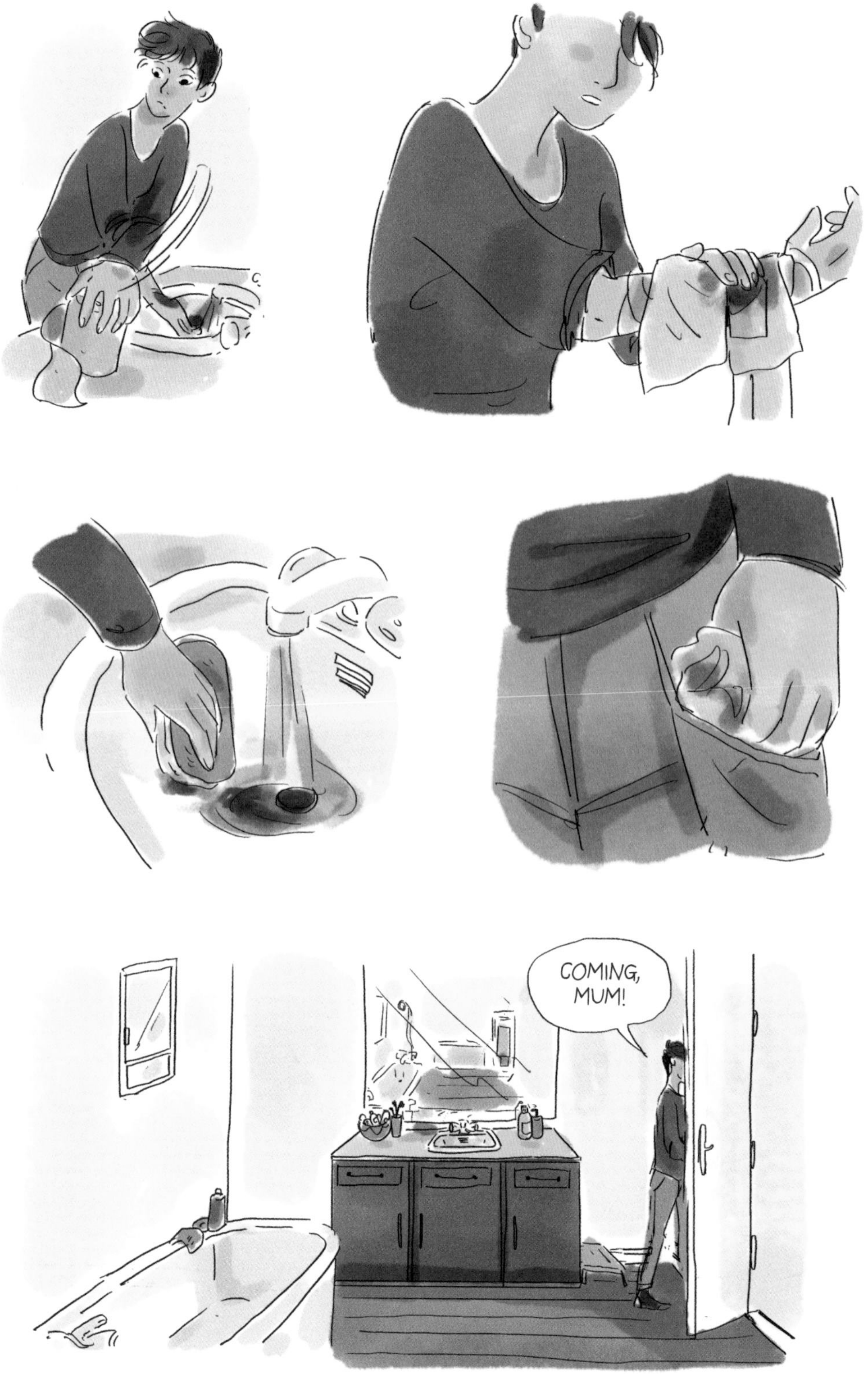
COMING, MUM!

I'm not normal. What's wrong with me? My parents call this a teen crisis.
That's cute, but it doesn't help me. What the hell is it?

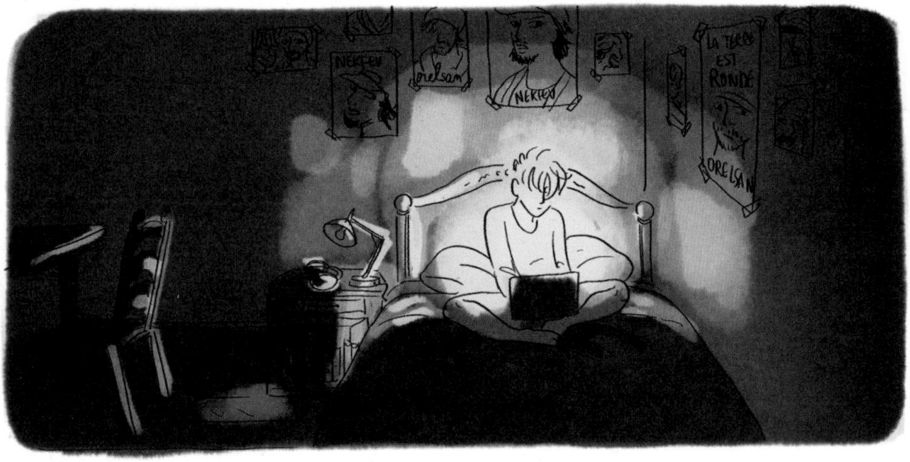
NEKFEU
Orelsan
NEKFEU
LA TERRE EST RONDE
ORELSAN

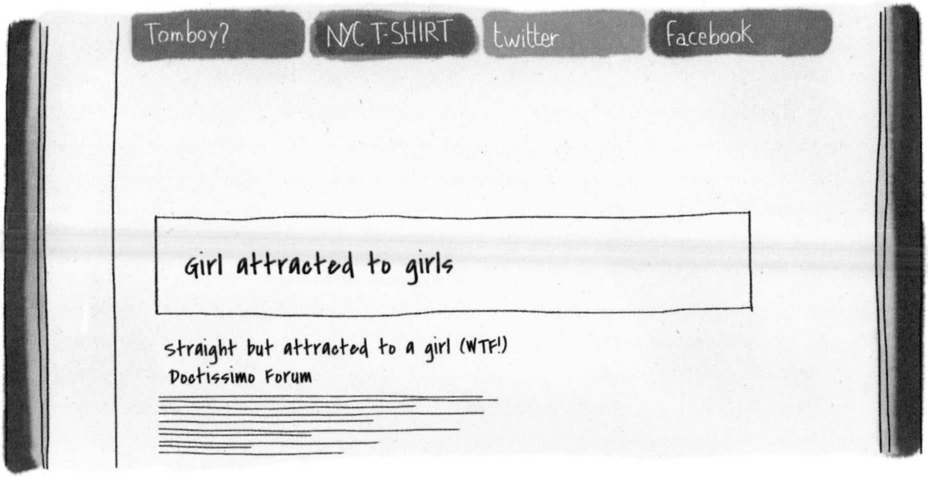
Tomboy?
NYC T-SHIRT
twitter
facebook
Girl attracted to girls
straight but attracted to a girl (WTF!)
Doctissimo Forum

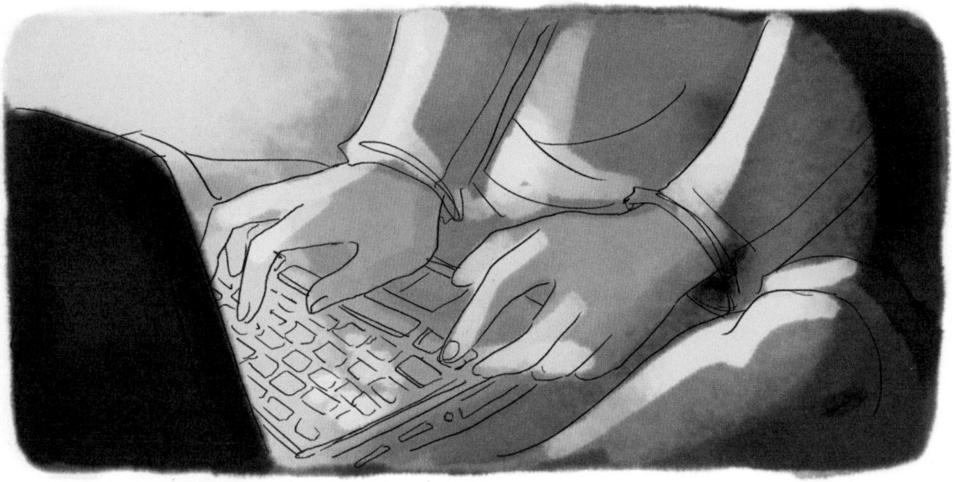

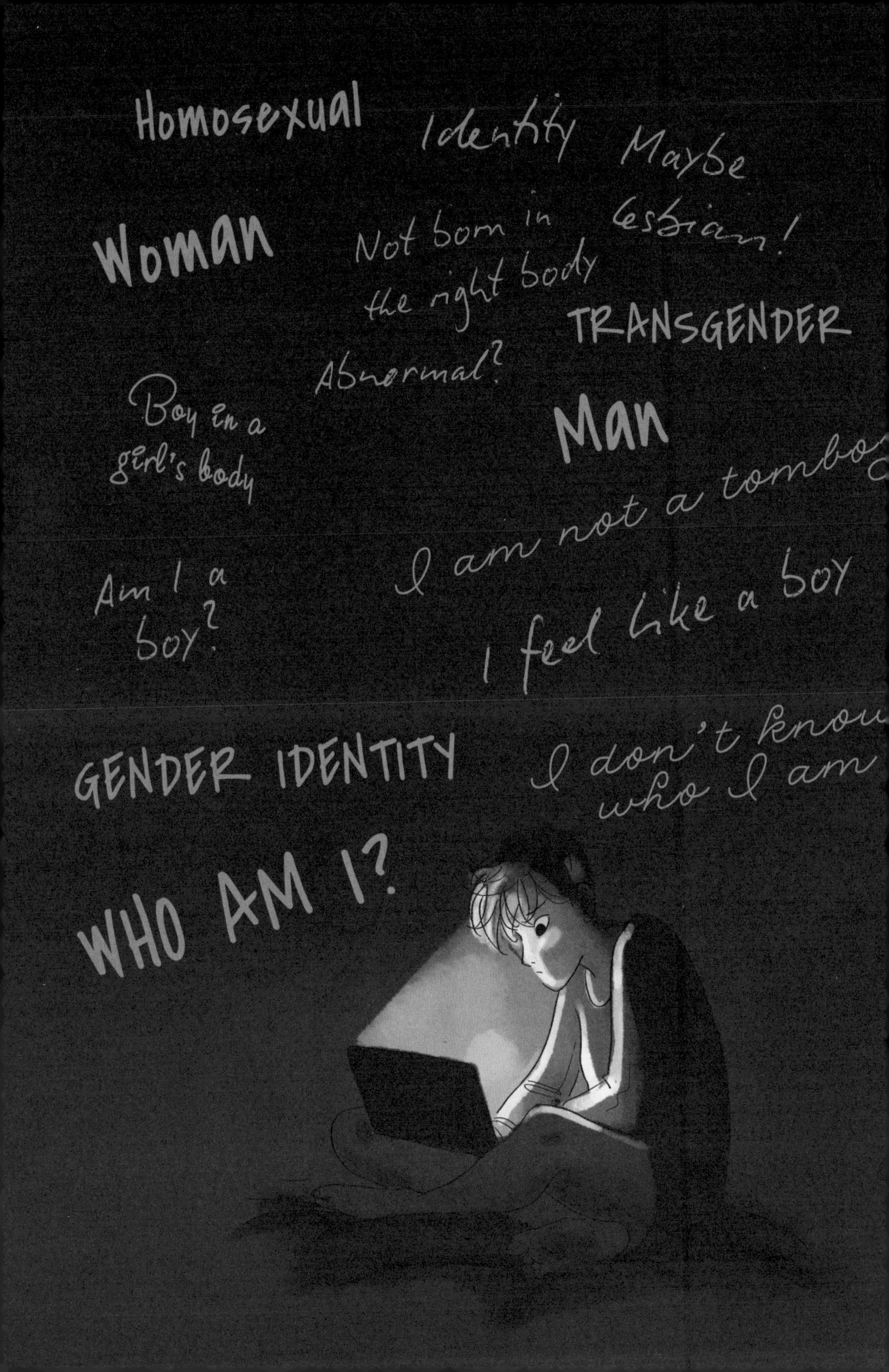
Homosexual
Identity
Maybe
Woman
Not born in the right body
lesbian!
TRANSGENDER
Abnormal?
Boy in a girl's body
Man
I am not a tombo
Am I a boy?
I feel like a boy
GENDER IDENTITY
I don't know who I am
WHO AM I?

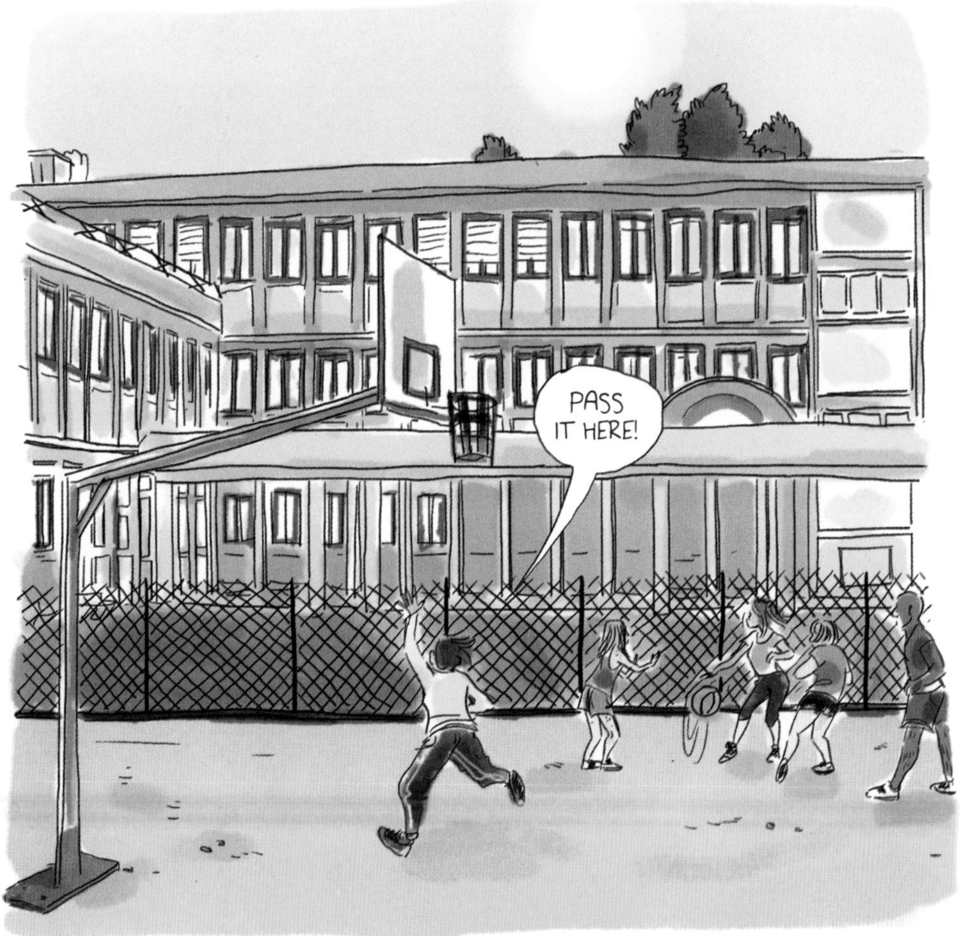
PASS
IT HERE!

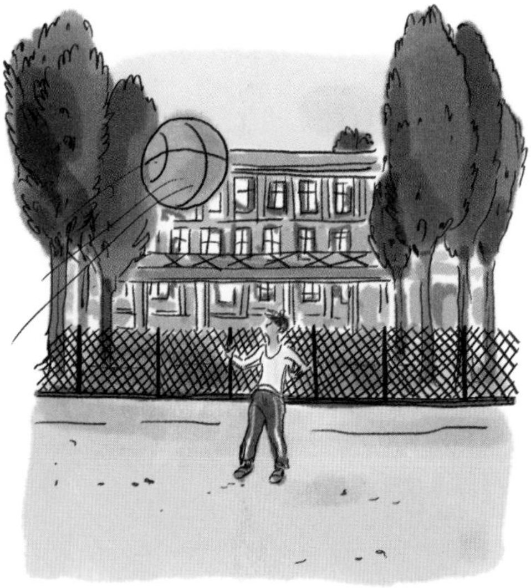

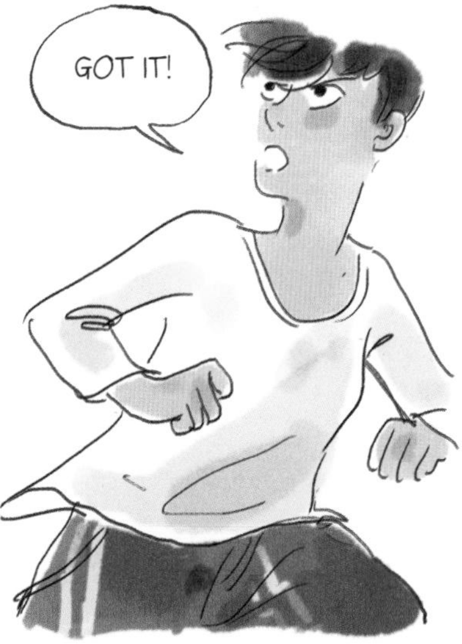
GOT IT!

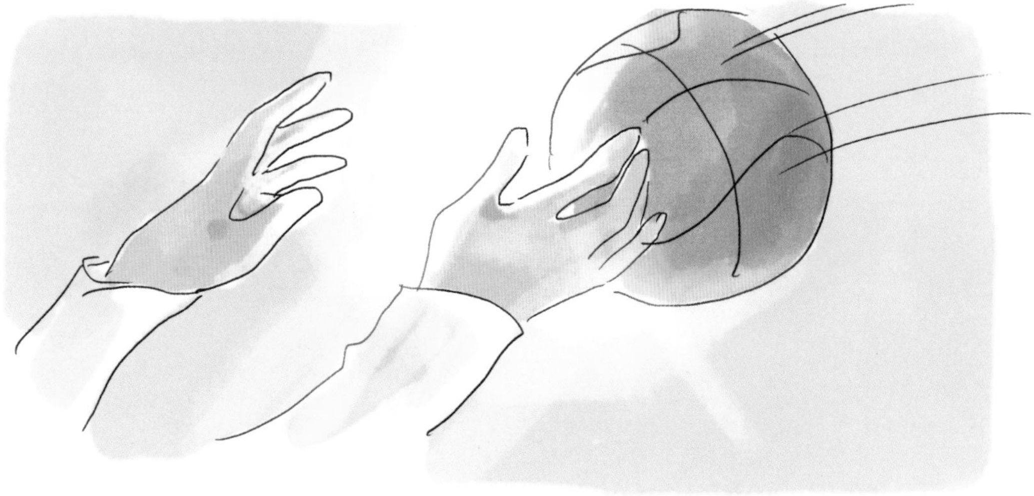

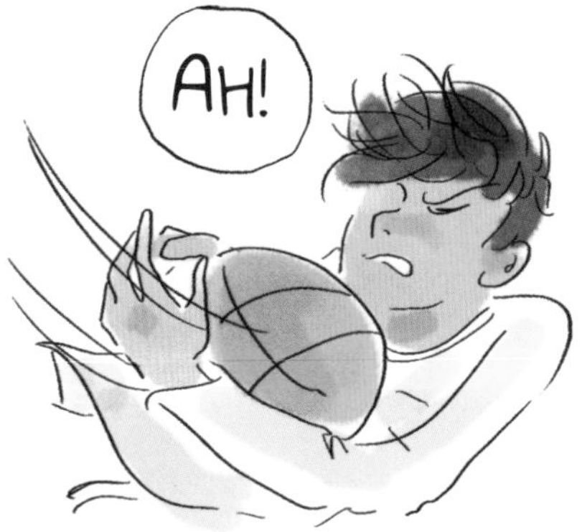
AH!

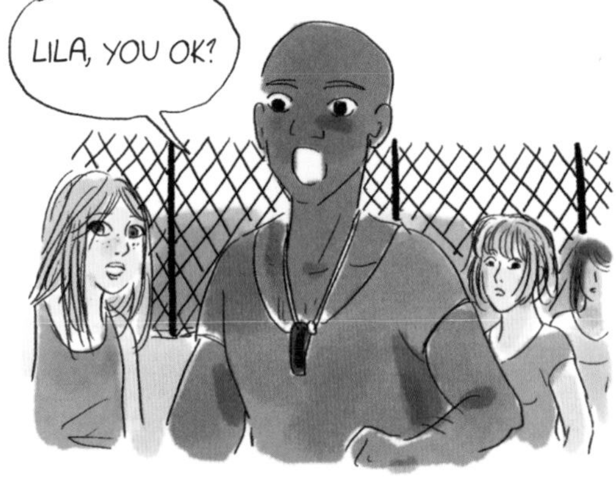
LILA, YOU OK?

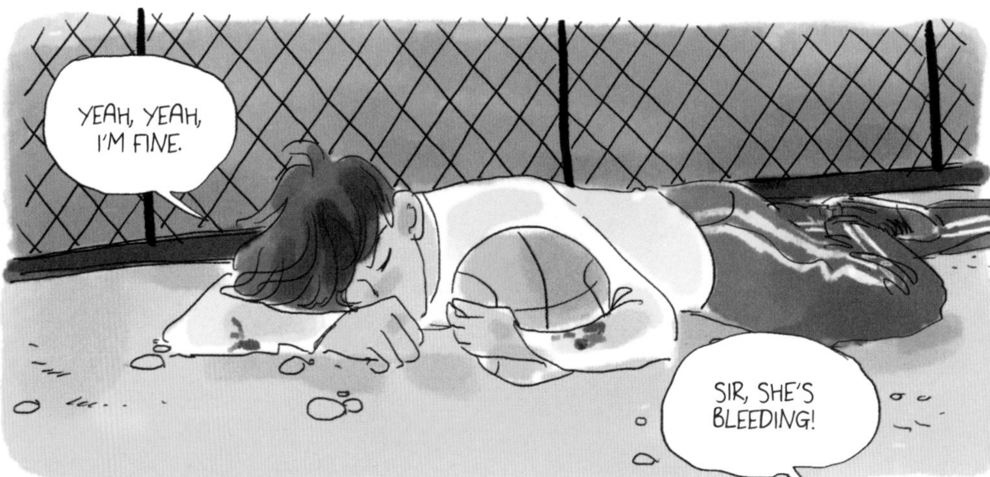
YEAH, YEAH, I'M FINE.
SIR, SHE'S BLEEDING!

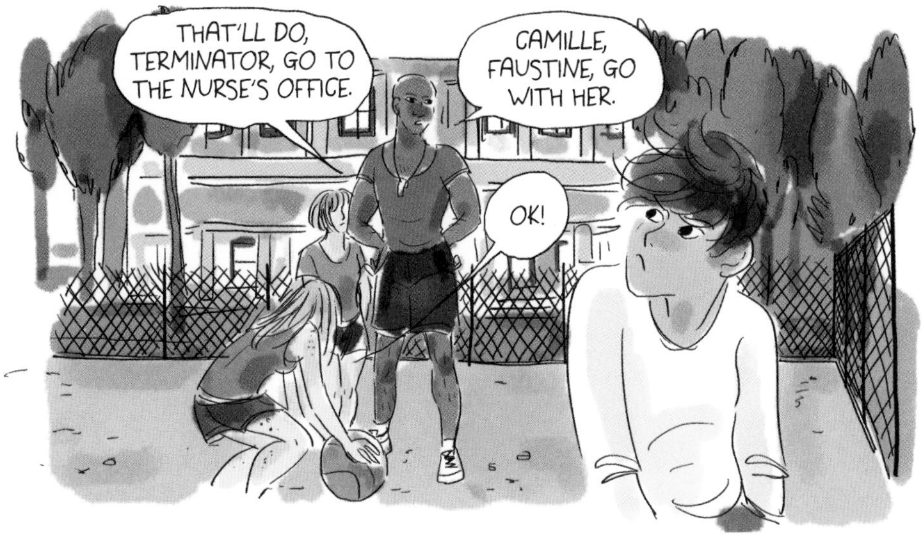
THAT'LL DO, TERMINATOR, GO TO THE NURSE'S OFFICE.
CAMILLE, FAUSTINE, GO WITH HER.
OK!

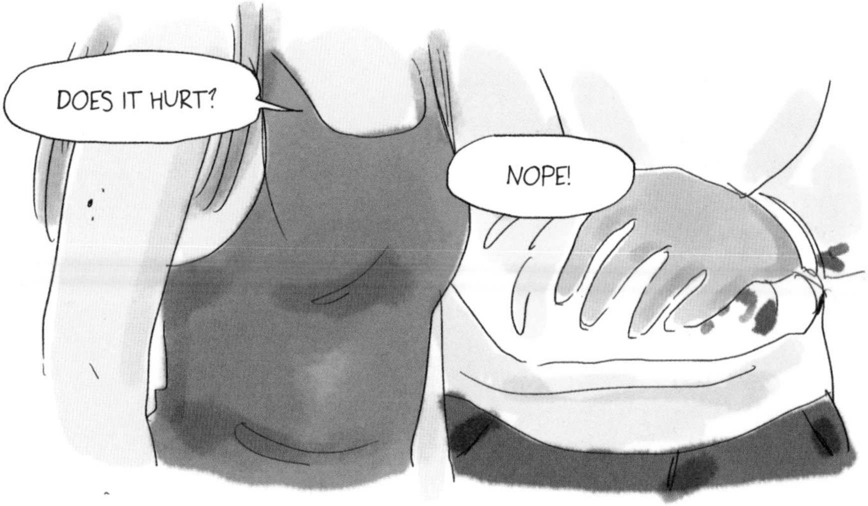
DOES IT HURT?
NOPE!

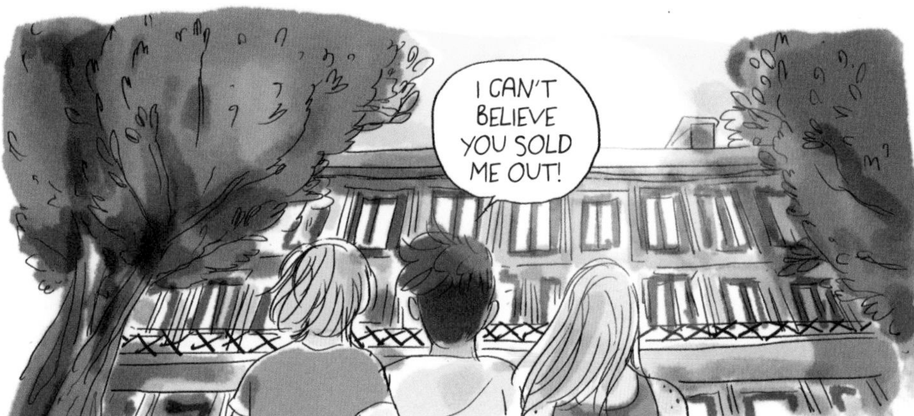
I CAN'T BELIEVE YOU SOLD ME OUT!

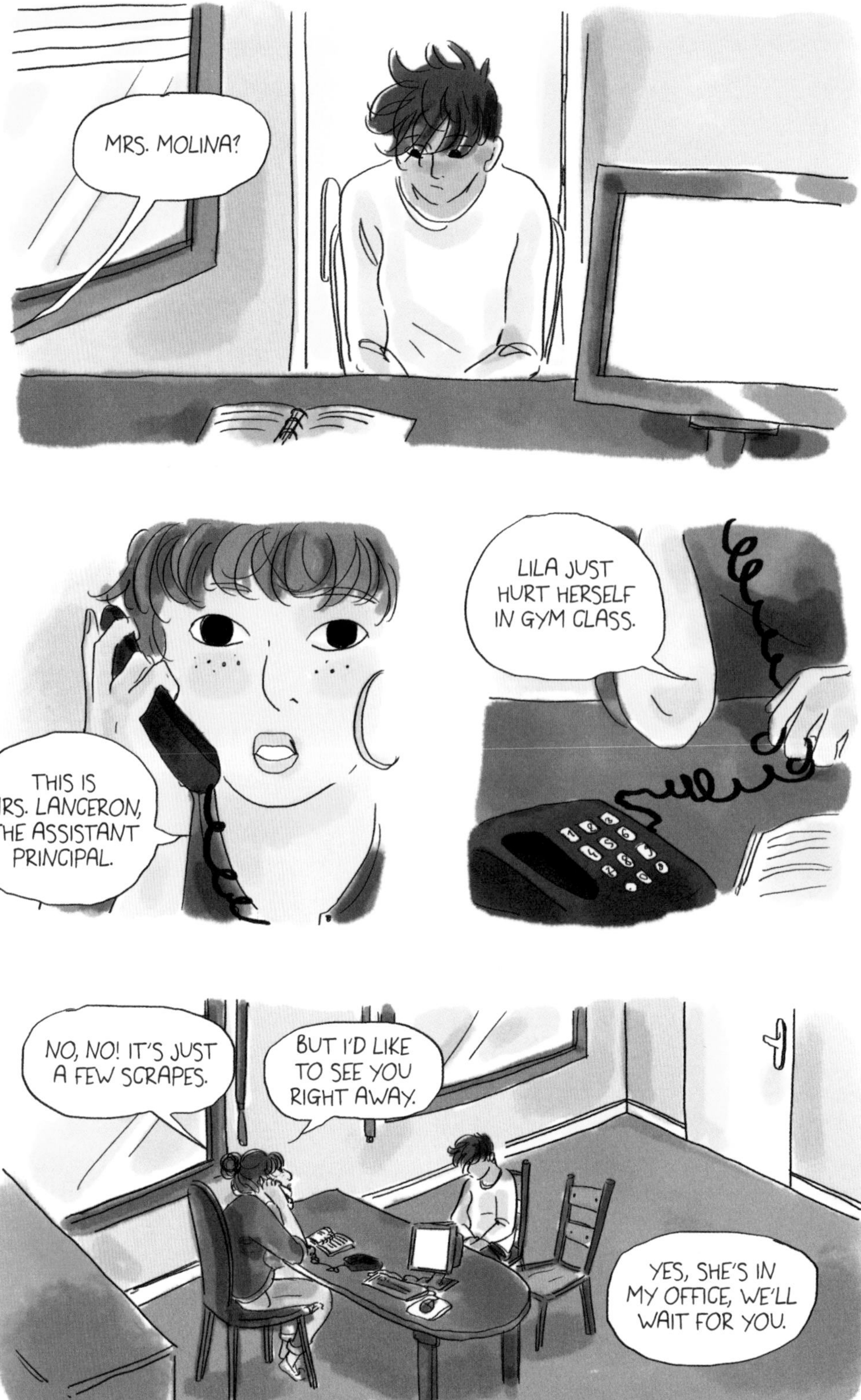
MRS. MOLINA?
THIS IS MRS. LANCERON, THE ASSISTANT PRINCIPAL.
LILA JUST HURT HERSELF IN GYM CLASS.
NO, NO! IT'S JUST A FEW SCRAPES.
BUT I'D LIKE TO SEE YOU RIGHT AWAY.
YES, SHE'S IN MY OFFICE, WE'LL WAIT FOR YOU.

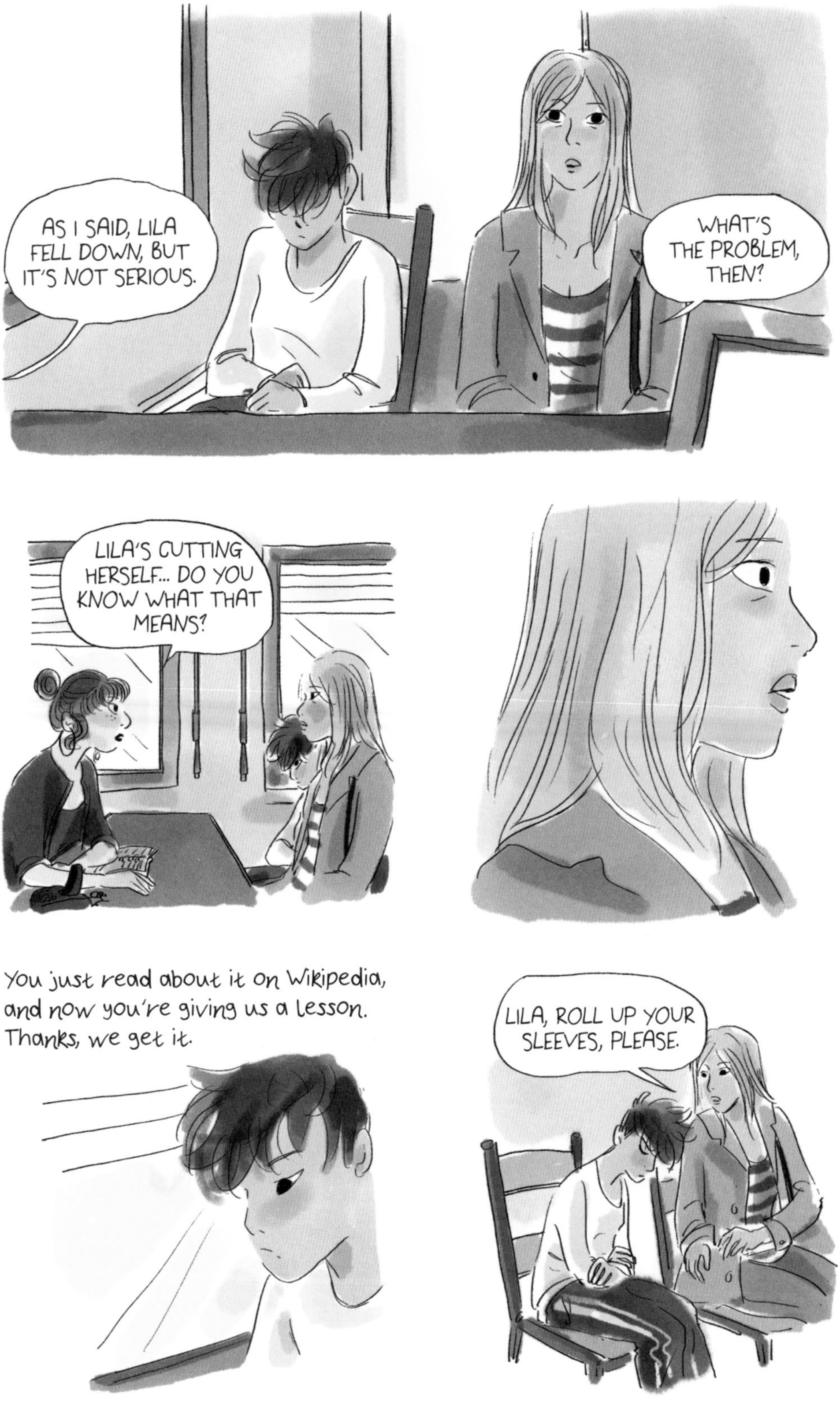
AS I SAID, LILA FELL DOWN, BUT IT'S NOT SERIOUS.
WHAT'S THE PROBLEM, THEN?
LILA'S CUTTING HERSELF... DO YOU KNOW WHAT THAT MEANS?
You just read about it on Wikipedia, and now you're giving us a lesson. Thanks, we get it.
LILA, ROLL UP YOUR SLEEVES, PLEASE.

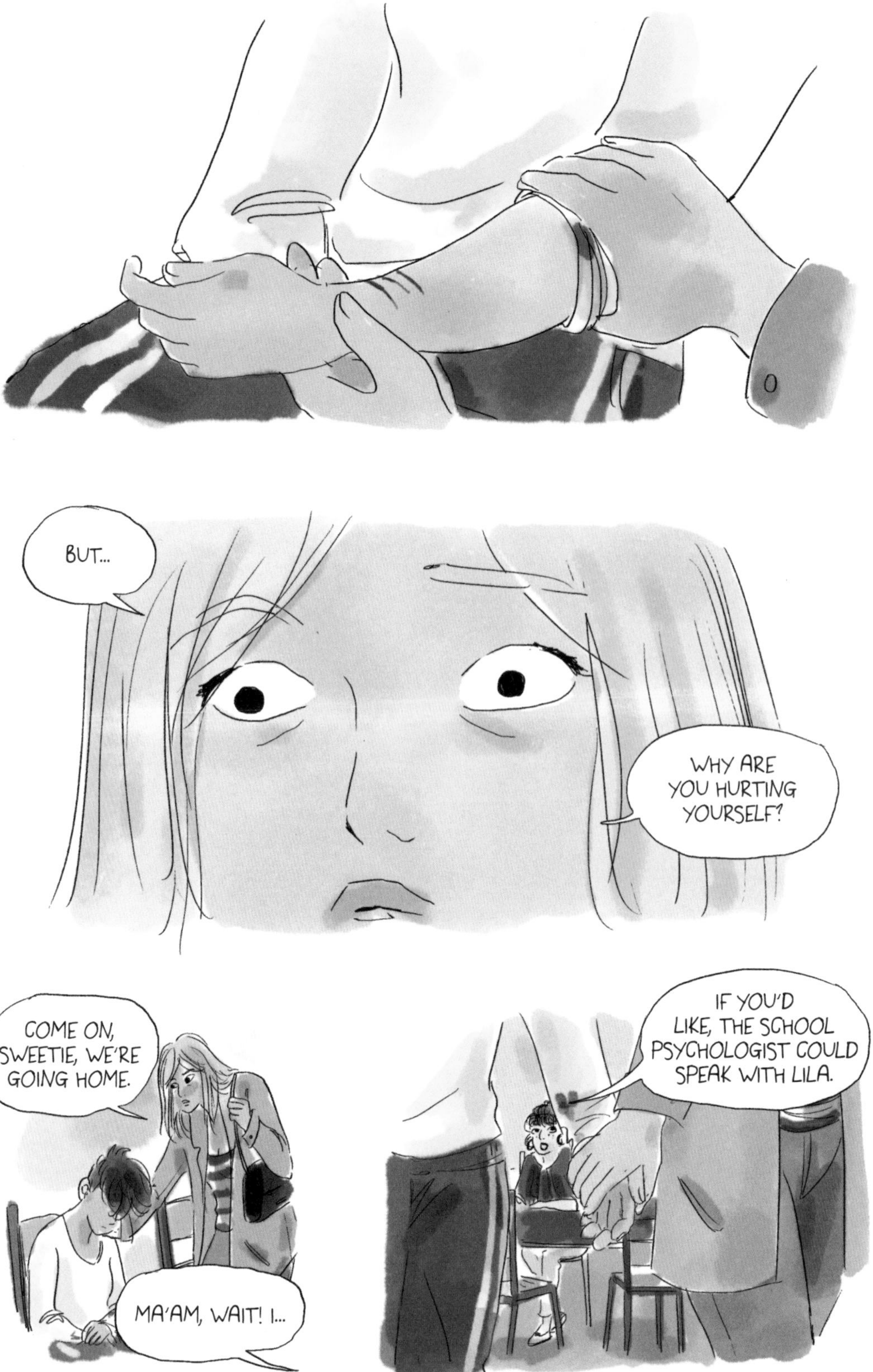
BUT...
WHY ARE YOU HURTING YOURSELF?
COME ON, SWEETIE, WE'RE GOING HOME.
MA'AM, WAIT! I...
IF YOU'D LIKE, THE SCHOOL PSYCHOLOGIST COULD SPEAK WITH LILA.

It's OK, guys, I'm not going to the loony bin, don't worry. But...

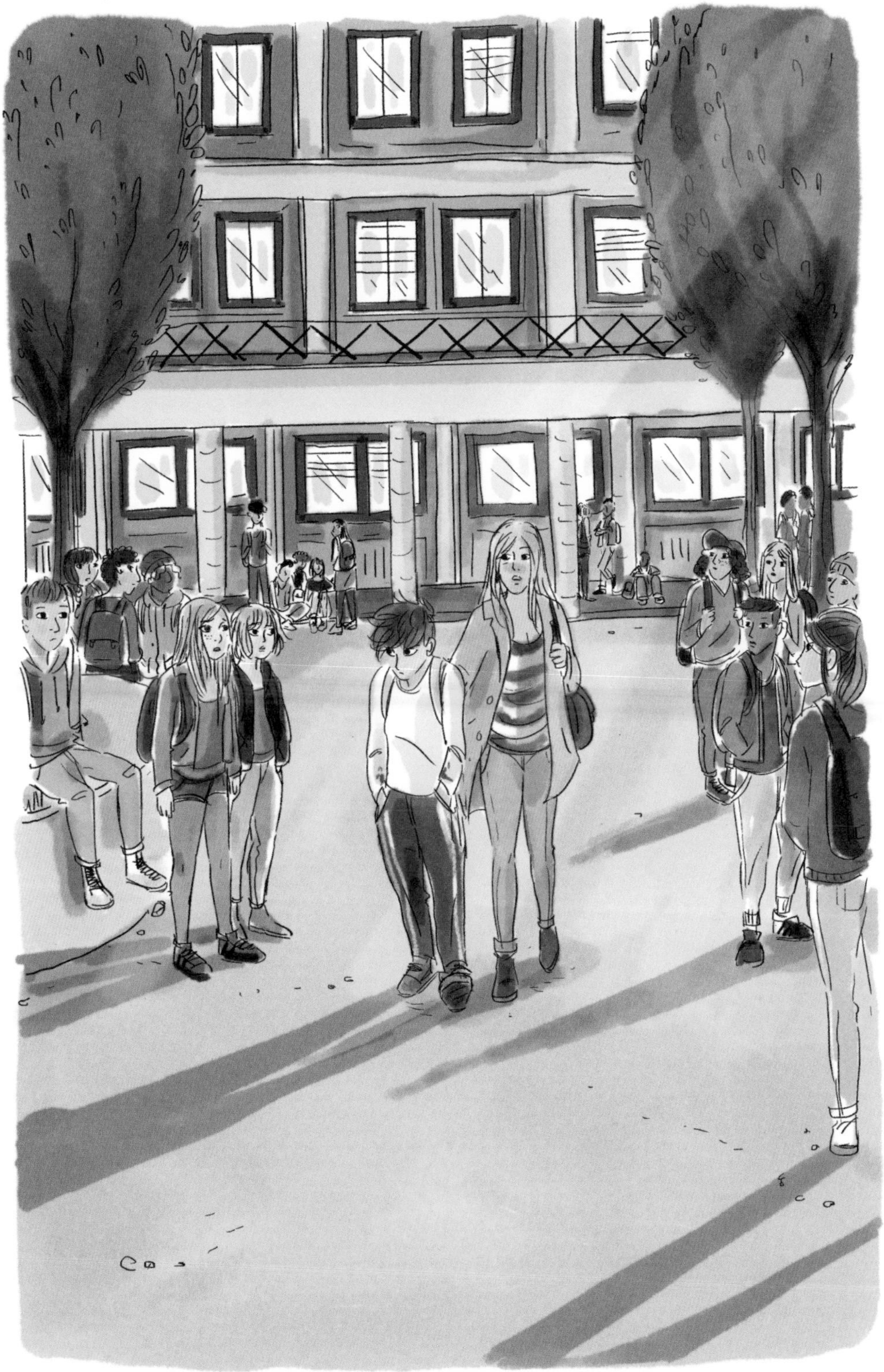

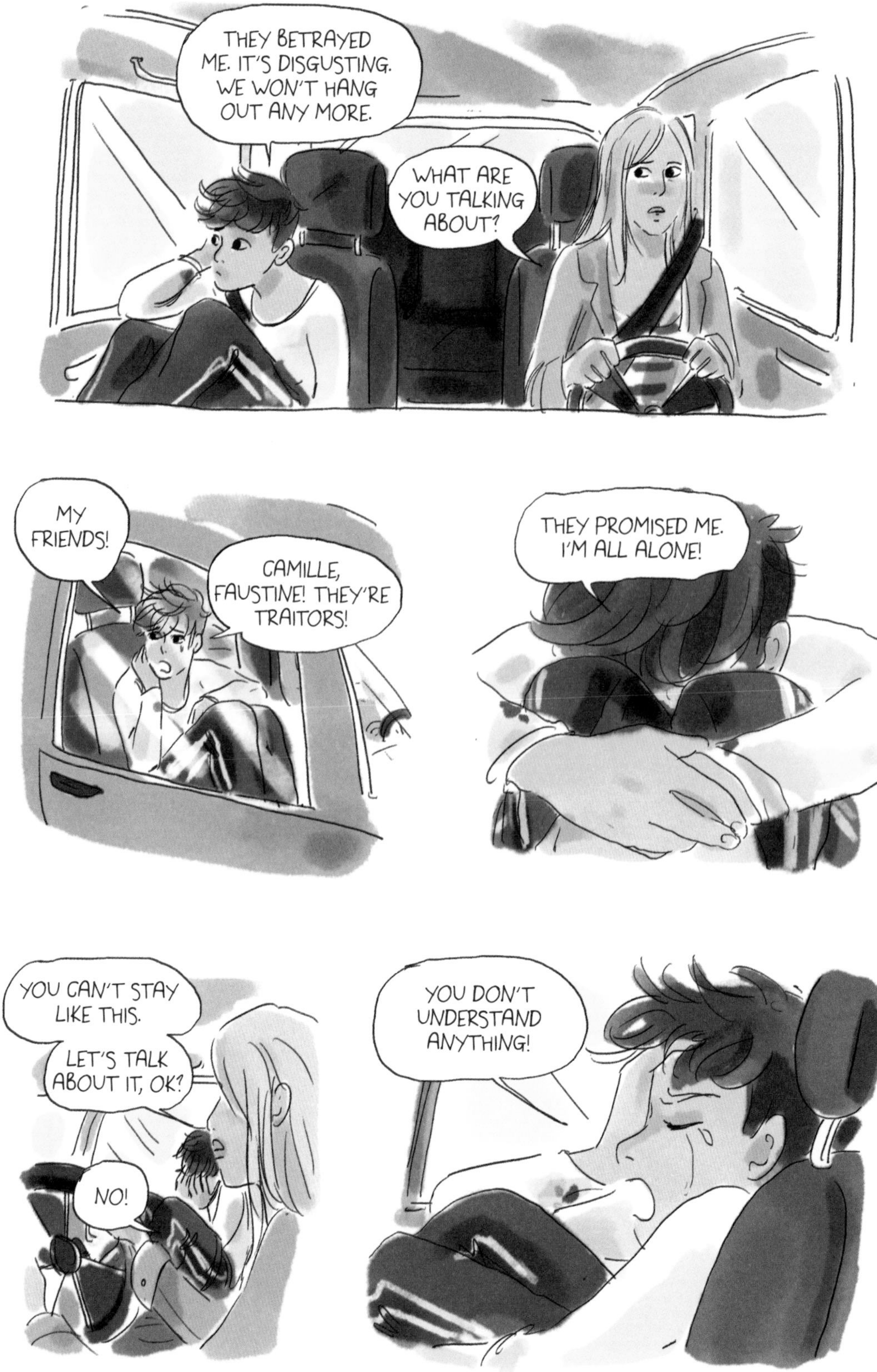
THEY BETRAYED ME. IT'S DISGUSTING. WE WON'T HANG OUT ANY MORE.
WHAT ARE YOU TALKING ABOUT?
MY FRIENDS!
CAMILLE, FAUSTINE! THEY'RE TRAITORS!
THEY PROMISED ME. I'M ALL ALONE!
YOU CAN'T STAY LIKE THIS.
LET'S TALK ABOUT IT, OK?
NO!
YOU DON'T UNDERSTAND ANYTHING!

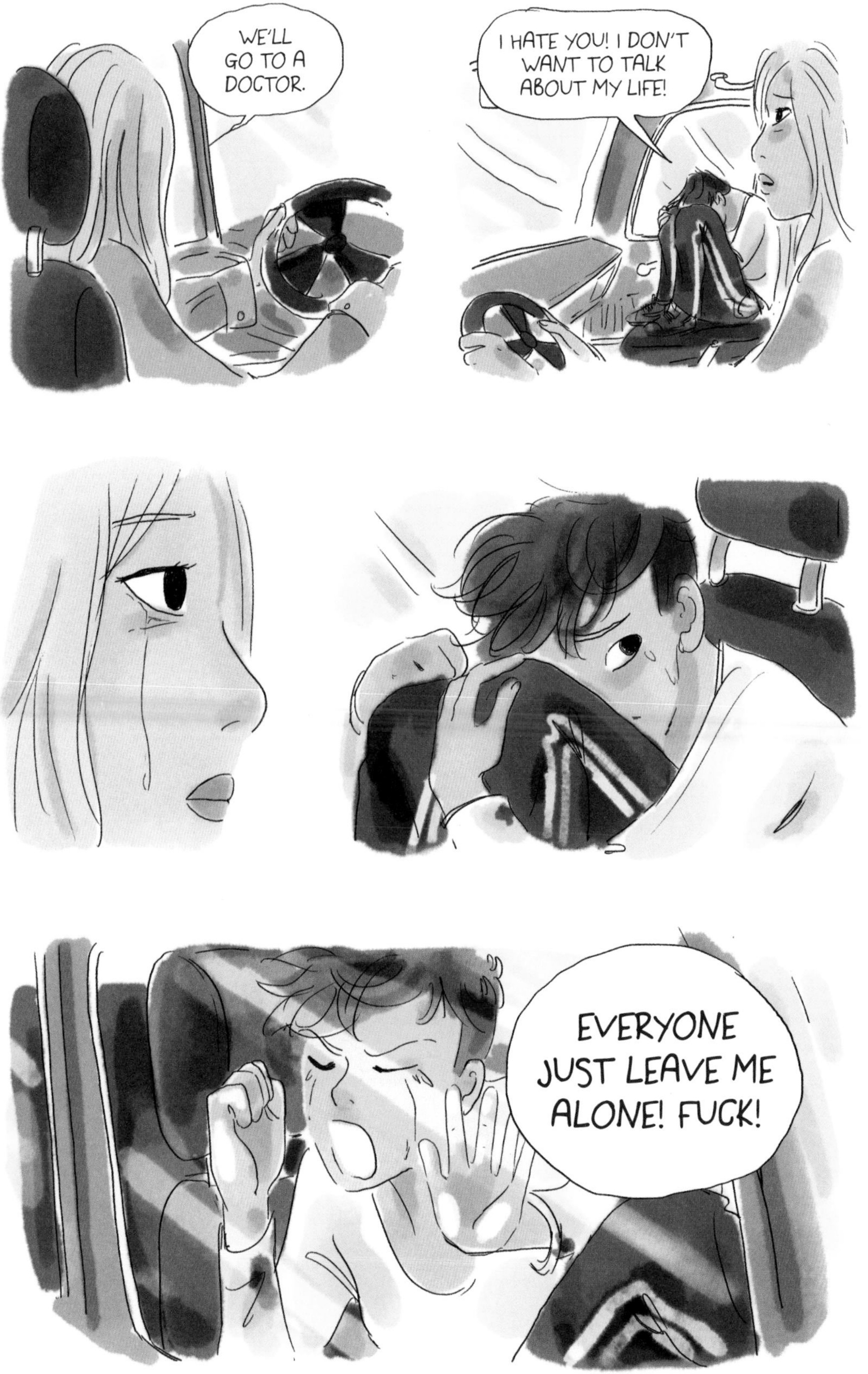
WE'LL GO TO A DOCTOR.
I HATE YOU! I DON'T WANT TO TALK ABOUT MY LIFE!
EVERYONE JUST LEAVE ME ALONE! FUCK!

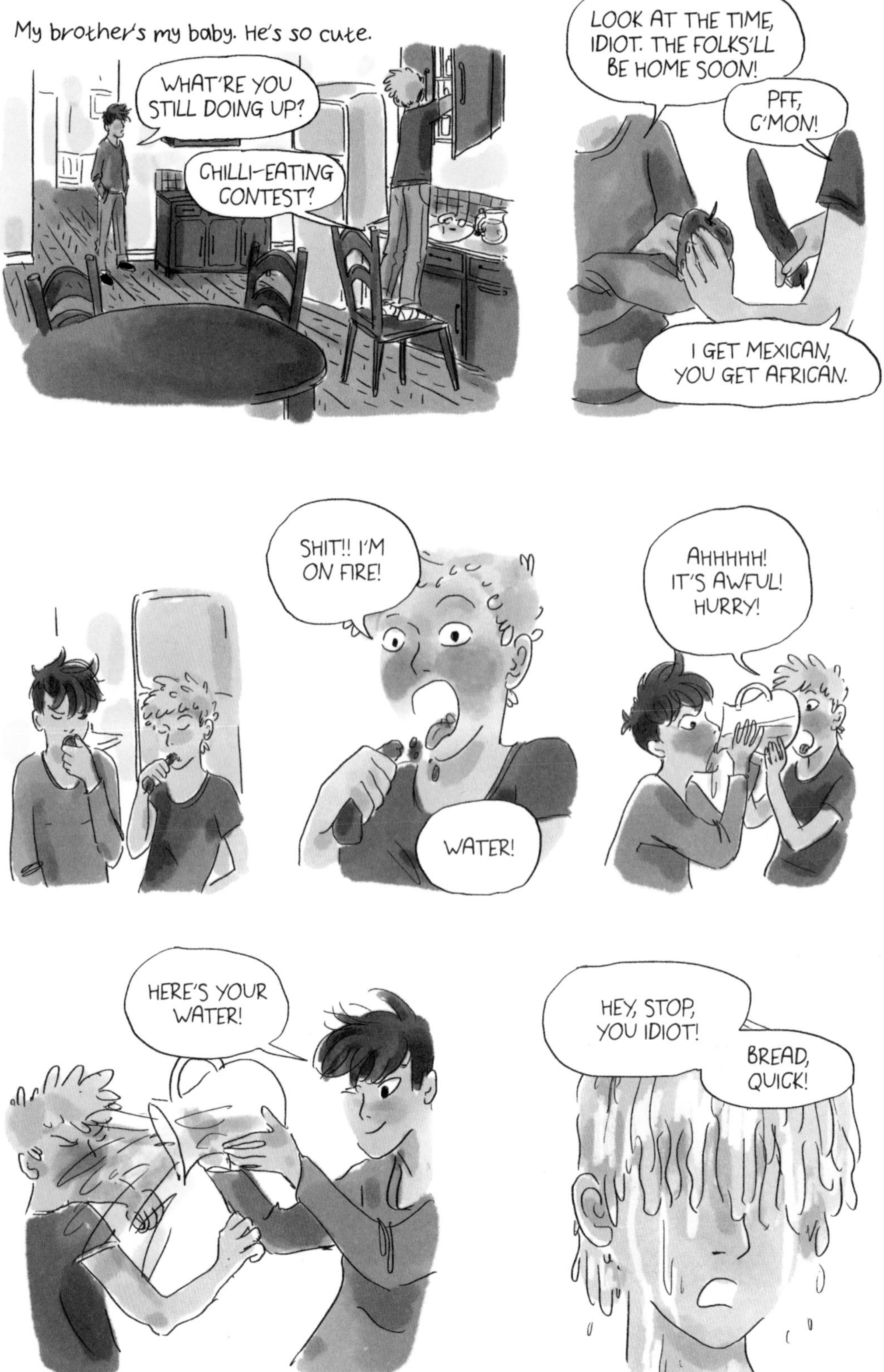

My brother's my baby. He's so cute.
WHAT'RE YOU STILL DOING UP?
CHILLI-EATING CONTEST?
LOOK AT THE TIME, IDIOT. THE FOLKS'LL BE HOME SOON!
PFF, C'MON!
I GET MEXICAN, YOU GET AFRICAN.
SHIT!! I'M ON FIRE!
WATER!
AHHHHH! IT'S AWFUL! HURRY!
HERE'S YOUR WATER!
HEY, STOP, YOU IDIOT!
BREAD, QUICK!

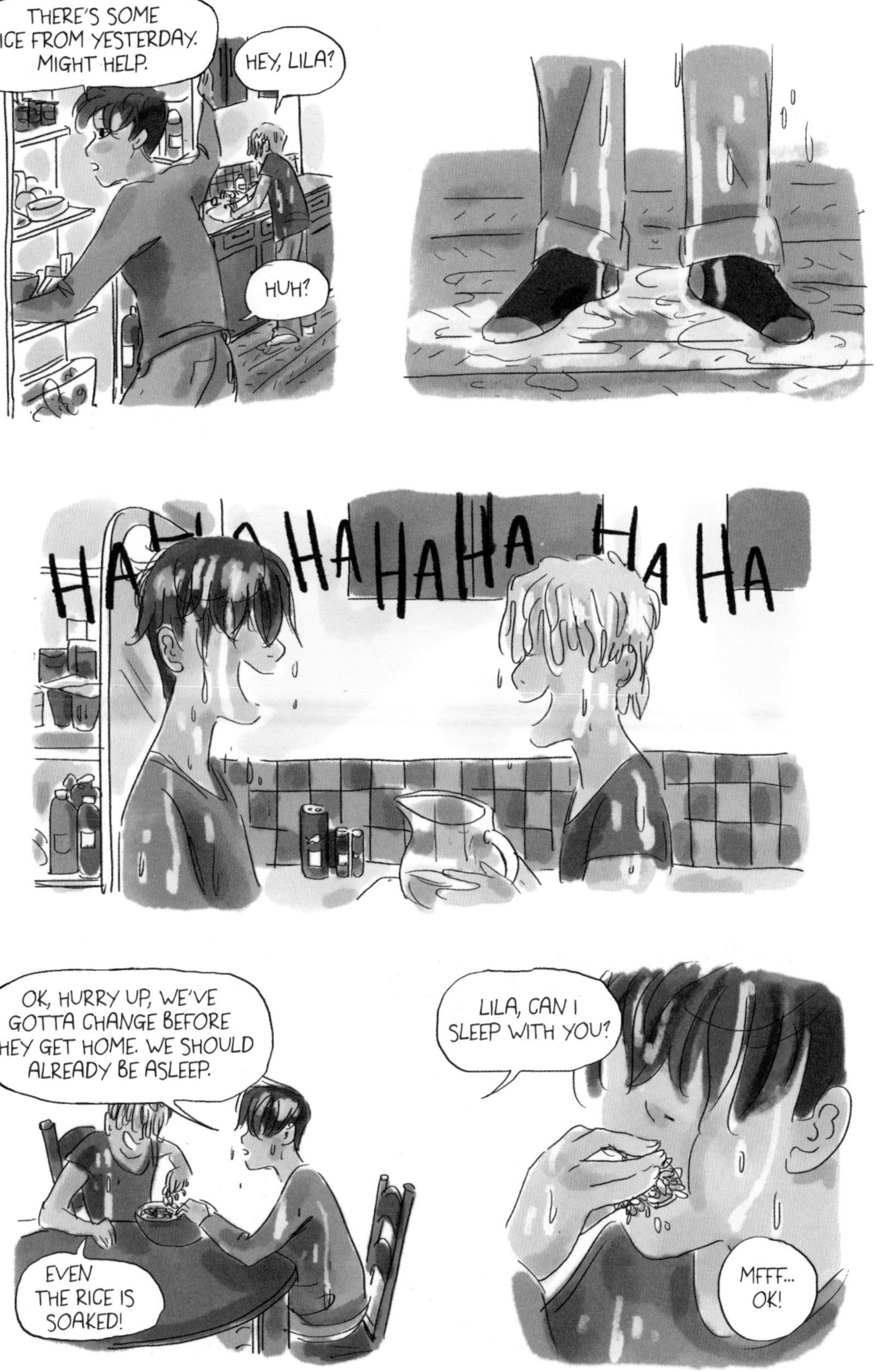
THERE'S SOME RICE FROM YESTERDAY. MIGHT HELP.
HEY, LILA?
HUH?
HAHAHAHAHAHA HAHA HA
OK, HURRY UP, WE'VE GOTTA CHANGE BEFORE THEY GET HOME. WE SHOULD ALREADY BE ASLEEP.
EVEN THE RICE IS SOAKED!
LILA, CAN I SLEEP WITH YOU?
MFFF... OK!

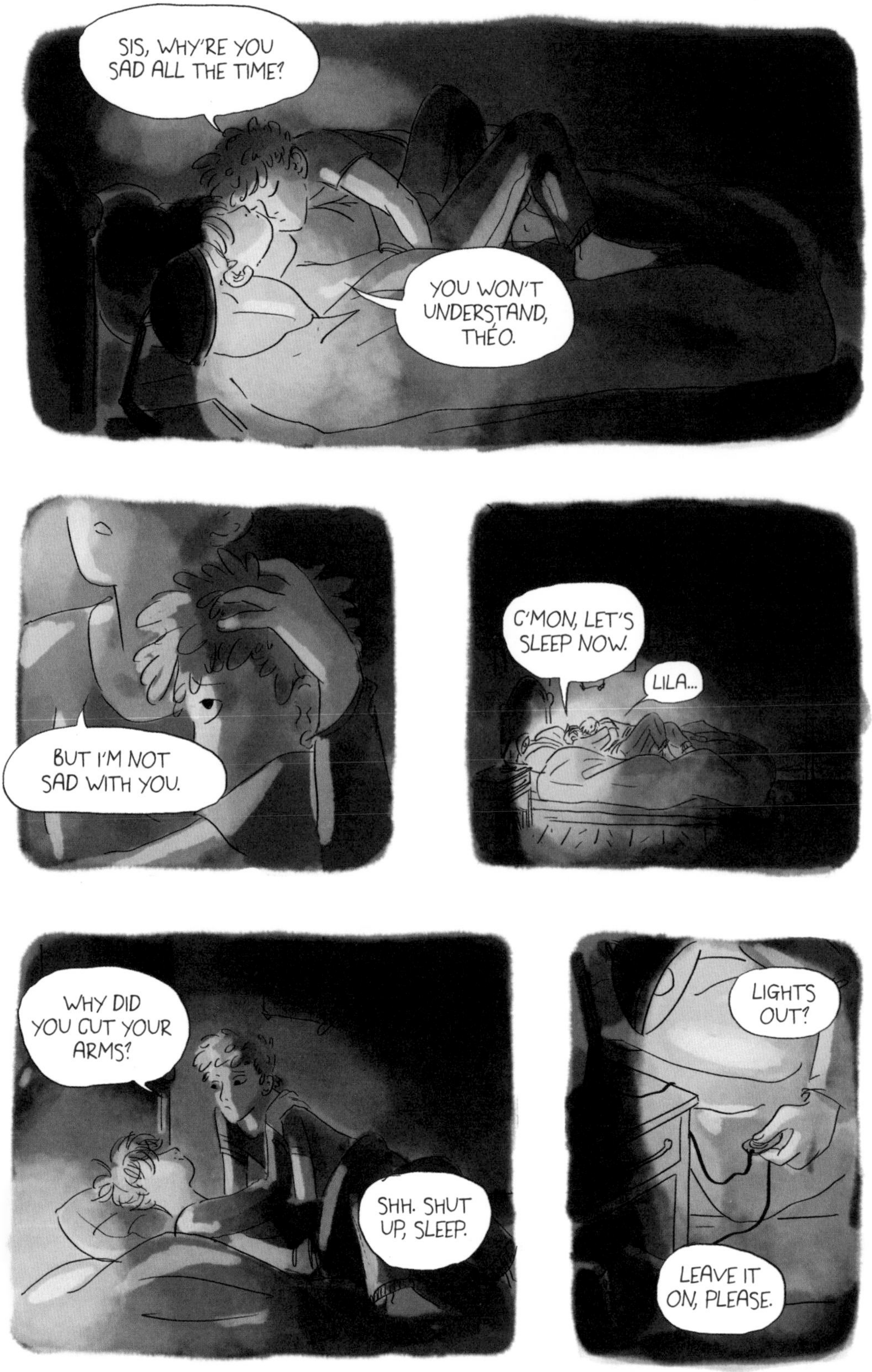
SIS, WHY'RE YOU SAD ALL THE TIME?
YOU WON'T UNDERSTAND, THÉO.
BUT I'M NOT SAD WITH YOU.
C'MON, LET'S SLEEP NOW.
LILA...
WHY DID YOU CUT YOUR ARMS?
SHH. SHUT UP, SLEEP.
LIGHTS OUT?
LEAVE IT ON, PLEASE.

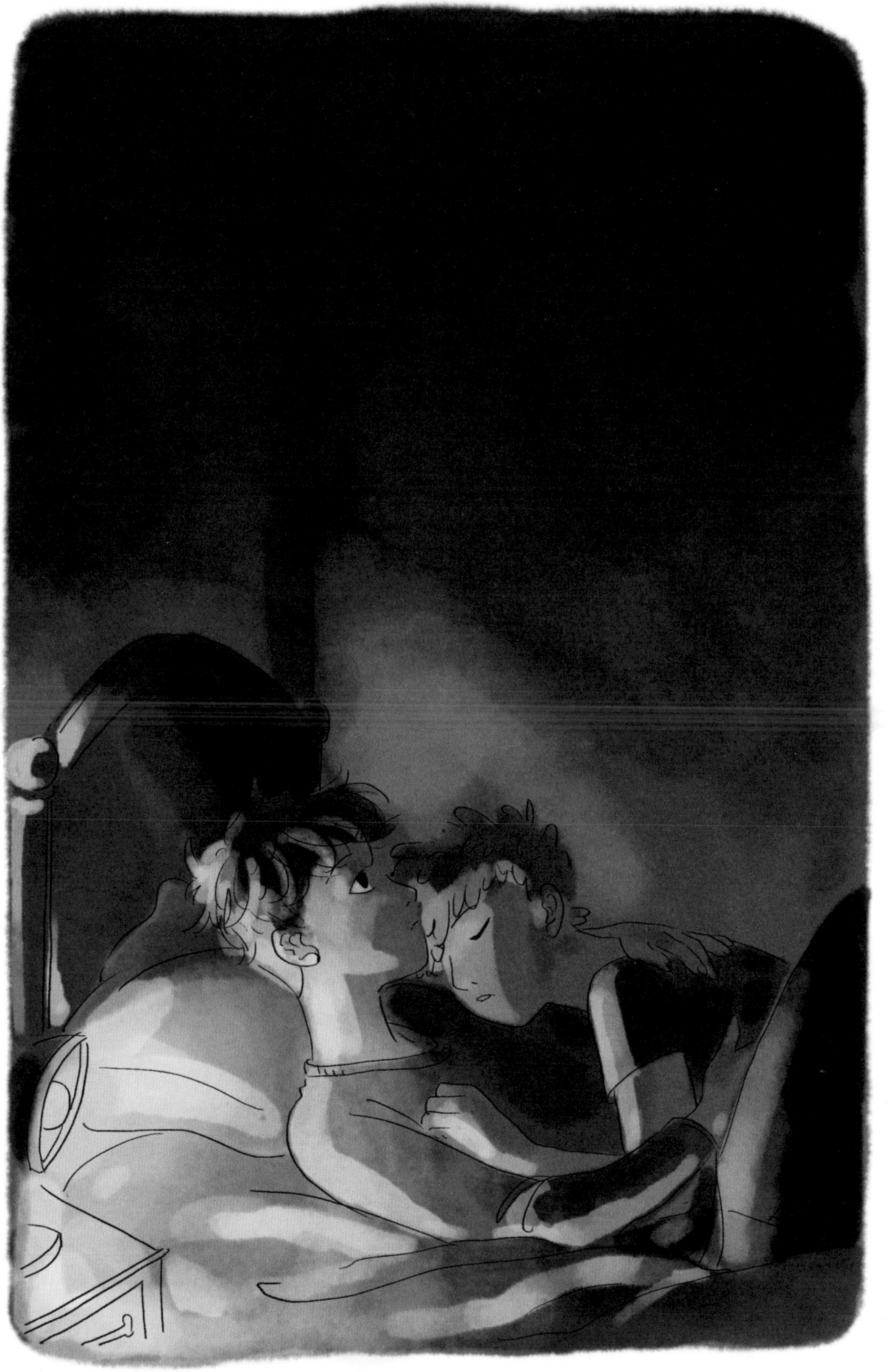

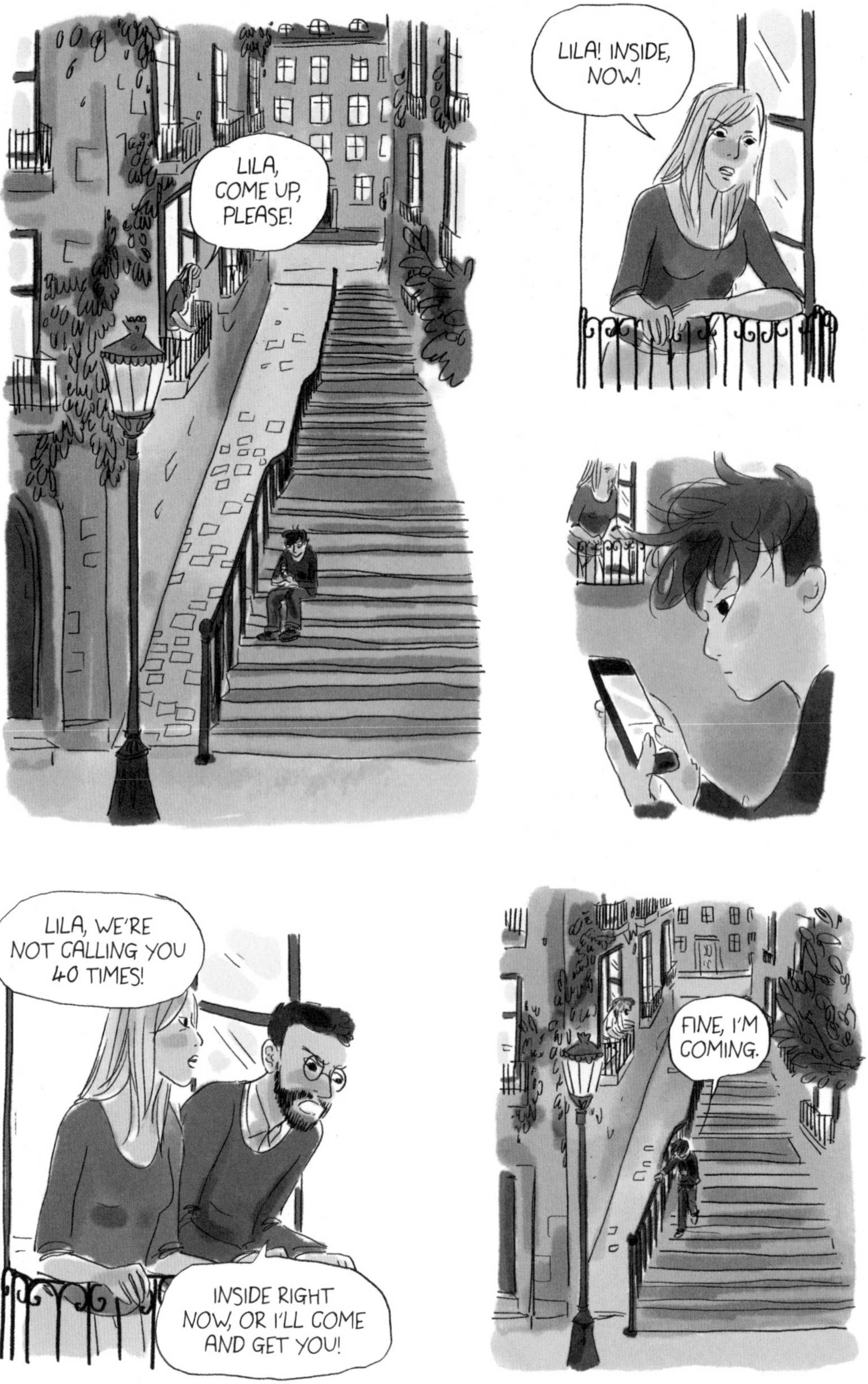
LILA, COME UP, PLEASE!
LILA! INSIDE, NOW!
LILA, WE'RE NOT CALLING YOU 40 TIMES!
INSIDE RIGHT NOW, OR I'LL COME AND GET YOU!
FINE, I'M COMING.

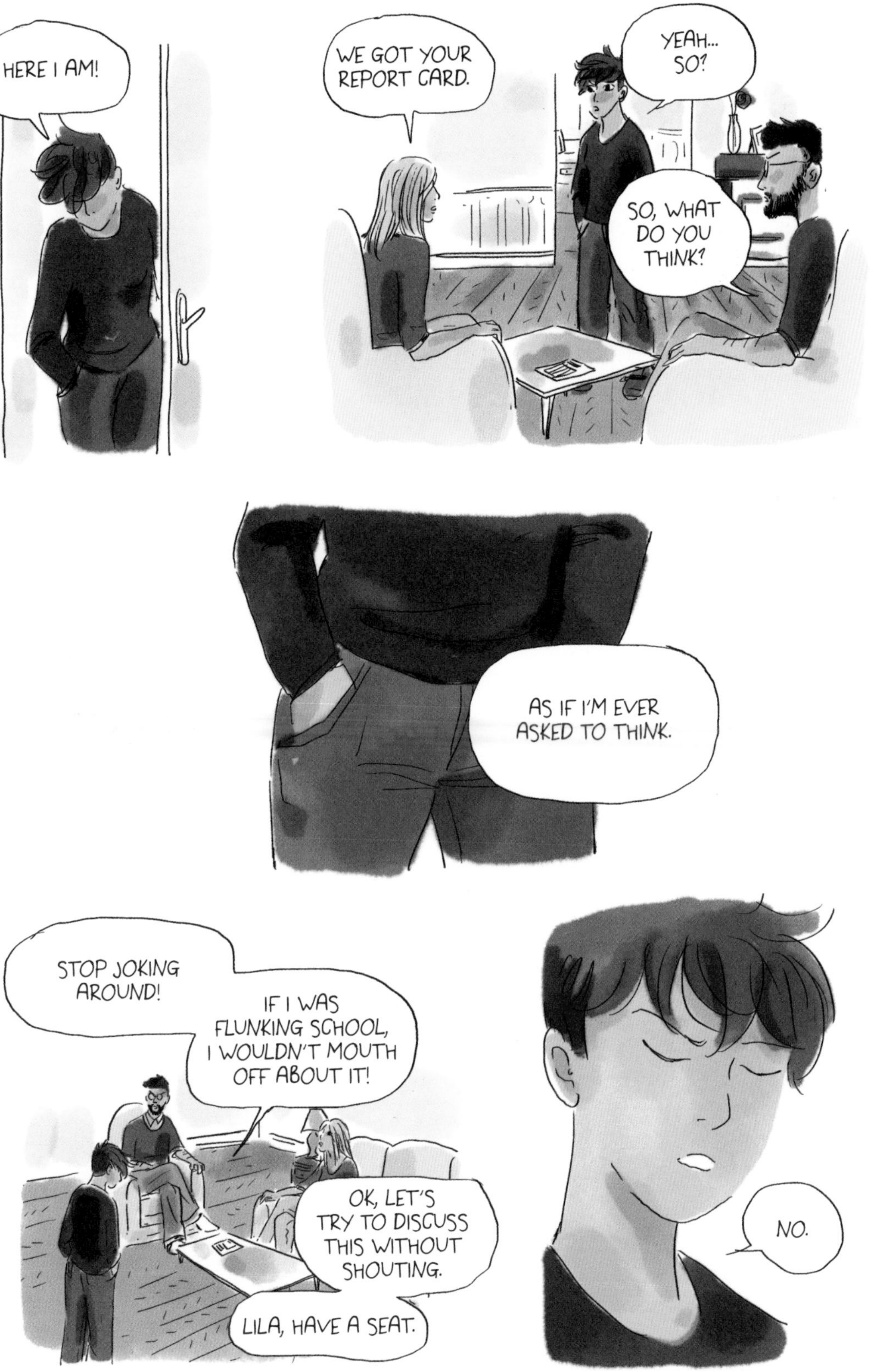
HERE I AM!
WE GOT YOUR REPORT CARD.
YEAH... SO?
SO, WHAT DO YOU THINK?
AS IF I'M EVER ASKED TO THINK.
STOP JOKING AROUND!
IF I WAS FLUNKING SCHOOL, I WOULDN'T MOUTH OFF ABOUT IT!
OK, LET'S TRY TO DISCUSS THIS WITHOUT SHOUTING.
LILA, HAVE A SEAT.
NO.

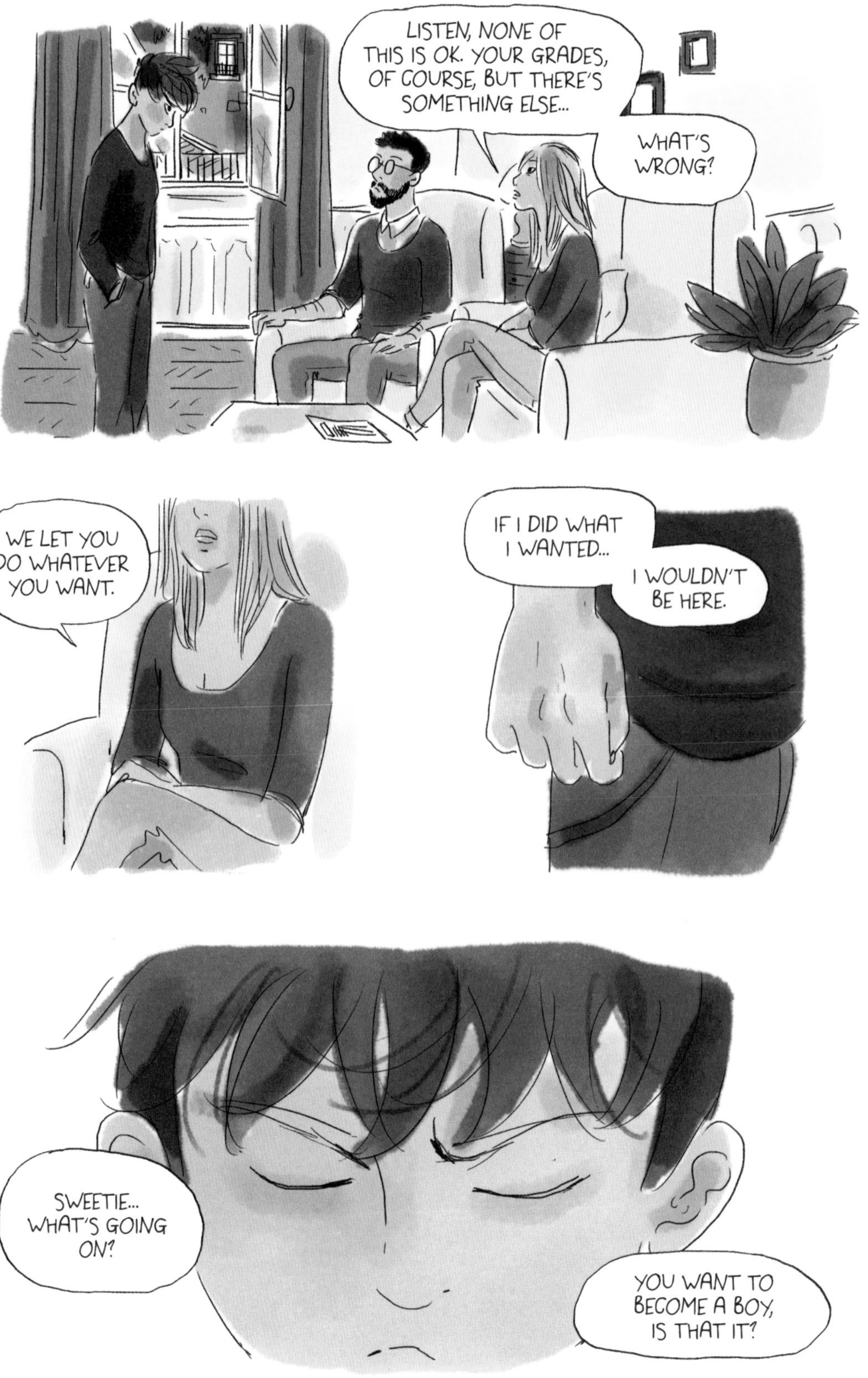
LISTEN, NONE OF THIS IS OK. YOUR GRADES, OF COURSE, BUT THERE'S SOMETHING ELSE...
WHAT'S WRONG?
WE LET YOU DO WHATEVER YOU WANT.
IF I DID WHAT I WANTED...
I WOULDN'T BE HERE.
SWEETIE... WHAT'S GOING ON?
YOU WANT TO BECOME A BOY, IS THAT IT?

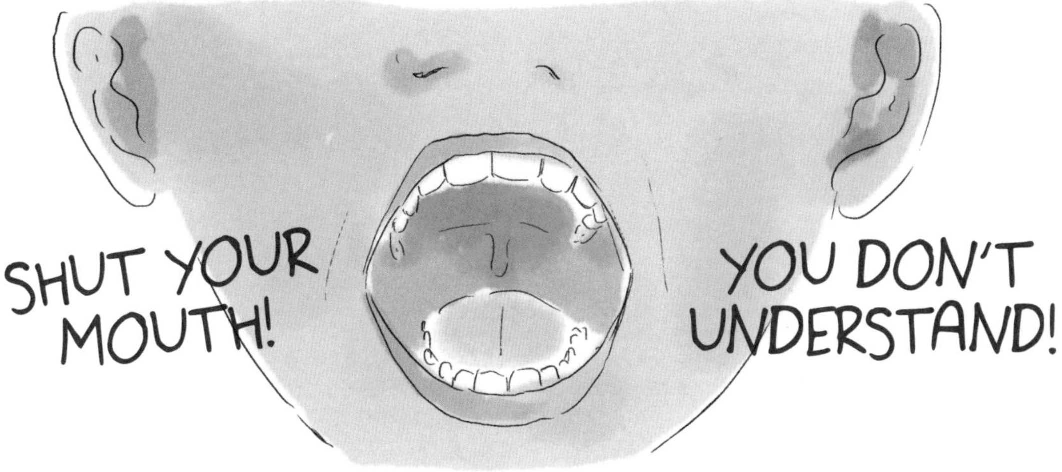
SHUT YOUR MOUTH!
YOU DON'T UNDERSTAND!

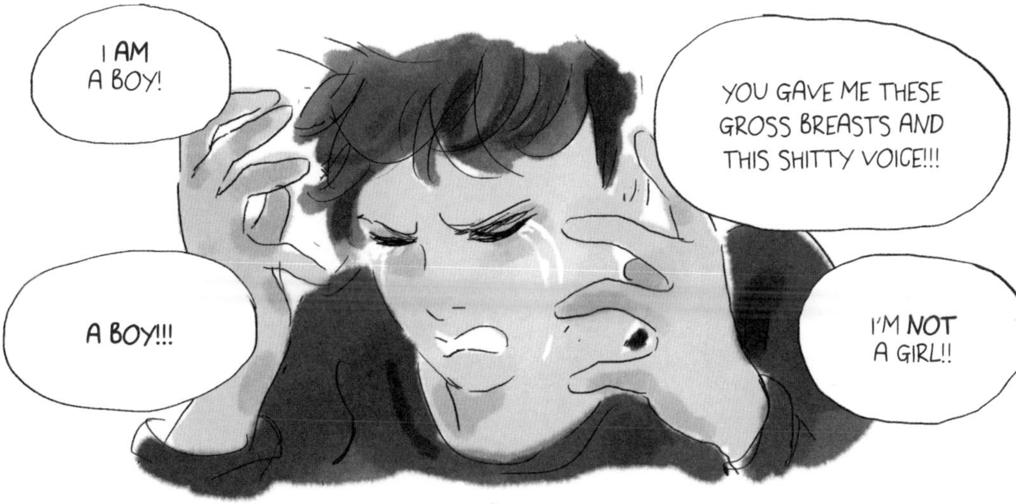
I AM A BOY!
YOU GAVE ME THESE GROSS BREASTS AND THIS SHITTY VOICE!!!
A BOY!!!
I'M NOT A GIRL!!

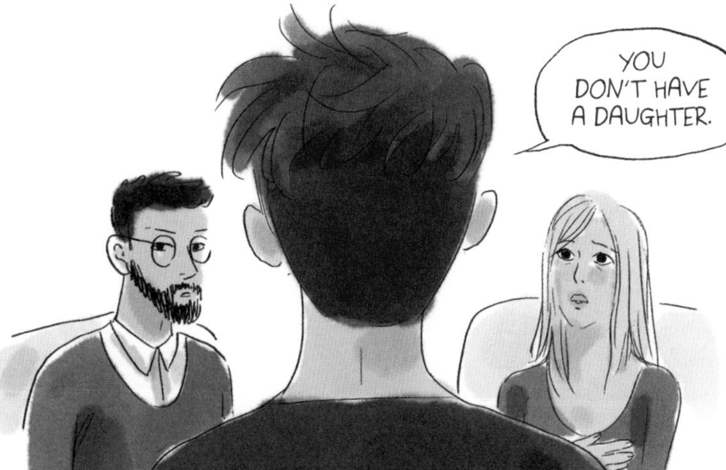
YOU DON'T HAVE A DAUGHTER.

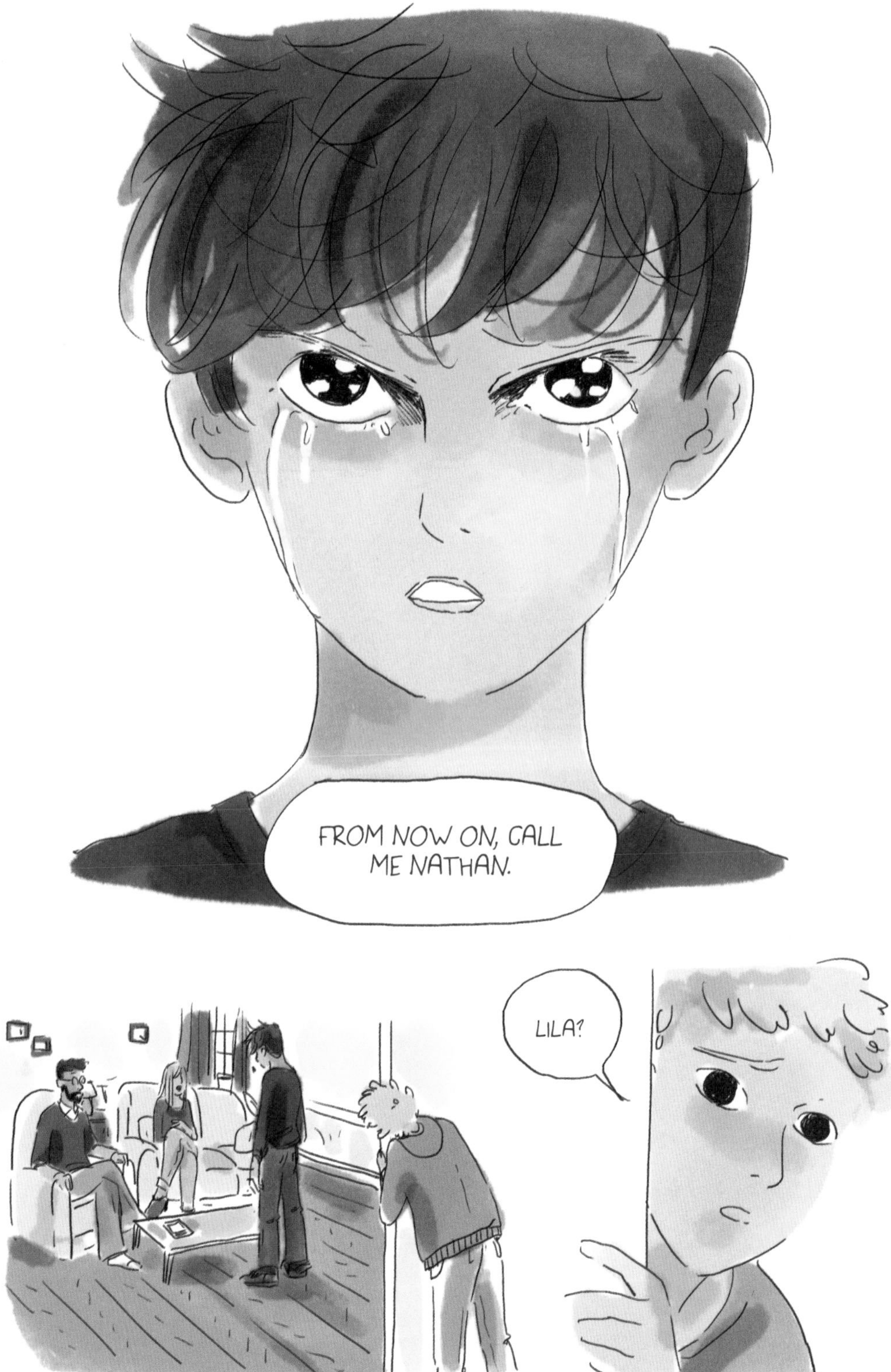
FROM NOW ON, CALL ME NATHAN.
LILA?

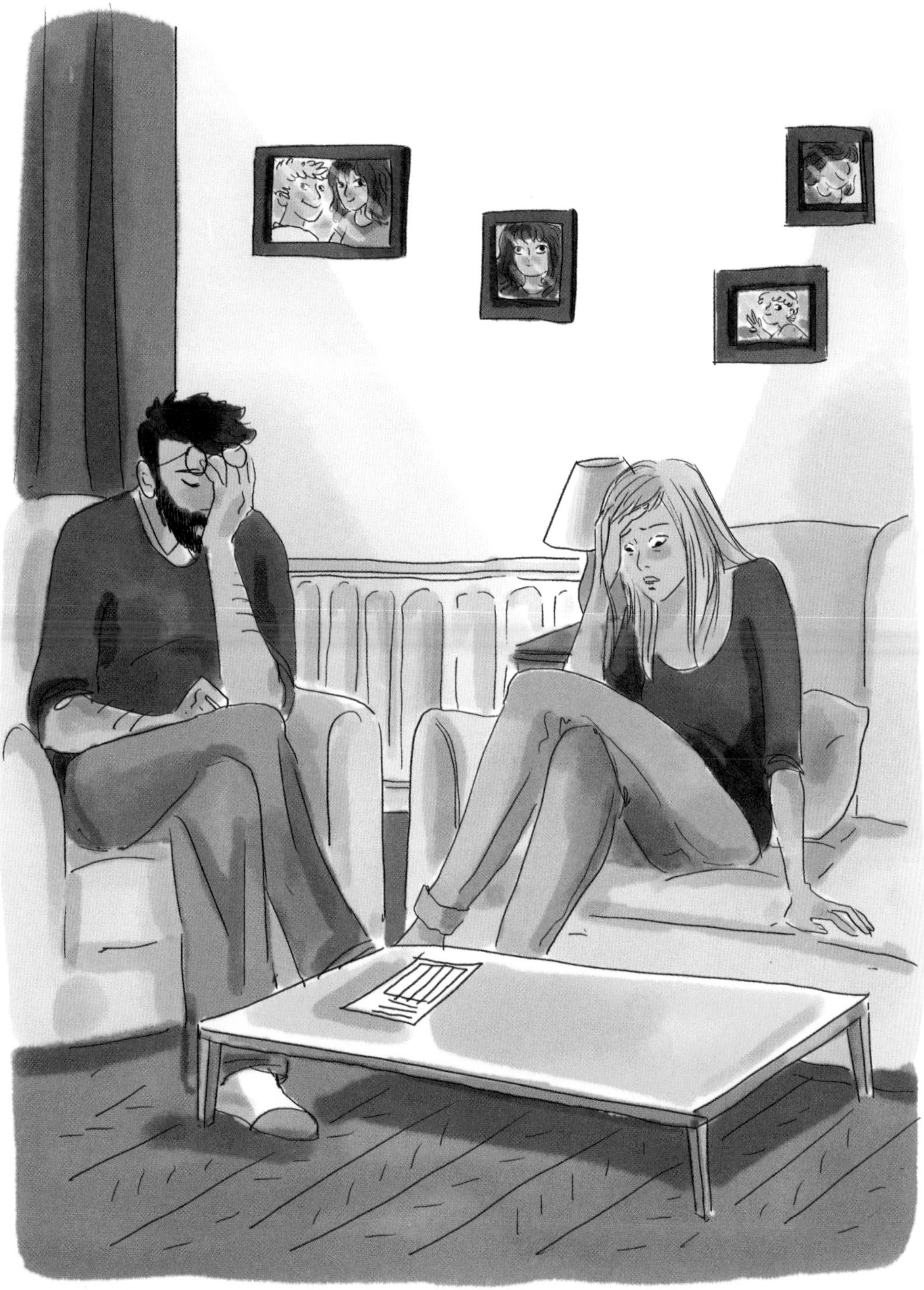

The party at my mother's childhood friend's place every 14 July always kicks off in style. These people are cool, the pool is, too, but we never see them in Paris.

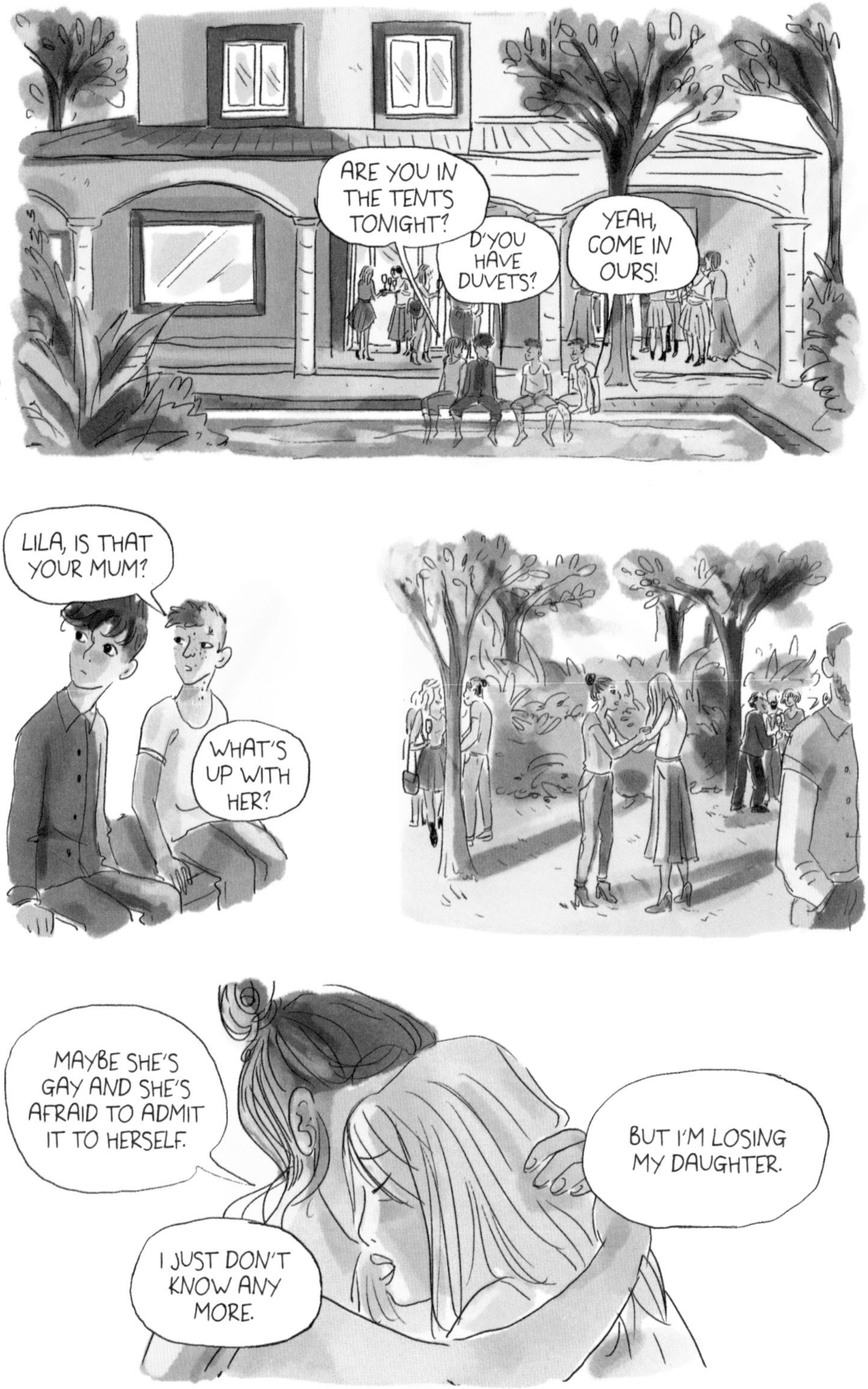
ARE YOU IN THE TENTS TONIGHT?
D'YOU HAVE DUVETS?
YEAH, COME IN OURS!
LILA, IS THAT YOUR MUM?
WHAT'S UP WITH HER?
MAYBE SHE'S GAY AND SHE'S AFRAID TO ADMIT IT TO HERSELF.
BUT I'M LOSING MY DAUGHTER.
I JUST DON'T KNOW ANY MORE.

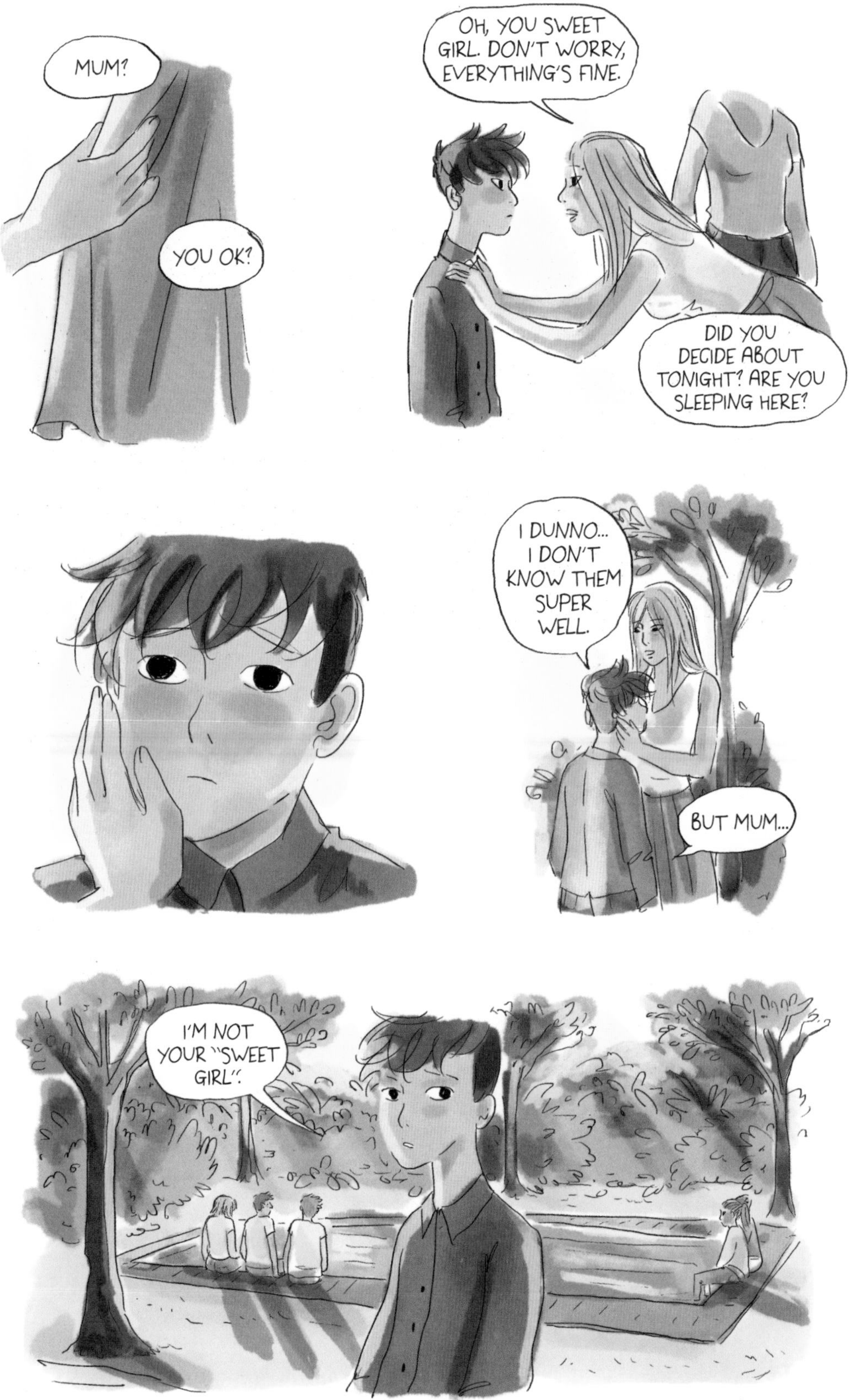
MUM?
YOU OK?
OH, YOU SWEET GIRL. DON'T WORRY, EVERYTHING'S FINE.
DID YOU DECIDE ABOUT TONIGHT? ARE YOU SLEEPING HERE?
I DUNNO... I DON'T KNOW THEM SUPER WELL.
BUT MUM...
I'M NOT YOUR "SWEET GIRL".
...your sweet boy.

This feeling with Sam and Noah is weird: we've known each other since we were kids, but we're strangers. They don't know anything about me, except that I was the only girl who played with them. Having to explain who I am, that's my weird life.

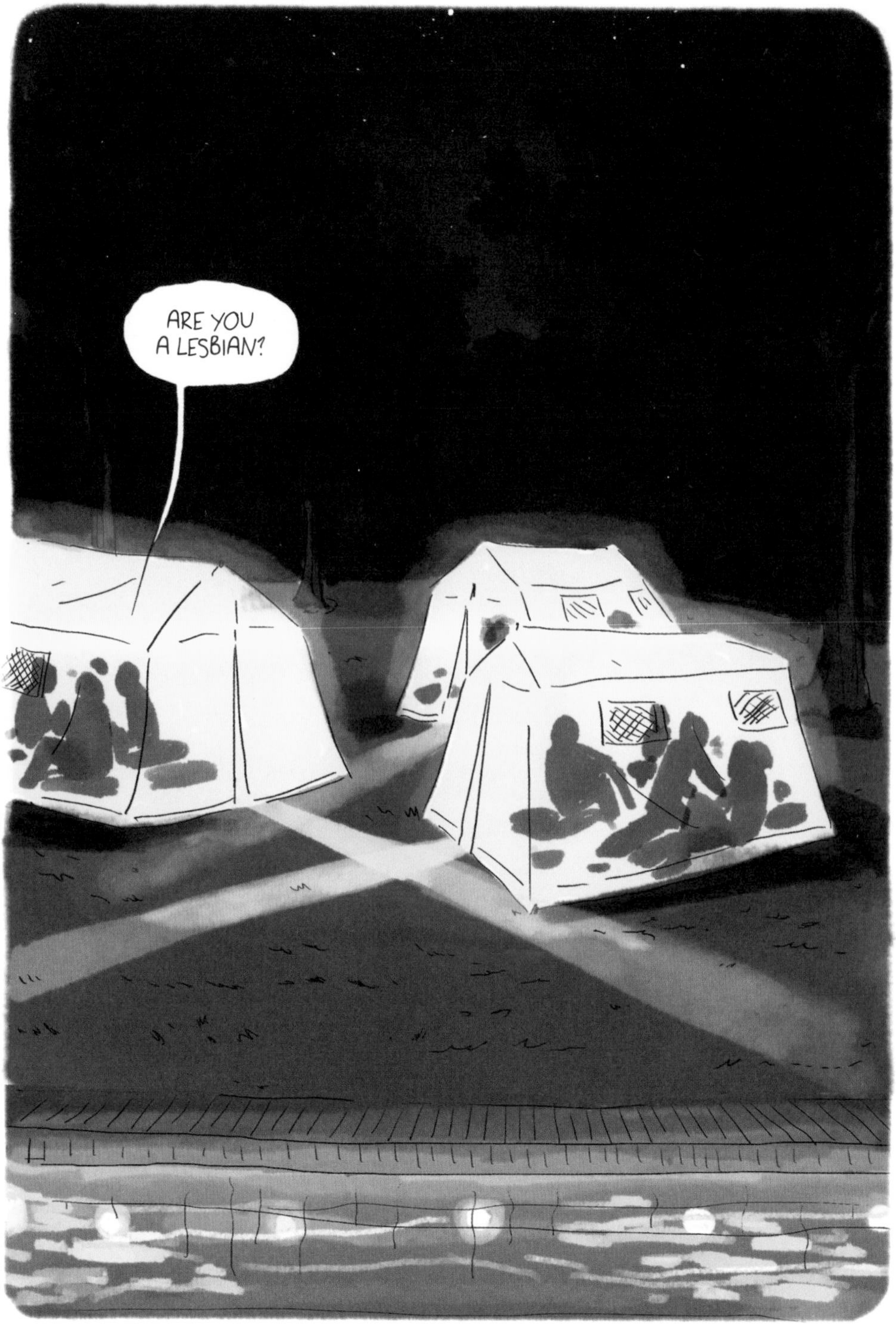
ARE YOU A LESBIAN?

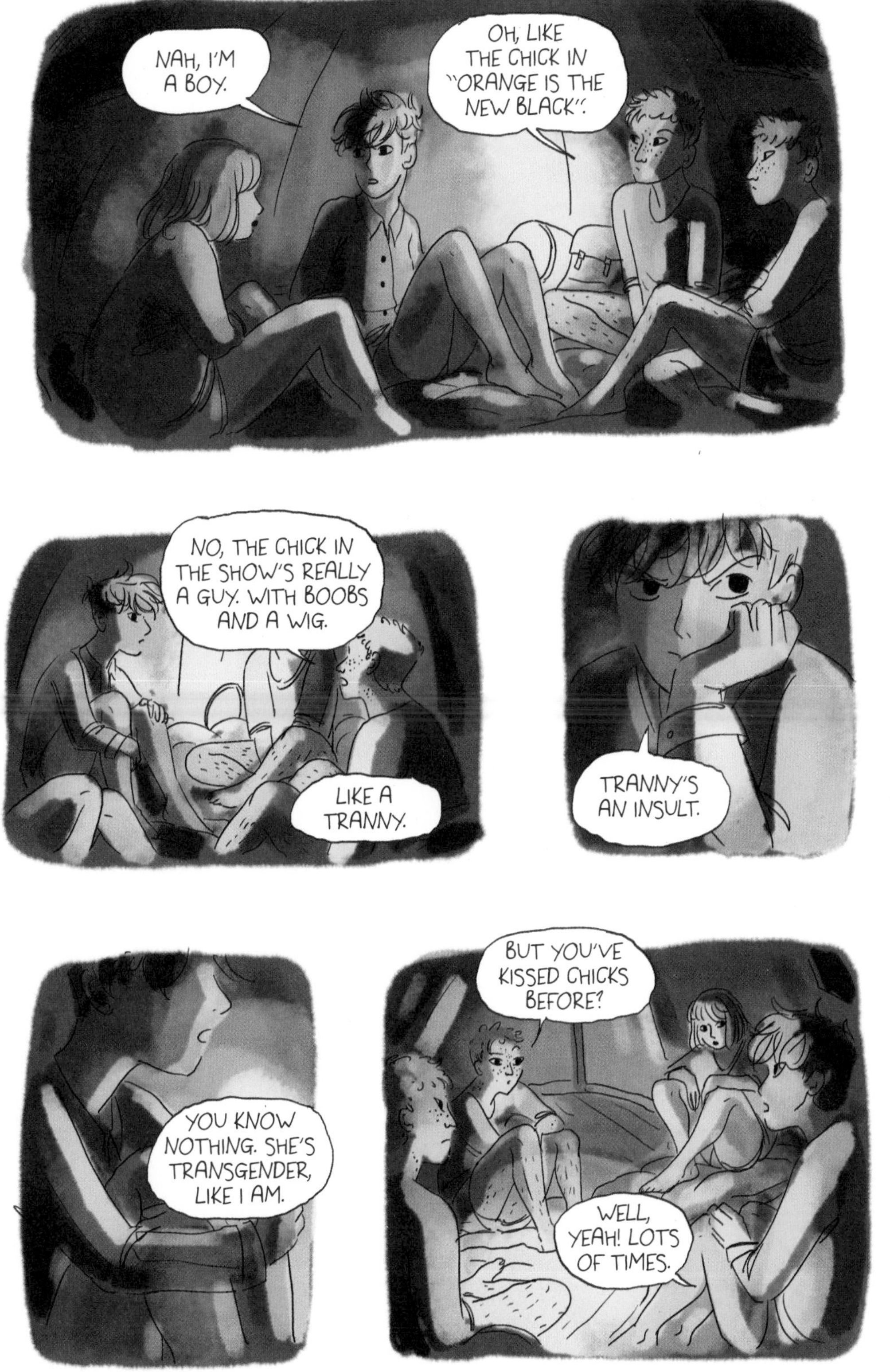
NAH, I'M A BOY.
OH, LIKE THE CHICK IN "ORANGE IS THE NEW BLACK".
NO, THE CHICK IN THE SHOW'S REALLY A GUY. WITH BOOBS AND A WIG.
LIKE A TRANNY.
TRANNY'S AN INSULT.
YOU KNOW NOTHING. SHE'S TRANSGENDER, LIKE I AM.
BUT YOU'VE KISSED CHICKS BEFORE?
WELL, YEAH! LOTS OF TIMES.

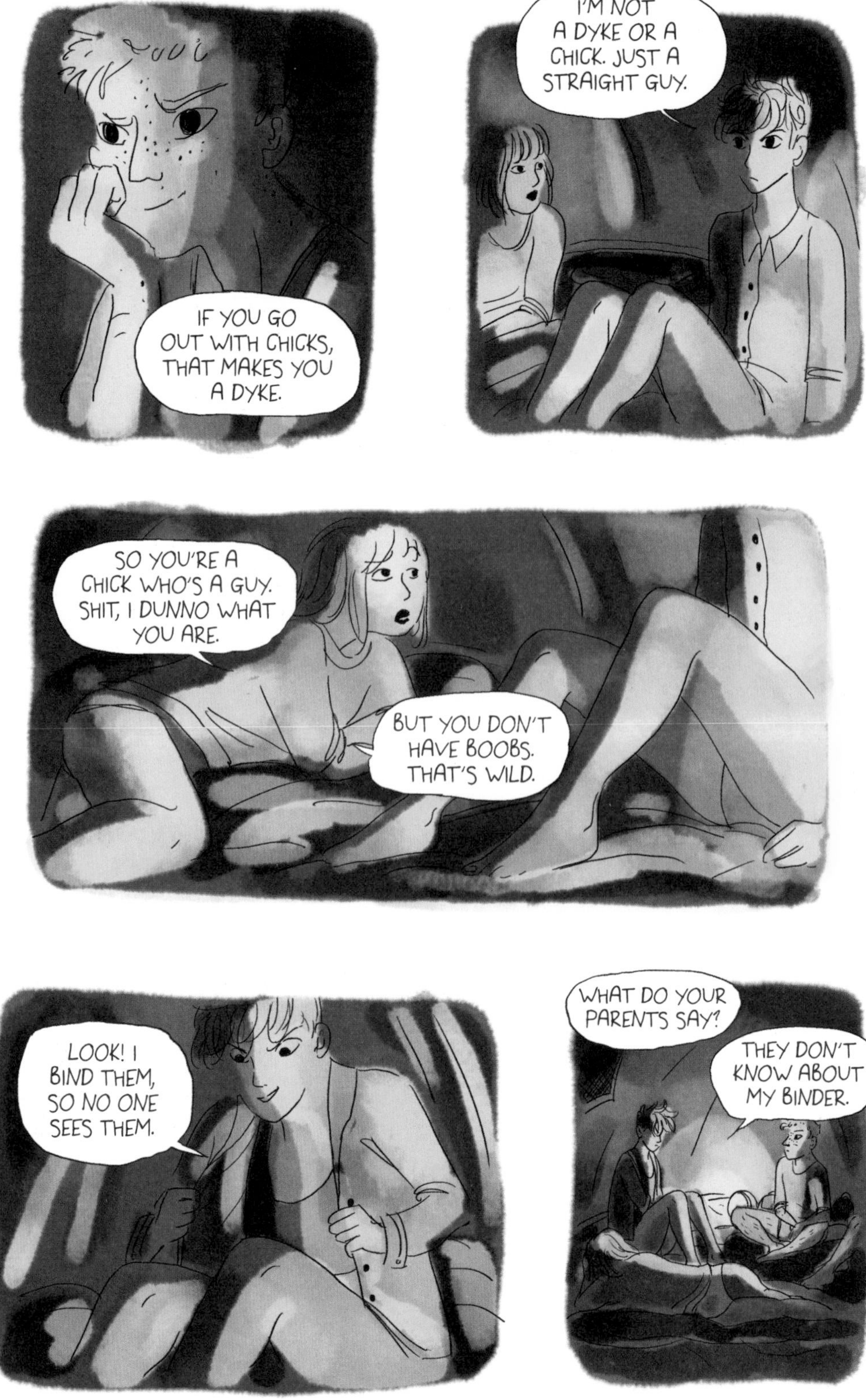
IF YOU GO OUT WITH CHICKS, THAT MAKES YOU A DYKE.
I'M NOT A DYKE OR A CHICK. JUST A STRAIGHT GUY.
SO YOU'RE A CHICK WHO'S A GUY. SHIT, I DUNNO WHAT YOU ARE.
BUT YOU DON'T HAVE BOOBS. THAT'S WILD.
LOOK! I BIND THEM, SO NO ONE SEES THEM.
WHAT DO YOUR PARENTS SAY?
THEY DON'T KNOW ABOUT MY BINDER.

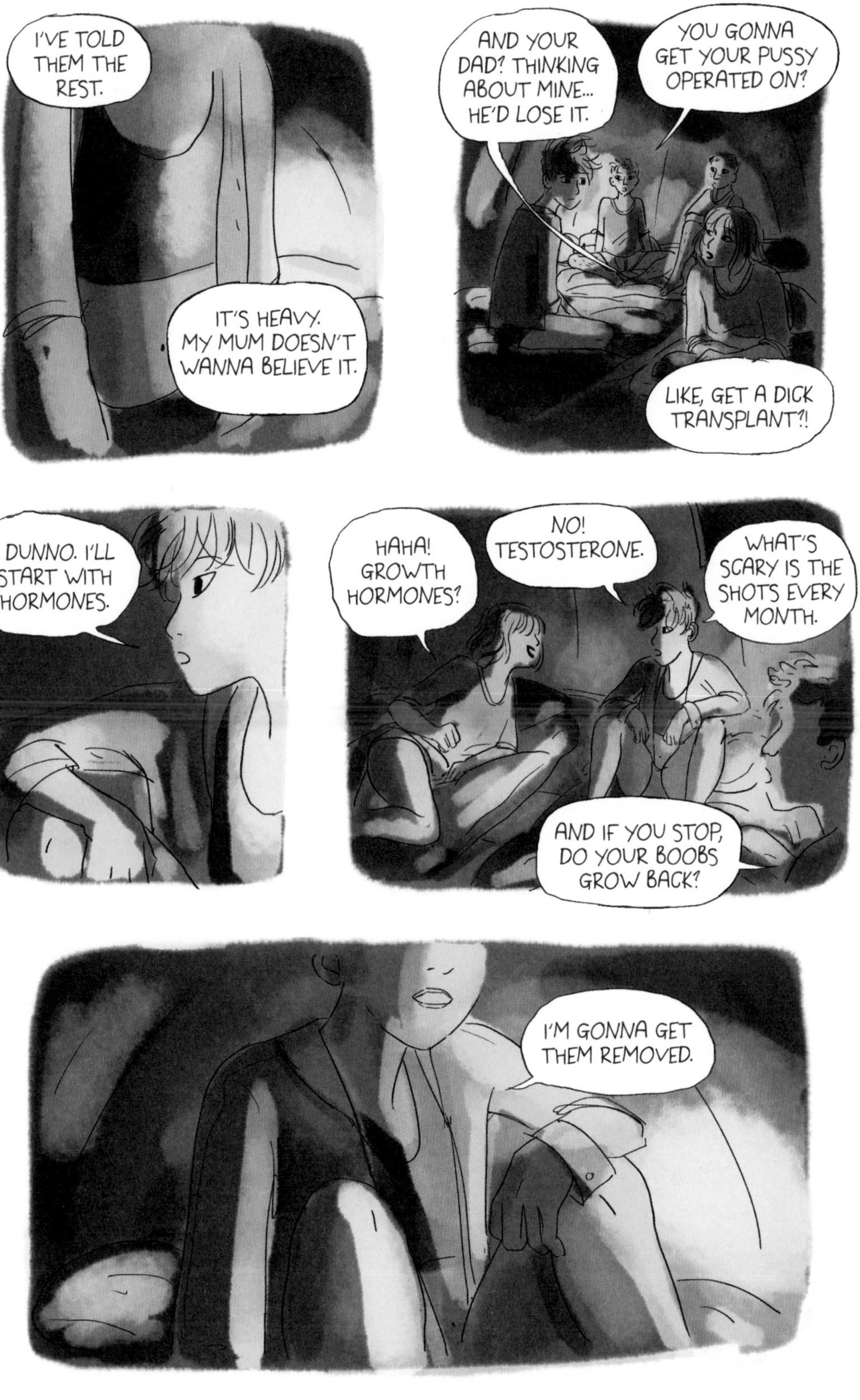
I'VE TOLD THEM THE REST.
IT'S HEAVY. MY MUM DOESN'T WANNA BELIEVE IT.
AND YOUR DAD? THINKING ABOUT MINE... HE'D LOSE IT.
YOU GONNA GET YOUR PUSSY OPERATED ON?
LIKE, GET A DICK TRANSPLANT?!
I DUNNO. I'LL START WITH HORMONES.
HAHA! GROWTH HORMONES?
NO! TESTOSTERONE.
WHAT'S SCARY IS THE SHOTS EVERY MONTH.
AND IF YOU STOP, DO YOUR BOOBS GROW BACK?
I'M GONNA GET THEM REMOVED.

My parents are worried. I hear them talking at night.
Théo's freaked out, too.

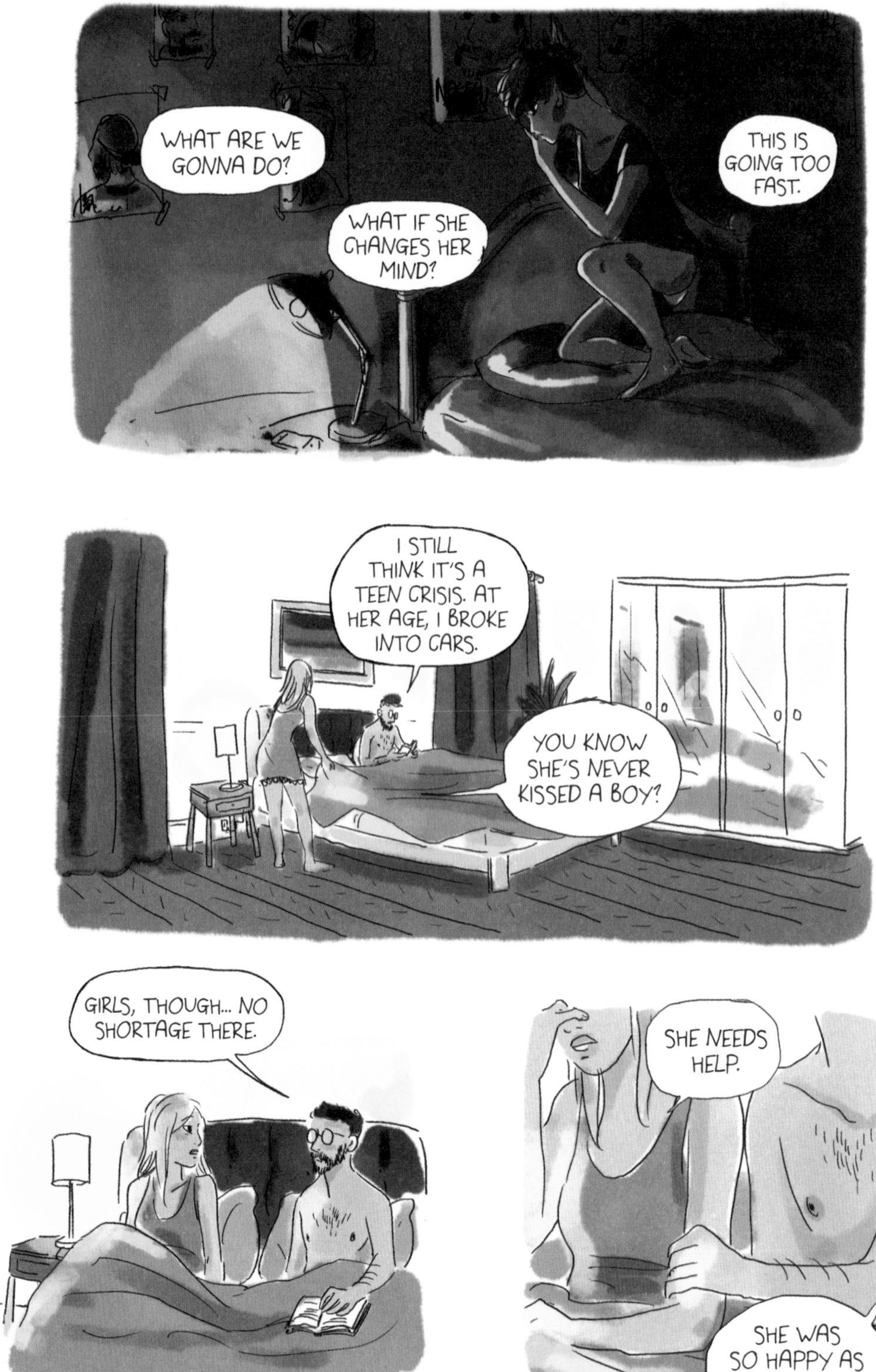
WHAT ARE WE GONNA DO?
WHAT IF SHE CHANGES HER MIND?
THIS IS GOING TOO FAST.
I STILL THINK IT'S A TEEN CRISIS. AT HER AGE, I BROKE INTO CARS.
YOU KNOW SHE'S NEVER KISSED A BOY?
GIRLS, THOUGH... NO SHORTAGE THERE.
SHE NEEDS HELP.
SHE WAS SO HAPPY AS A KID.

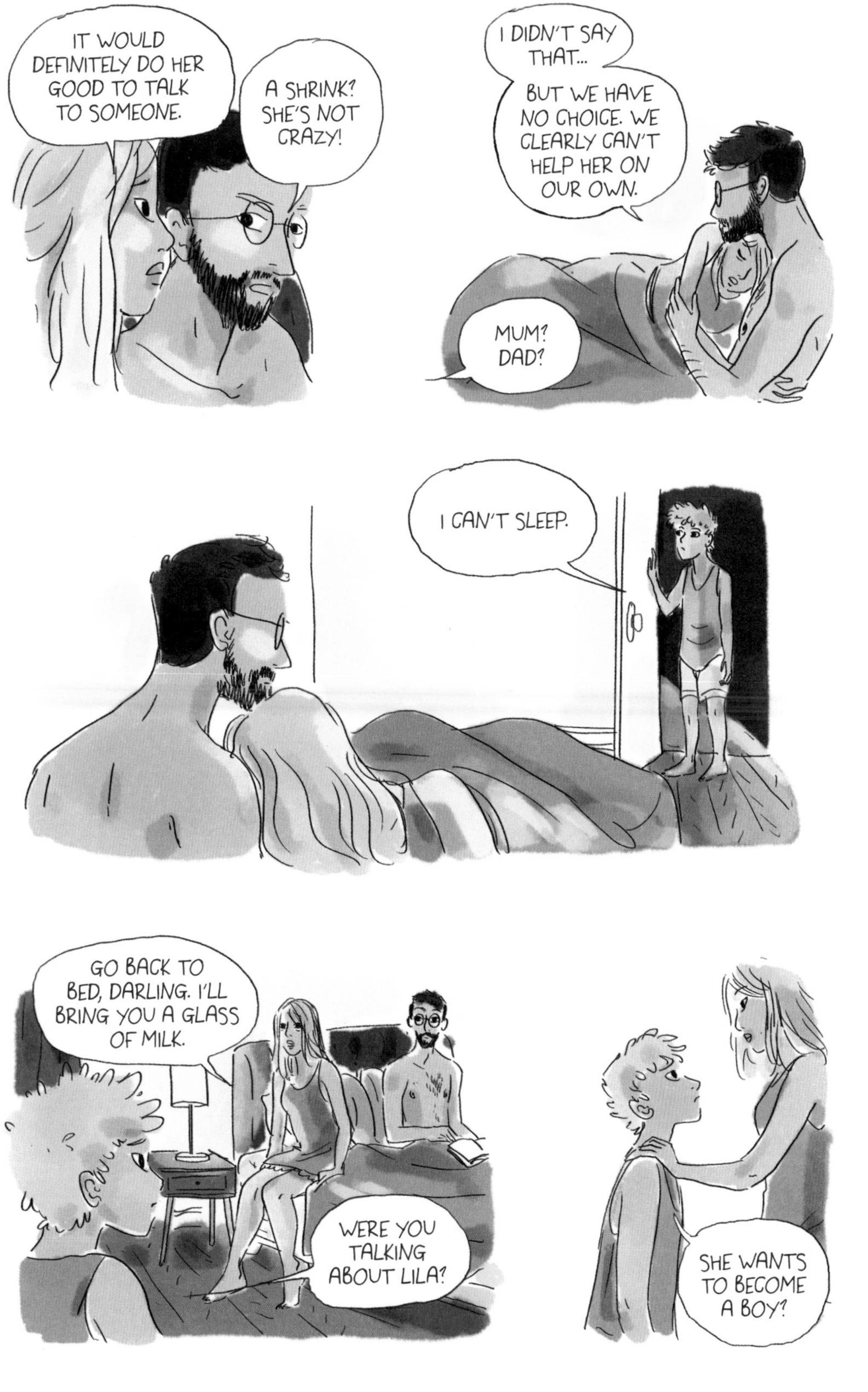
IT WOULD DEFINITELY DO HER GOOD TO TALK TO SOMEONE.
A SHRINK? SHE'S NOT CRAZY!
I DIDN'T SAY THAT...
BUT WE HAVE NO CHOICE. WE CLEARLY CAN'T HELP HER ON OUR OWN.
MUM? DAD?
I CAN'T SLEEP.
GO BACK TO BED, DARLING. I'LL BRING YOU A GLASS OF MILK.
WERE YOU TALKING ABOUT LILA?
SHE WANTS TO BECOME A BOY?

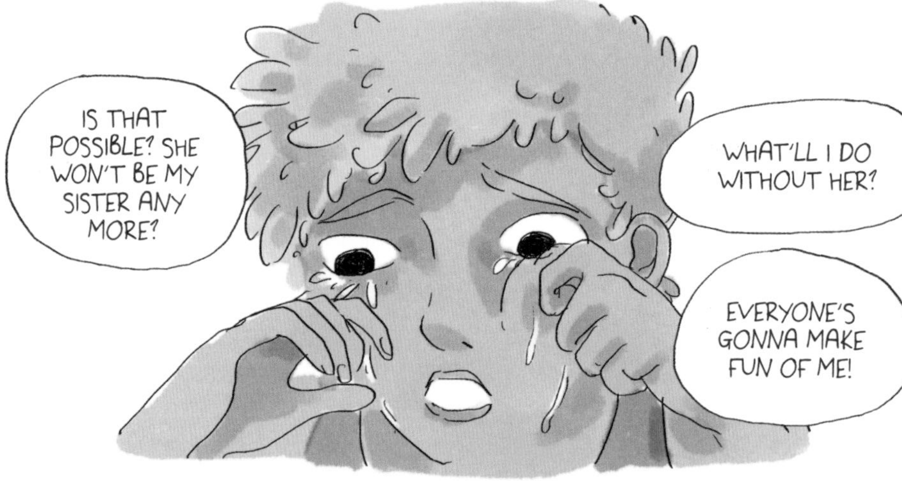
IS THAT POSSIBLE? SHE WON'T BE MY SISTER ANY MORE?
WHAT'LL I DO WITHOUT HER?
EVERYONE'S GONNA MAKE FUN OF ME!

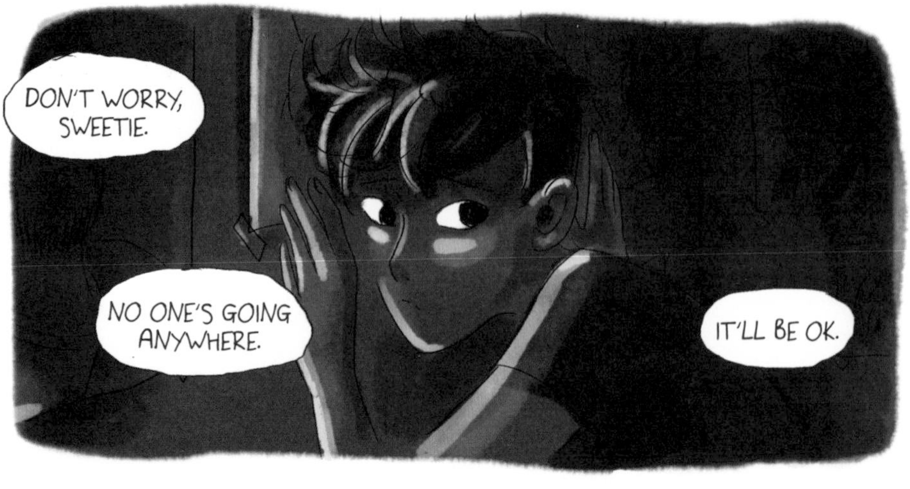
DON'T WORRY, SWEETIE.
NO ONE'S GOING ANYWHERE.
IT'LL BE OK.

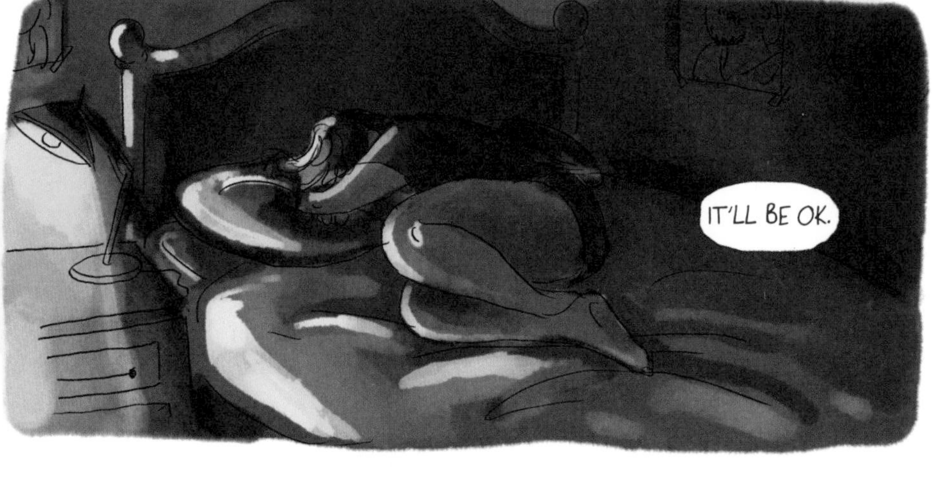
IT'LL BE OK.

At school, the teachers are cool with me. I think they understand.

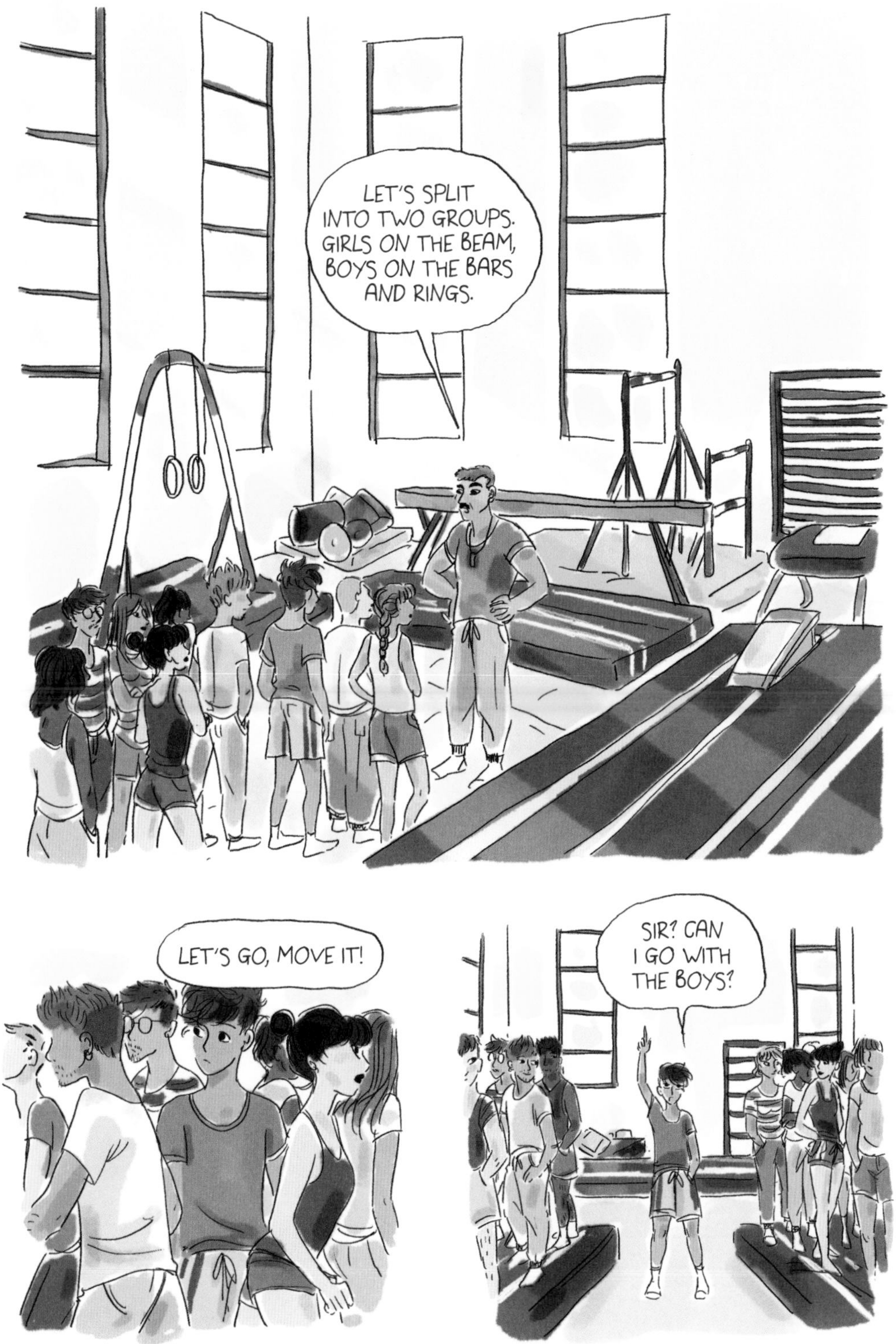
LET'S SPLIT INTO TWO GROUPS. GIRLS ON THE BEAM, BOYS ON THE BARS AND RINGS.
LET'S GO, MOVE IT!
SIR? CAN I GO WITH THE BOYS?

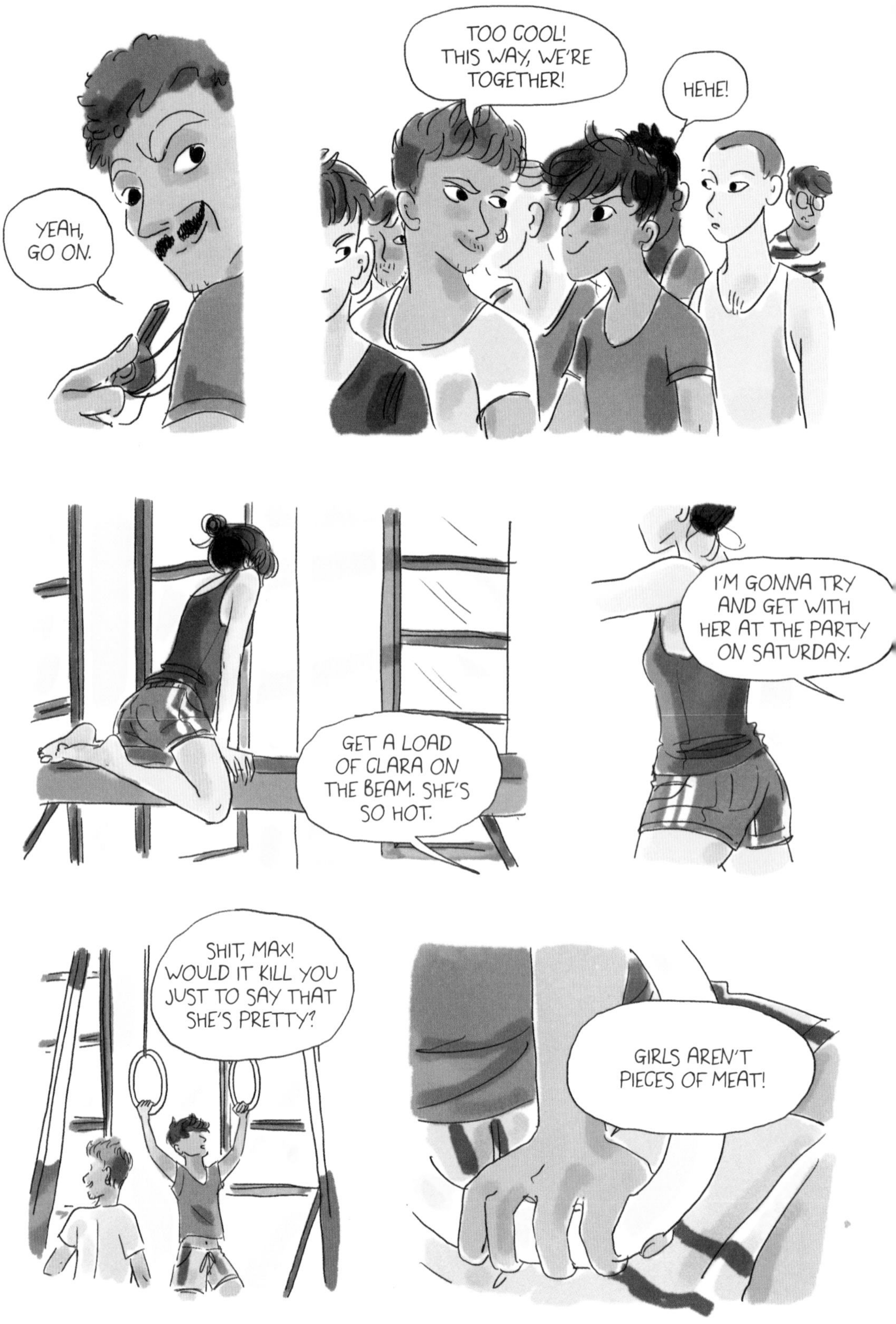
YEAH, GO ON.
TOO COOL! THIS WAY, WE'RE TOGETHER!
HEHE!
GET A LOAD OF CLARA ON THE BEAM. SHE'S SO HOT.
I'M GONNA TRY AND GET WITH HER AT THE PARTY ON SATURDAY.
SHIT, MAX! WOULD IT KILL YOU JUST TO SAY THAT SHE'S PRETTY?
GIRLS AREN'T PIECES OF MEAT!

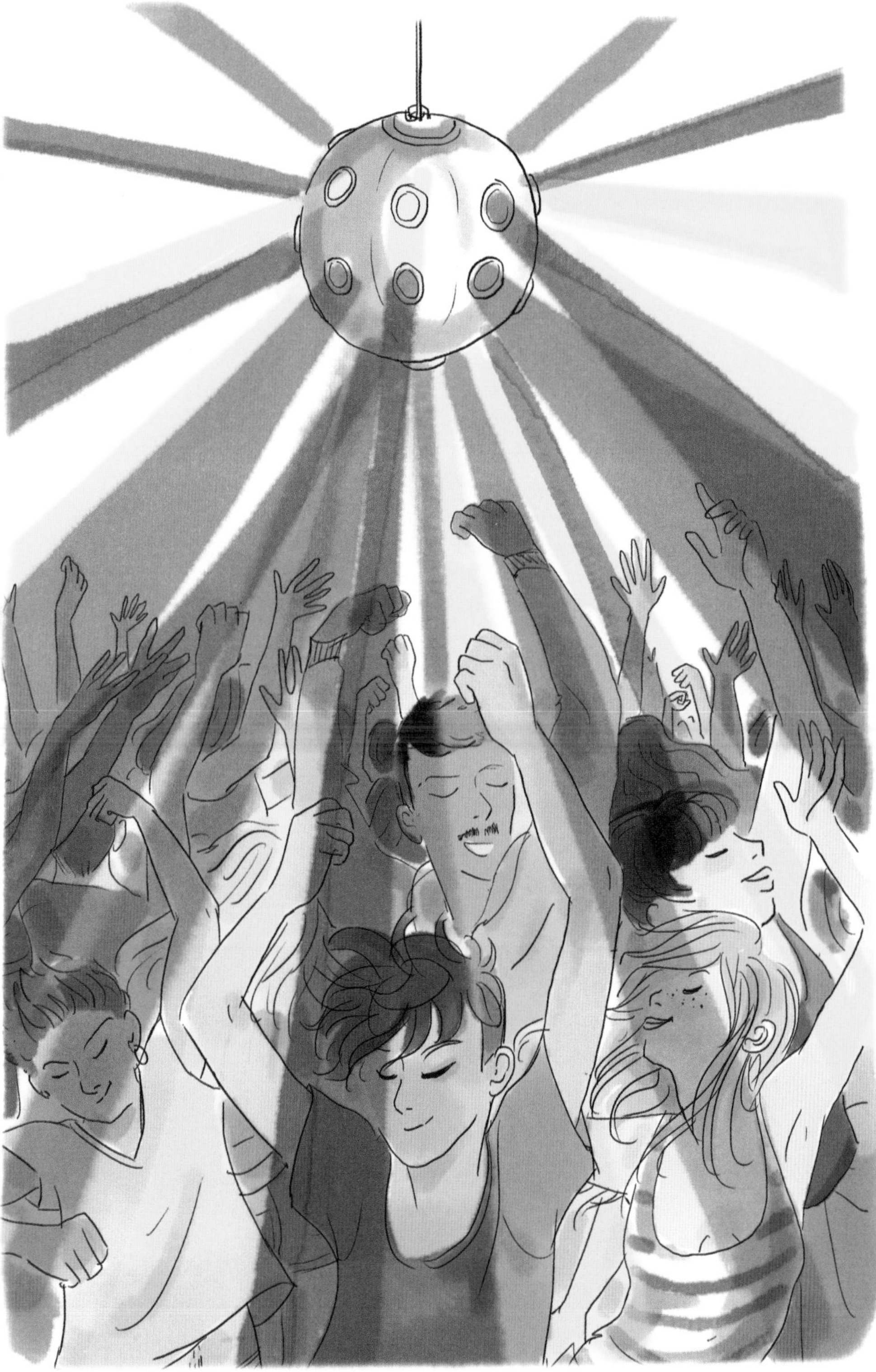

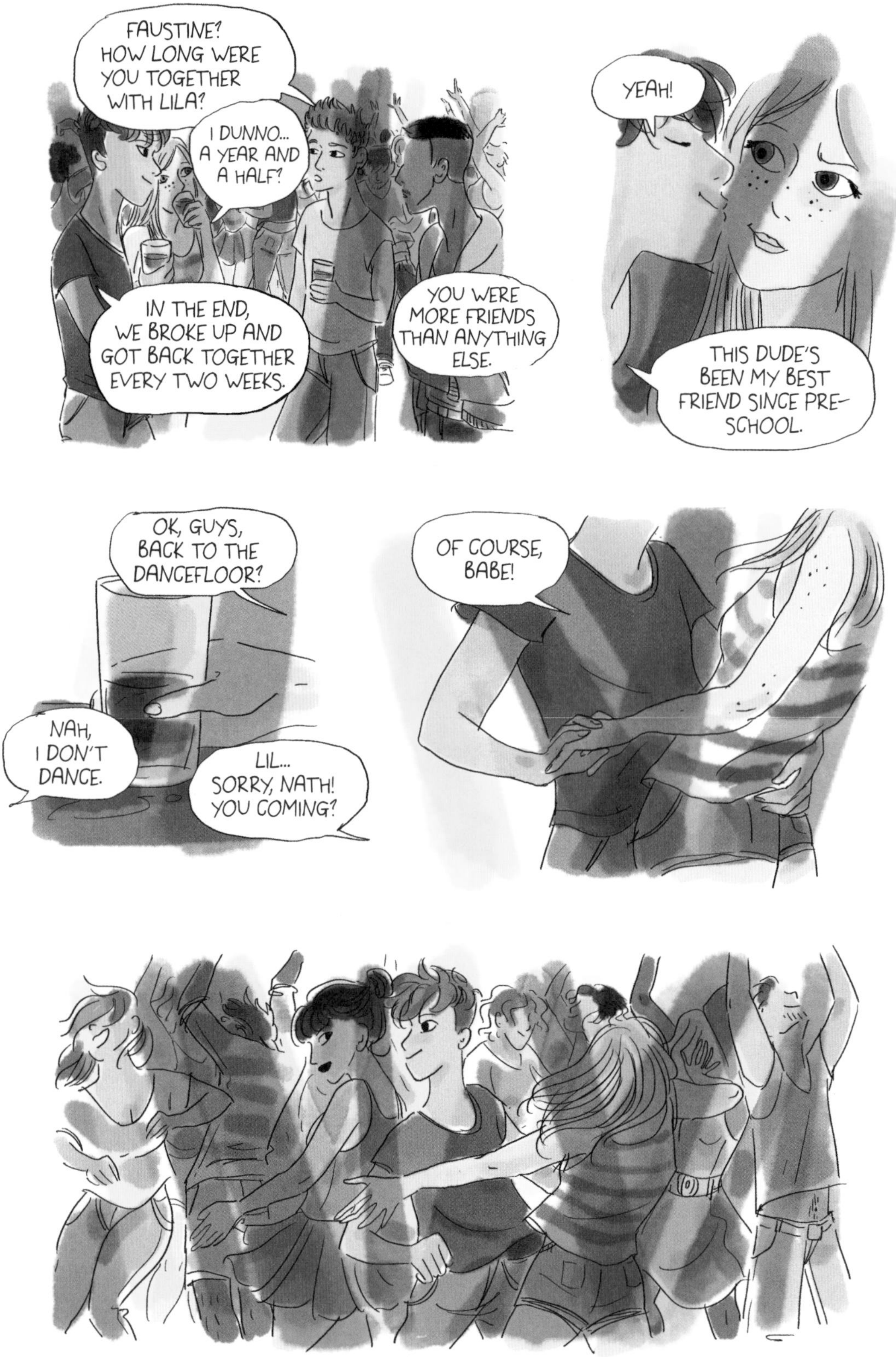
FAUSTINE? HOW LONG WERE YOU TOGETHER WITH LILA?
I DUNNO... A YEAR AND A HALF?
IN THE END, WE BROKE UP AND GOT BACK TOGETHER EVERY TWO WEEKS.
YOU WERE MORE FRIENDS THAN ANYTHING ELSE.
YEAH!
THIS DUDE'S BEEN MY BEST FRIEND SINCE PRE-SCHOOL.
OK, GUYS, BACK TO THE DANCEFLOOR?
NAH, I DON'T DANCE.
LIL... SORRY, NATH! YOU COMING?
OF COURSE, BABE!

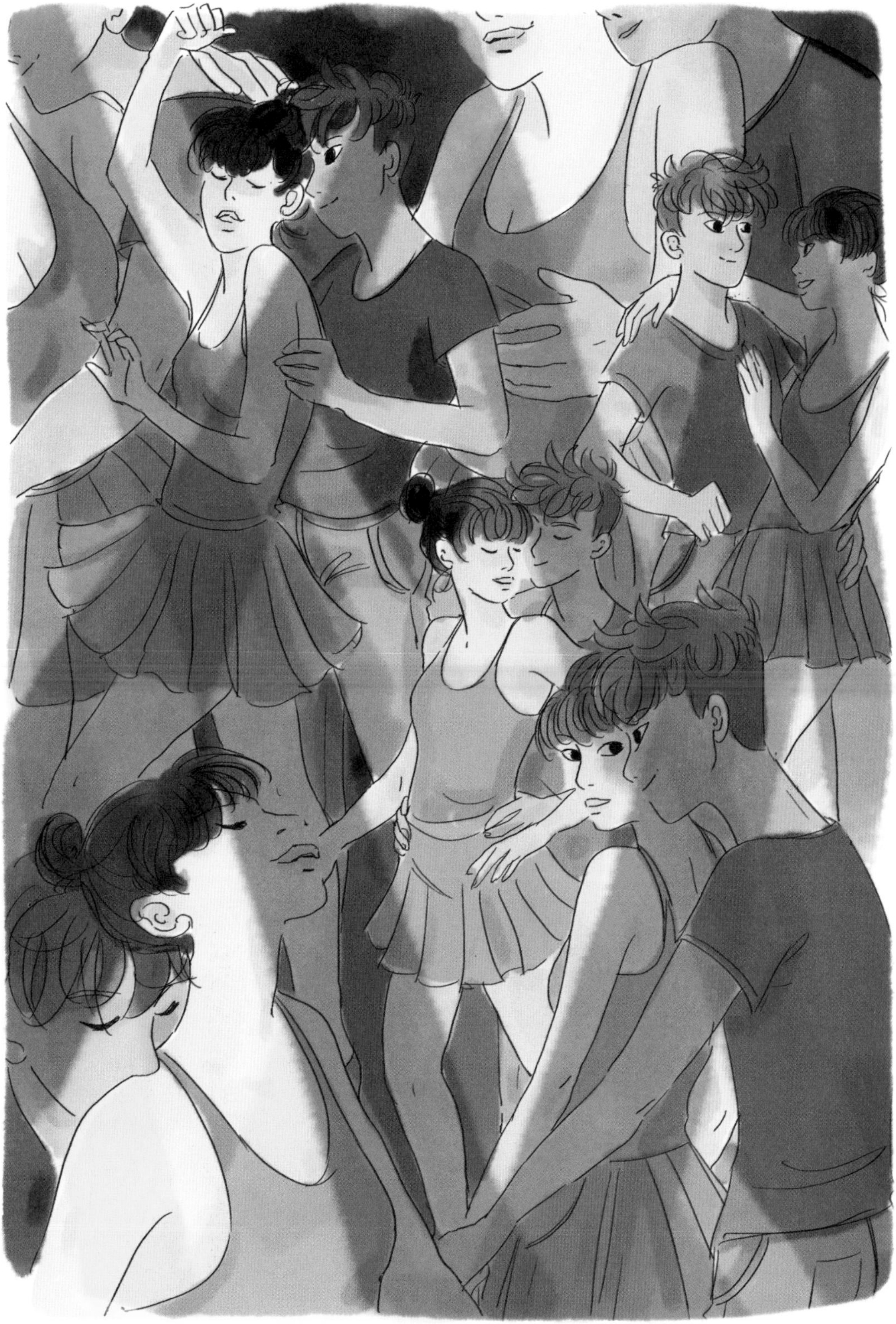

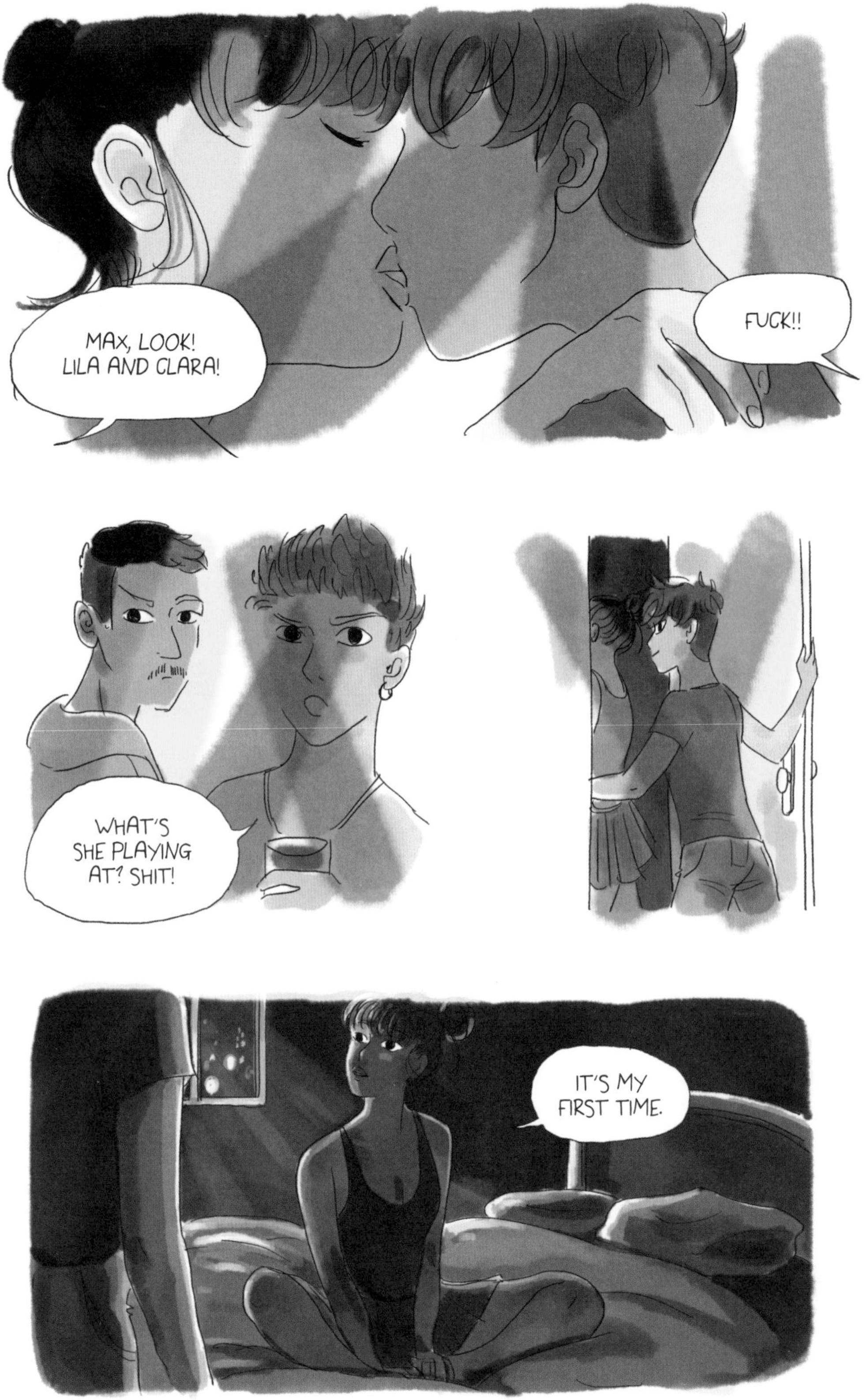
MAX, LOOK! LILA AND CLARA!
FUCK!!
WHAT'S SHE PLAYING AT? SHIT!
IT'S MY FIRST TIME.

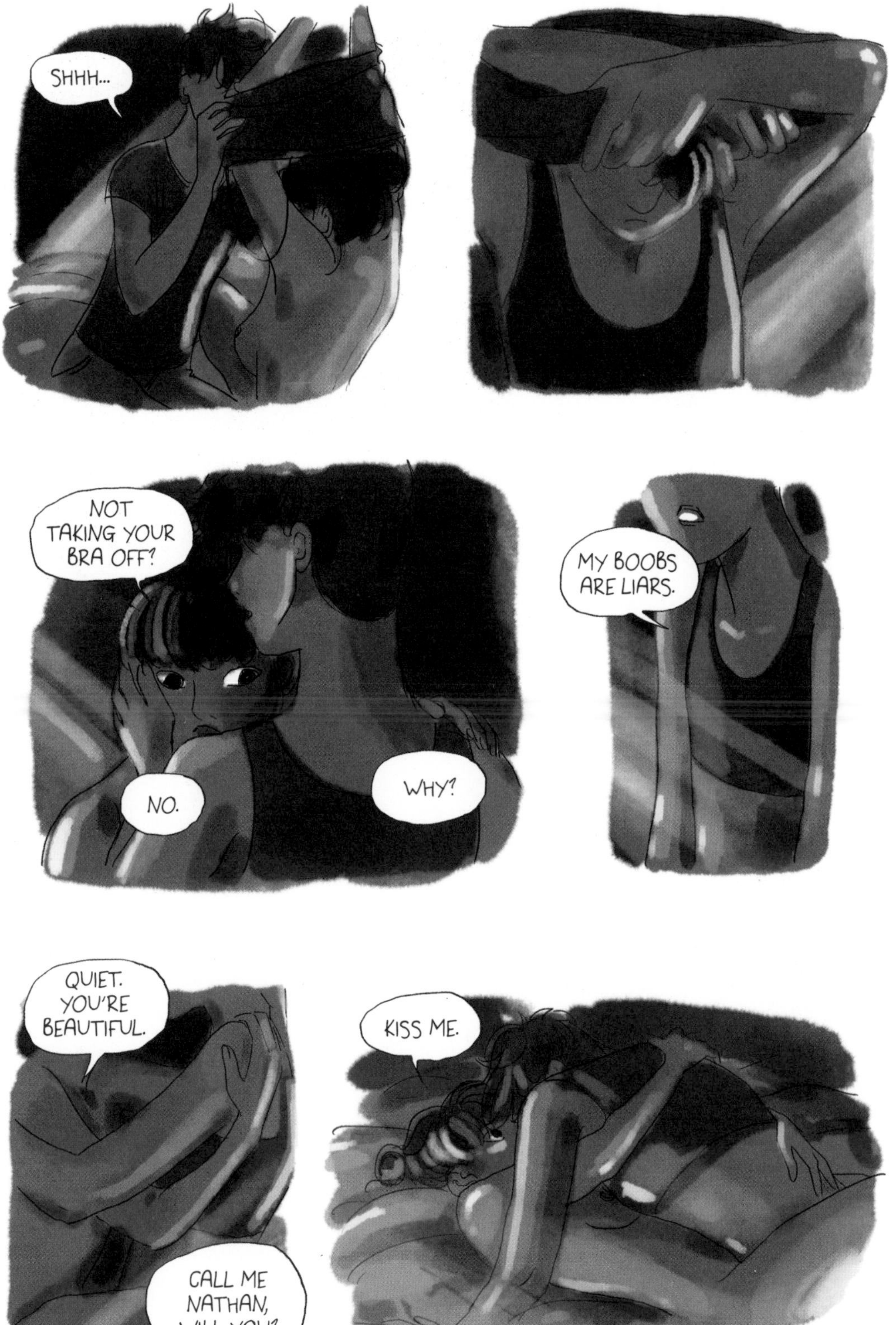
SHHH...
NOT TAKING YOUR BRA OFF?
NO.
WHY?
MY BOOBS ARE LIARS.
QUIET. YOU'RE BEAUTIFUL.
CALL ME NATHAN, WILL YOU?
KISS ME.

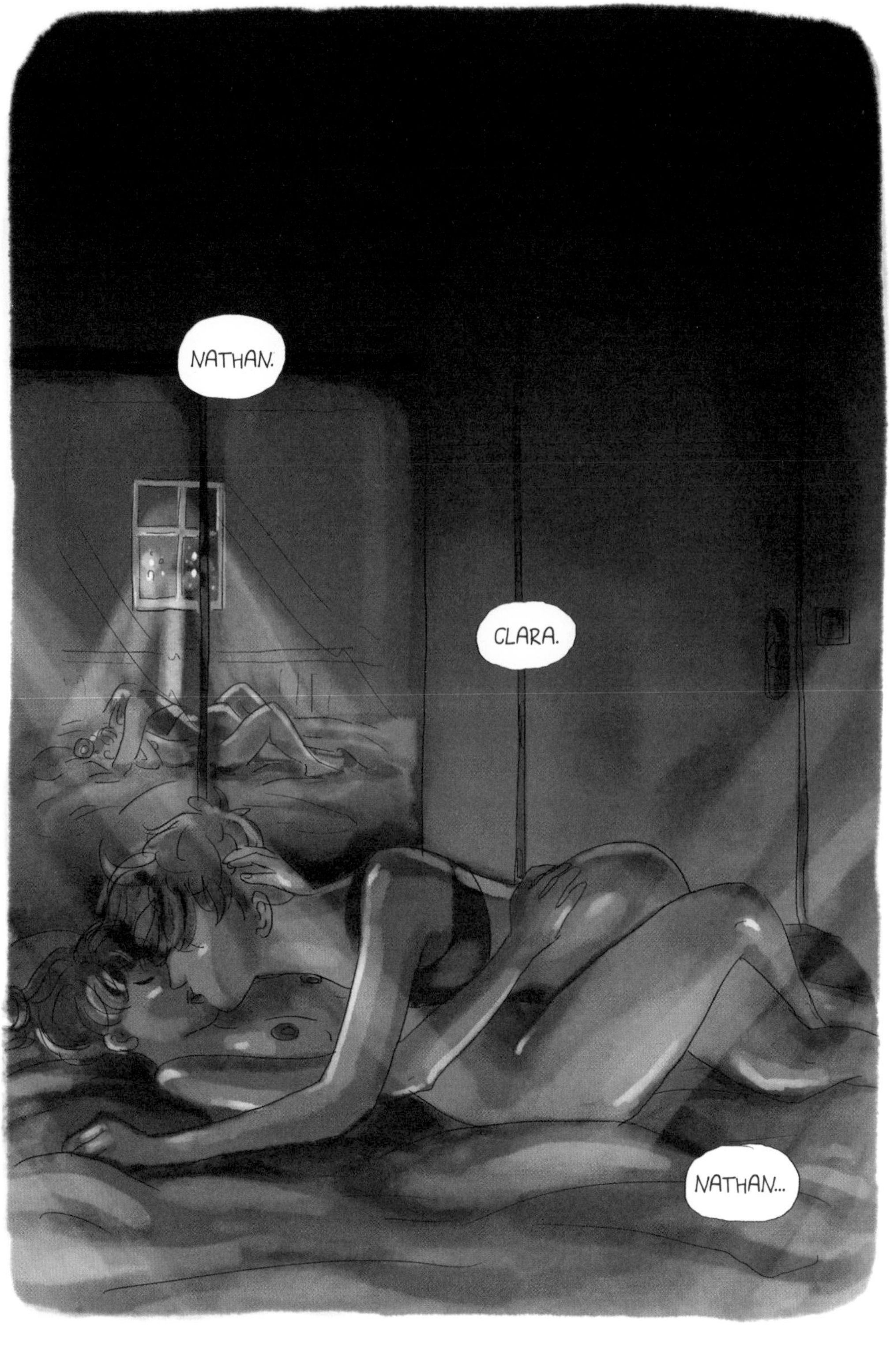
NATHAN.
CLARA.
NATHAN...

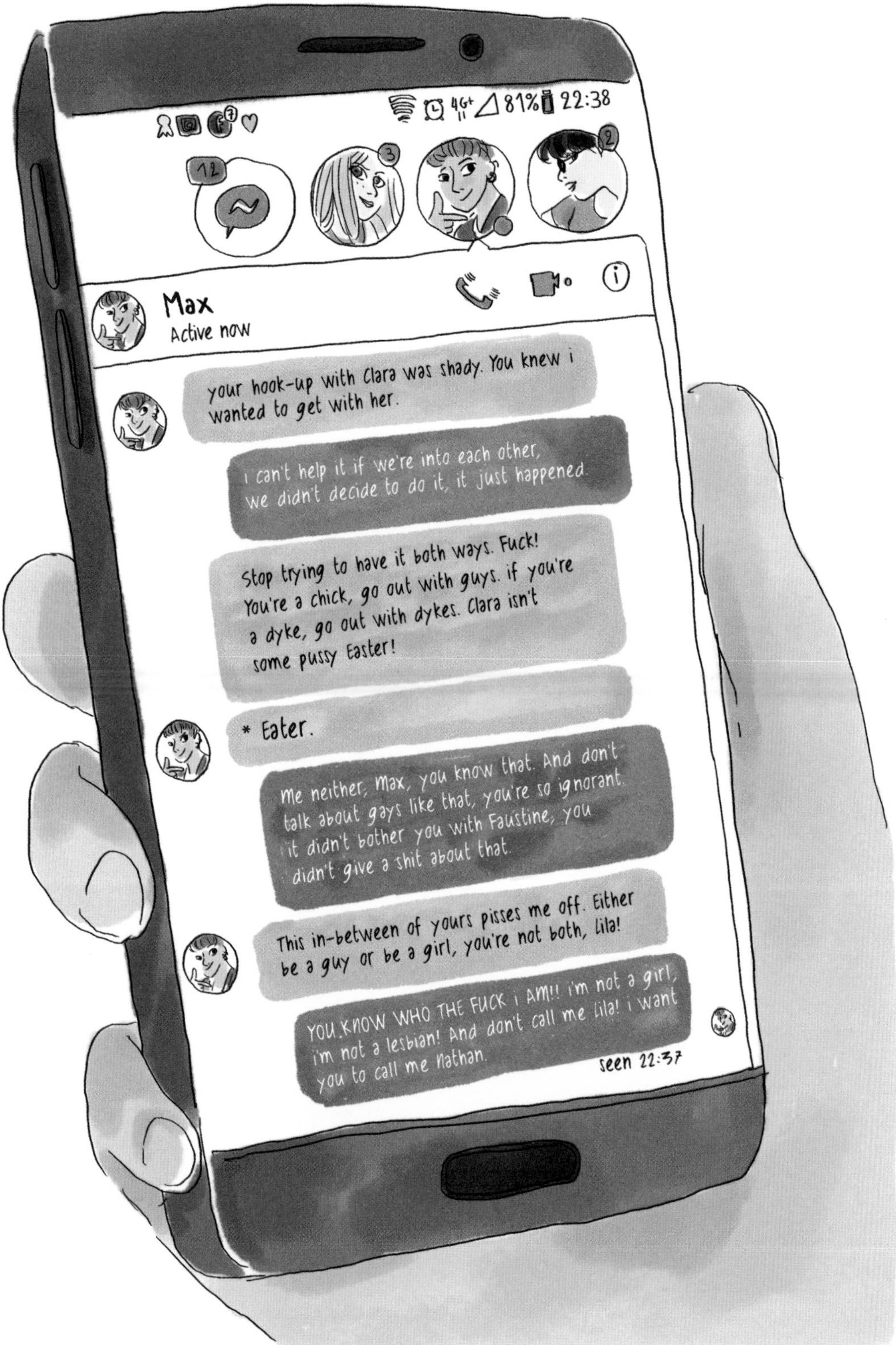
81% 22:38
Max
Active now
your hook-up with Clara was shady. You knew i wanted to get with her.
i can't help it if we're into each other, we didn't decide to do it, it just happened.
Stop trying to have it both ways. Fuck! You're a chick, go out with guys. if you're a dyke, go out with dykes. Clara isn't some pussy Easter!
* Eater.
Me neither, Max, you know that. And don't talk about gays like that, you're so ignorant. it didn't bother you with Faustine, you didn't give a shit about that.
This in-between of yours pisses me off. Either be a guy or be a girl, you're not both, Lila!
YOU KNOW WHO THE FUCK i AM!! i'm not a girl, i'm not a lesbian! And don't call me Lila! i want you to call me Nathan.
seen 22:37

Dr. Danglard: he's like the old man with the shell from "Dragon Ball Z".
I like him. He acts like a friend. I see him for an hour per week.

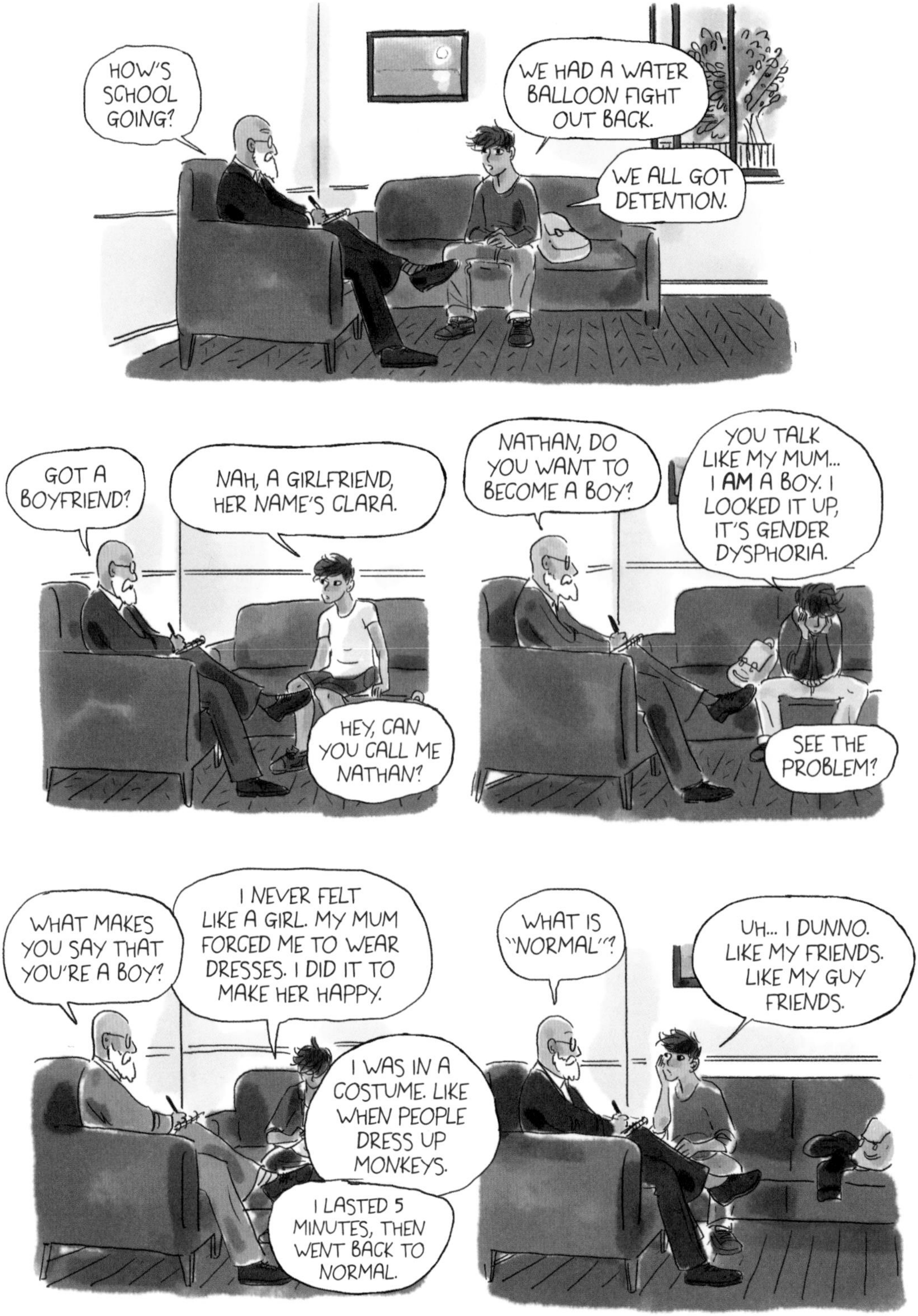
HOW'S SCHOOL GOING?
WE HAD A WATER BALLOON FIGHT OUT BACK.
WE ALL GOT DETENTION.
GOT A BOYFRIEND?
NAH, A GIRLFRIEND, HER NAME'S CLARA.
HEY, CAN YOU CALL ME NATHAN?
NATHAN, DO YOU WANT TO BECOME A BOY?
YOU TALK LIKE MY MUM... I **AM** A BOY. I LOOKED IT UP, IT'S GENDER DYSPHORIA.
SEE THE PROBLEM?
WHAT MAKES YOU SAY THAT YOU'RE A BOY?
I NEVER FELT LIKE A GIRL. MY MUM FORCED ME TO WEAR DRESSES. I DID IT TO MAKE HER HAPPY.
I WAS IN A COSTUME. LIKE WHEN PEOPLE DRESS UP MONKEYS.
I LASTED 5 MINUTES, THEN WENT BACK TO NORMAL.
WHAT IS "NORMAL"?
UH... I DUNNO. LIKE MY FRIENDS. LIKE MY GUY FRIENDS.

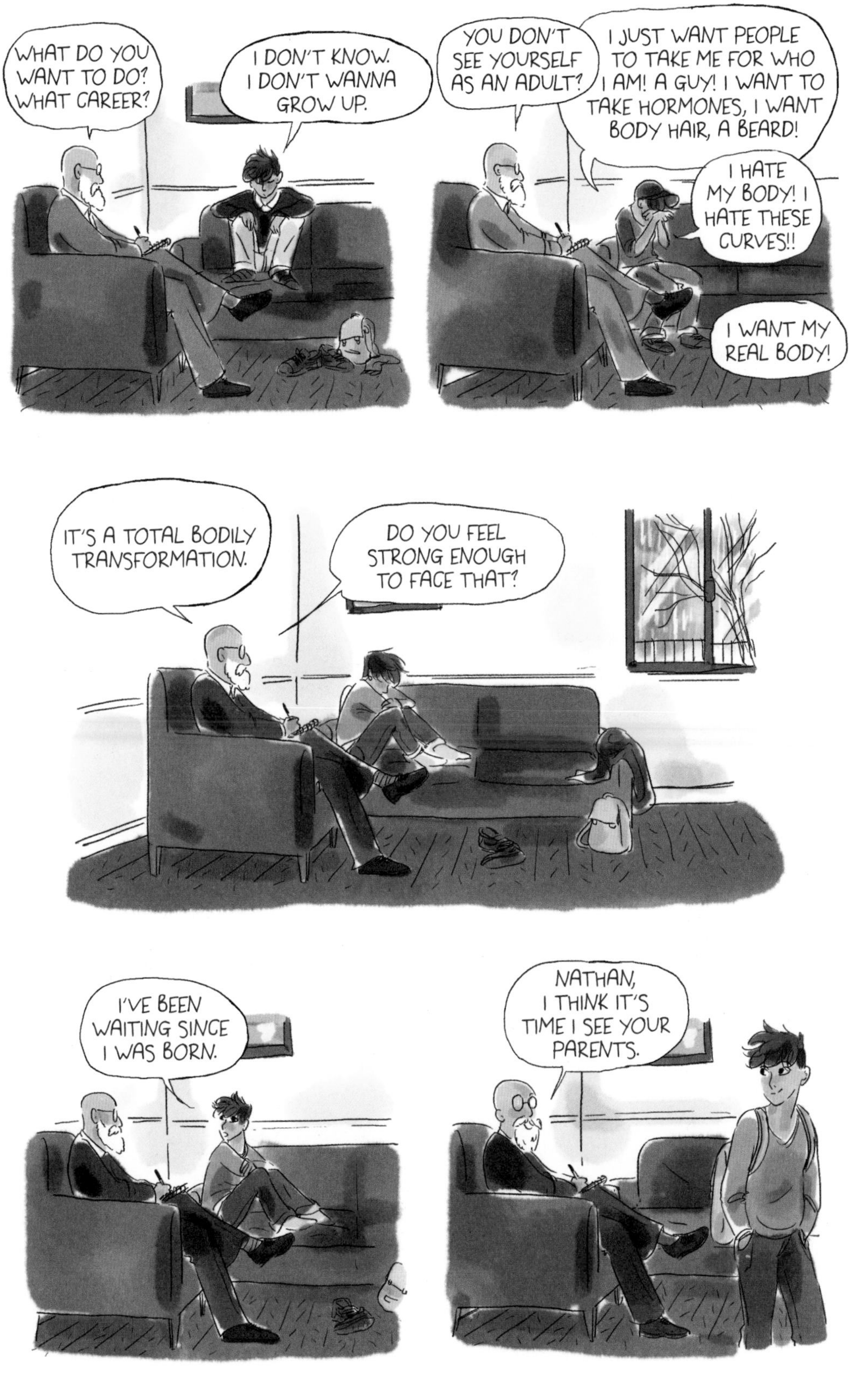
WHAT DO YOU WANT TO DO? WHAT CAREER?
I DON'T KNOW. I DON'T WANNA GROW UP.
YOU DON'T SEE YOURSELF AS AN ADULT?
I JUST WANT PEOPLE TO TAKE ME FOR WHO I AM! A GUY! I WANT TO TAKE HORMONES, I WANT BODY HAIR, A BEARD!
I HATE MY BODY! I HATE THESE CURVES!!
I WANT MY REAL BODY!
IT'S A TOTAL BODILY TRANSFORMATION.
DO YOU FEEL STRONG ENOUGH TO FACE THAT?
I'VE BEEN WAITING SINCE I WAS BORN.
NATHAN, I THINK IT'S TIME I SEE YOUR PARENTS.

Official diagnosis: I'm not crazy.

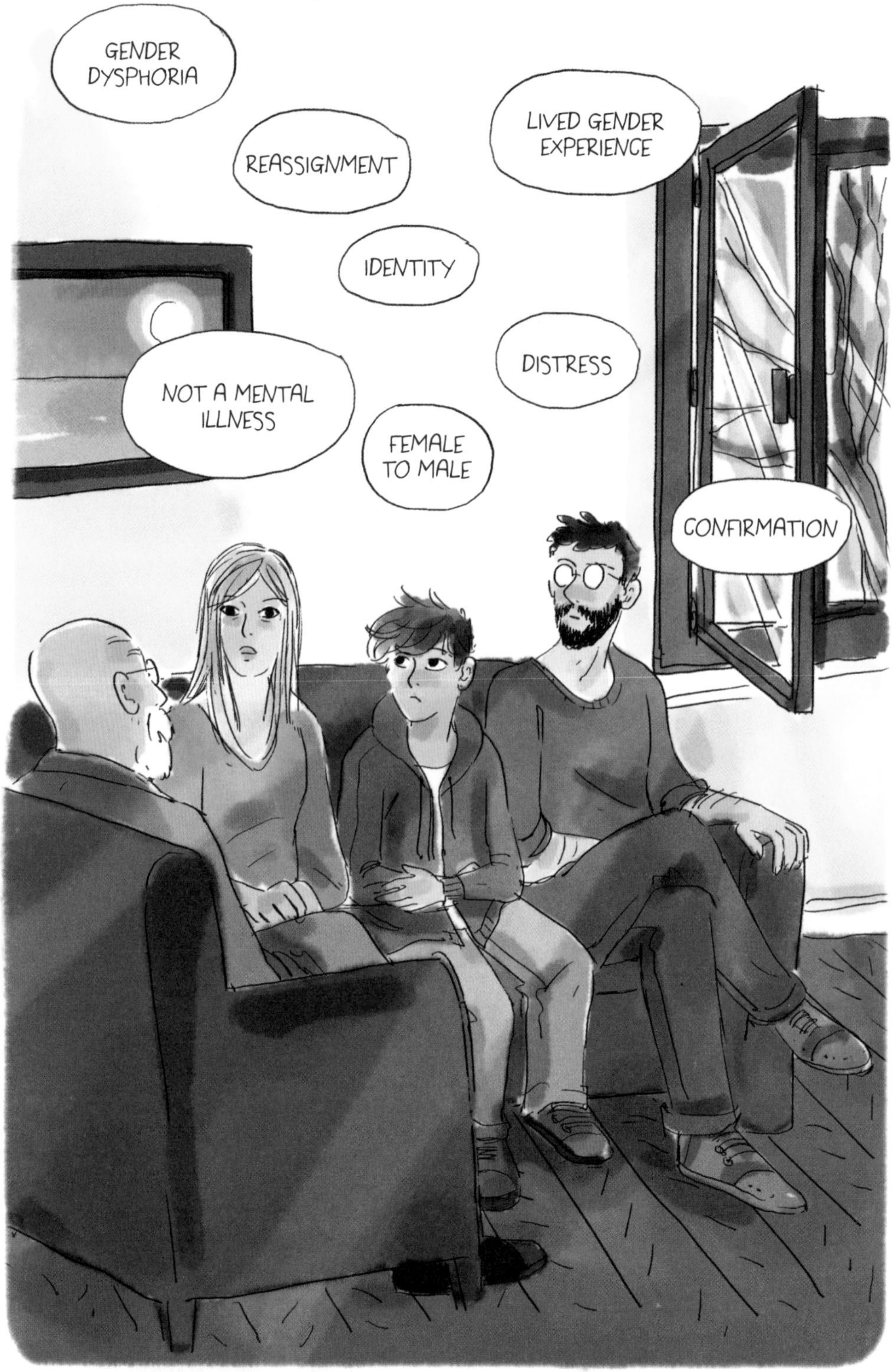
GENDER DYSPHORIA
REASSIGNMENT
LIVED GENDER EXPERIENCE
IDENTITY
DISTRESS
NOT A MENTAL ILLNESS
FEMALE TO MALE
CONFIRMATION

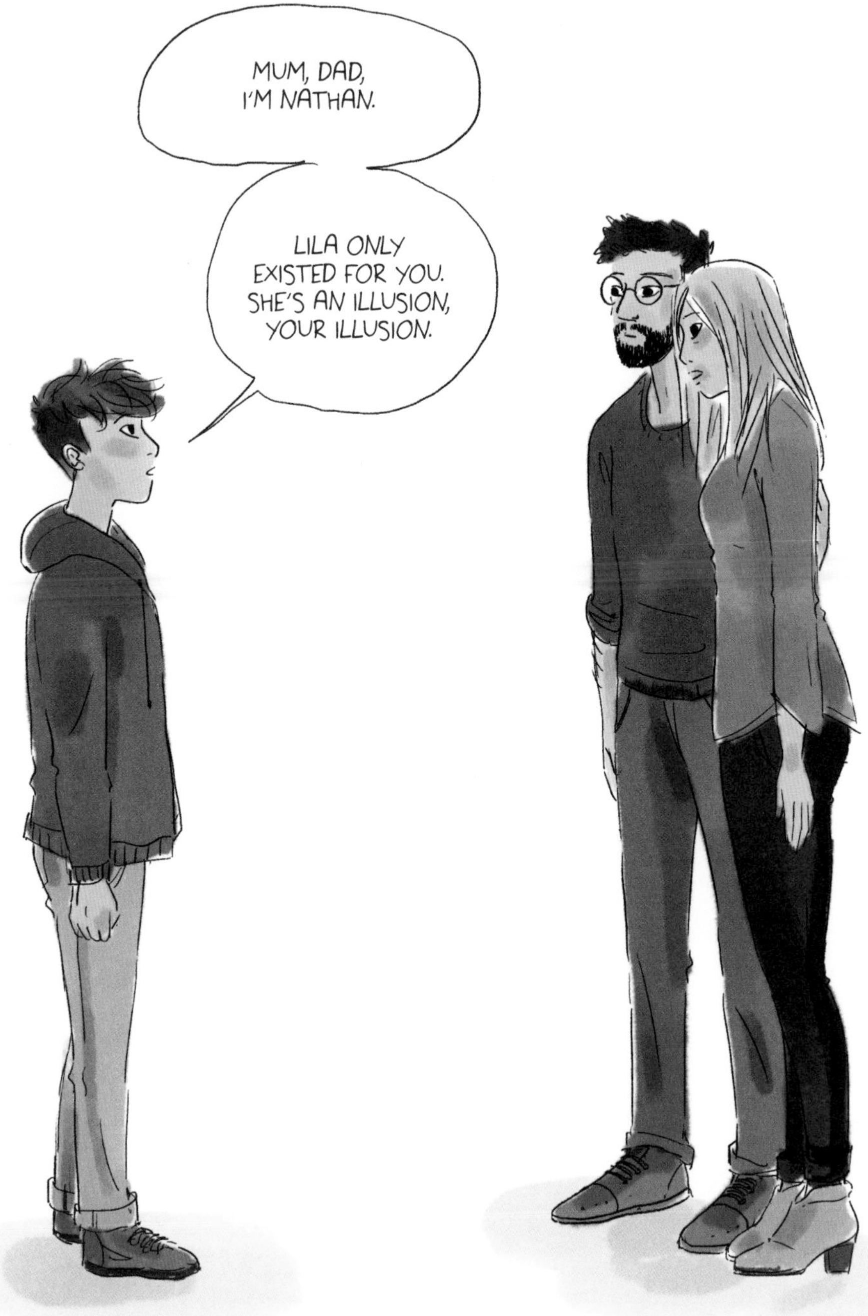
MUM, DAD,
I'M NATHAN.
LILA ONLY
EXISTED FOR YOU.
SHE'S AN ILLUSION,
YOUR ILLUSION.

Thankfully, I've got exercise to help clear my head.
Kicking a ball. Like a brute...

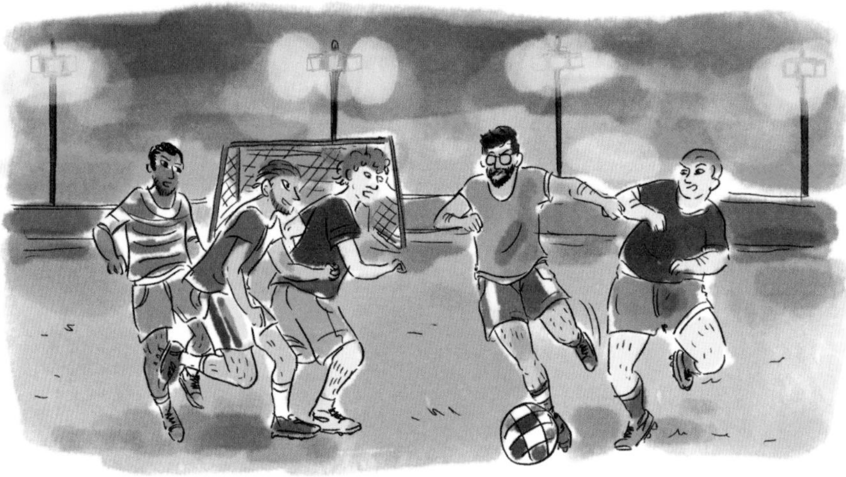

Wow! That feels good.

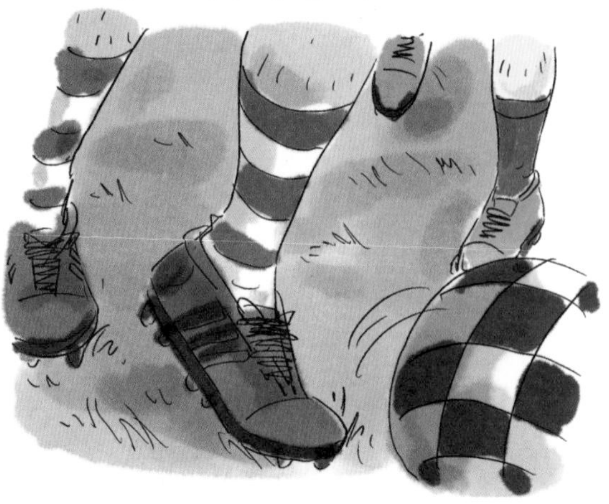

Lila played so well
as a little girl...

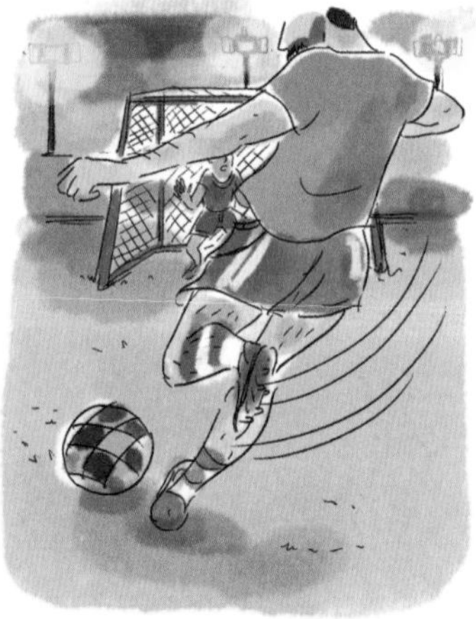

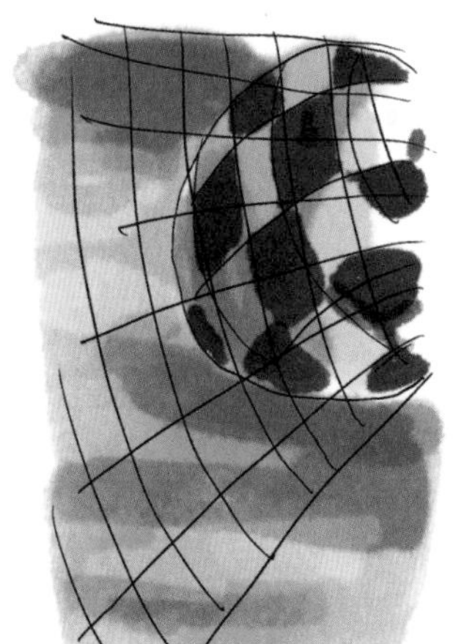

Lila, shit... get out of my head.

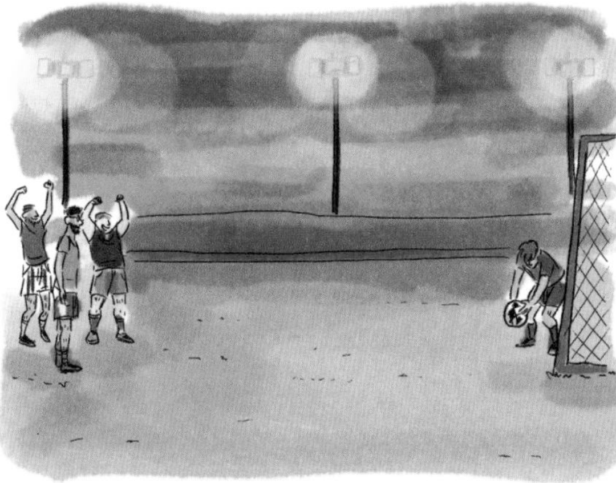

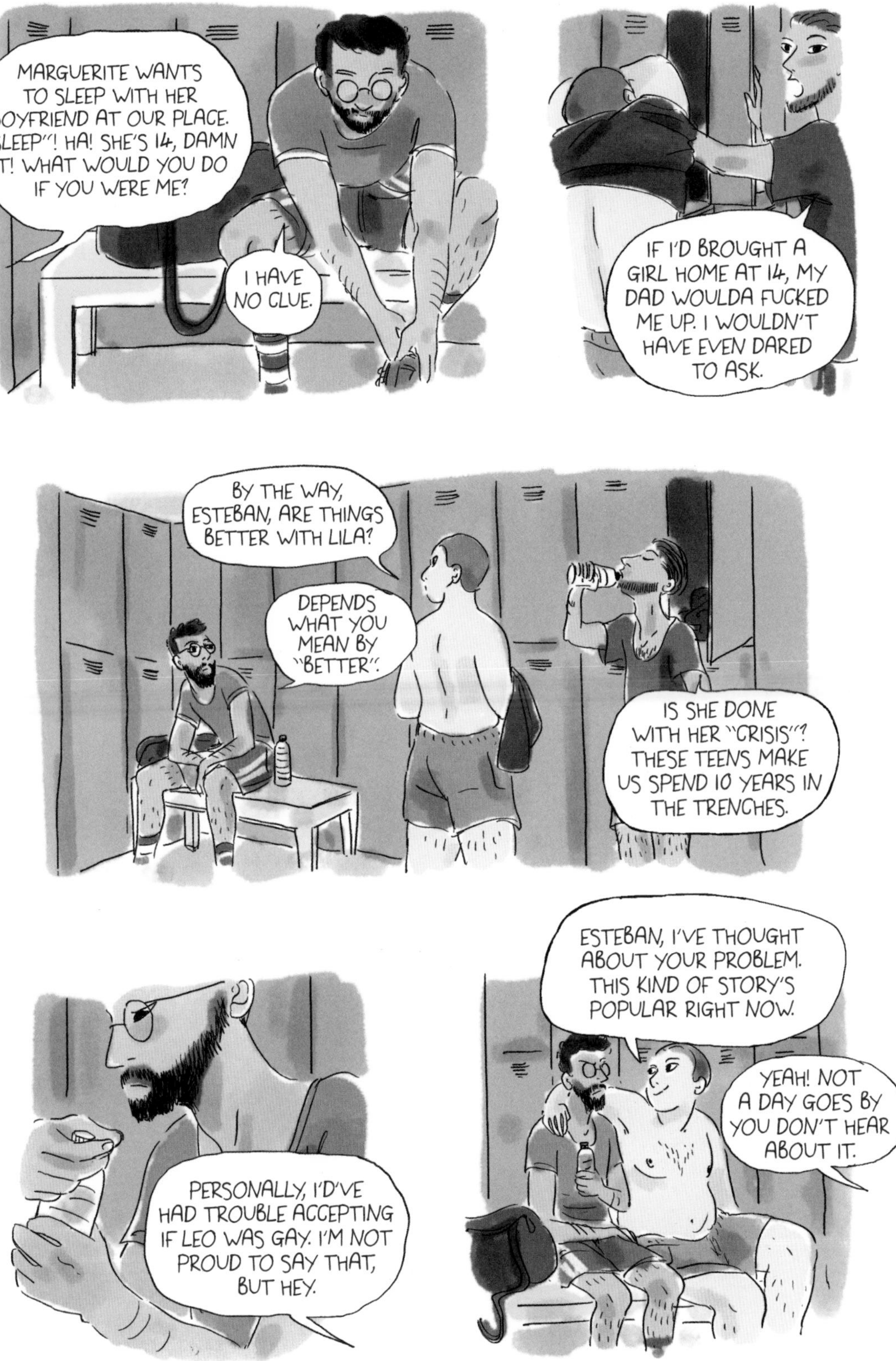
MARGUERITE WANTS TO SLEEP WITH HER BOYFRIEND AT OUR PLACE. "SLEEP"! HA! SHE'S 14, DAMN IT! WHAT WOULD YOU DO IF YOU WERE ME?
I HAVE NO CLUE.
IF I'D BROUGHT A GIRL HOME AT 14, MY DAD WOULDA FUCKED ME UP. I WOULDN'T HAVE EVEN DARED TO ASK.
BY THE WAY, ESTEBAN, ARE THINGS BETTER WITH LILA?
DEPENDS WHAT YOU MEAN BY "BETTER".
IS SHE DONE WITH HER "CRISIS"? THESE TEENS MAKE US SPEND 10 YEARS IN THE TRENCHES.
PERSONALLY, I'D'VE HAD TROUBLE ACCEPTING IF LEO WAS GAY. I'M NOT PROUD TO SAY THAT, BUT HEY.
ESTEBAN, I'VE THOUGHT ABOUT YOUR PROBLEM. THIS KIND OF STORY'S POPULAR RIGHT NOW.
YEAH! NOT A DAY GOES BY YOU DON'T HEAR ABOUT IT.

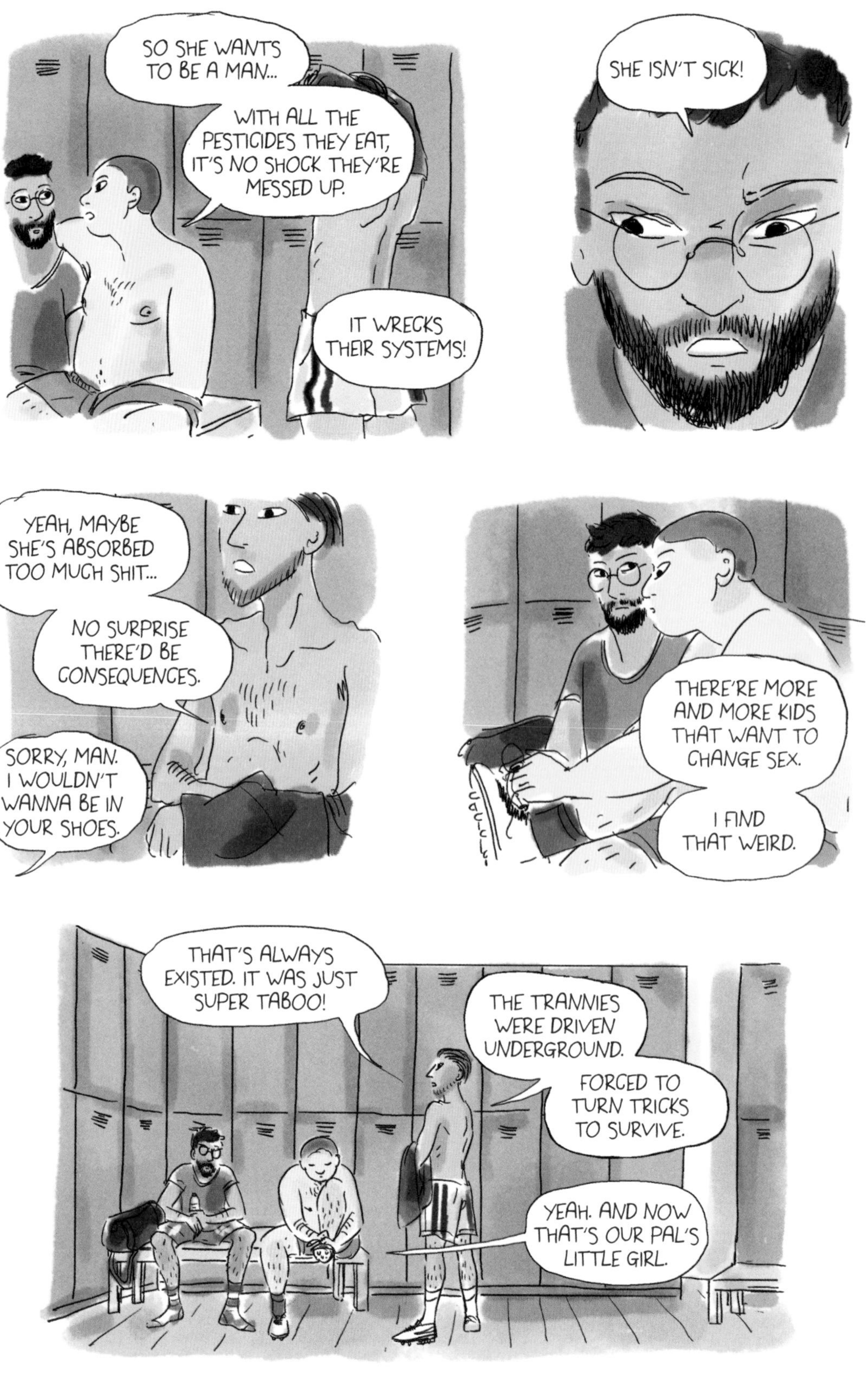
SO SHE WANTS TO BE A MAN...
WITH ALL THE PESTICIDES THEY EAT, IT'S NO SHOCK THEY'RE MESSED UP.
IT WRECKS THEIR SYSTEMS!
SHE ISN'T SICK!
YEAH, MAYBE SHE'S ABSORBED TOO MUCH SHIT...
NO SURPRISE THERE'D BE CONSEQUENCES.
SORRY, MAN. I WOULDN'T WANNA BE IN YOUR SHOES.
THERE'RE MORE AND MORE KIDS THAT WANT TO CHANGE SEX.
I FIND THAT WEIRD.
THAT'S ALWAYS EXISTED. IT WAS JUST SUPER TABOO!
THE TRANNIES WERE DRIVEN UNDERGROUND.
FORCED TO TURN TRICKS TO SURVIVE.
YEAH. AND NOW THAT'S OUR PAL'S LITTLE GIRL.

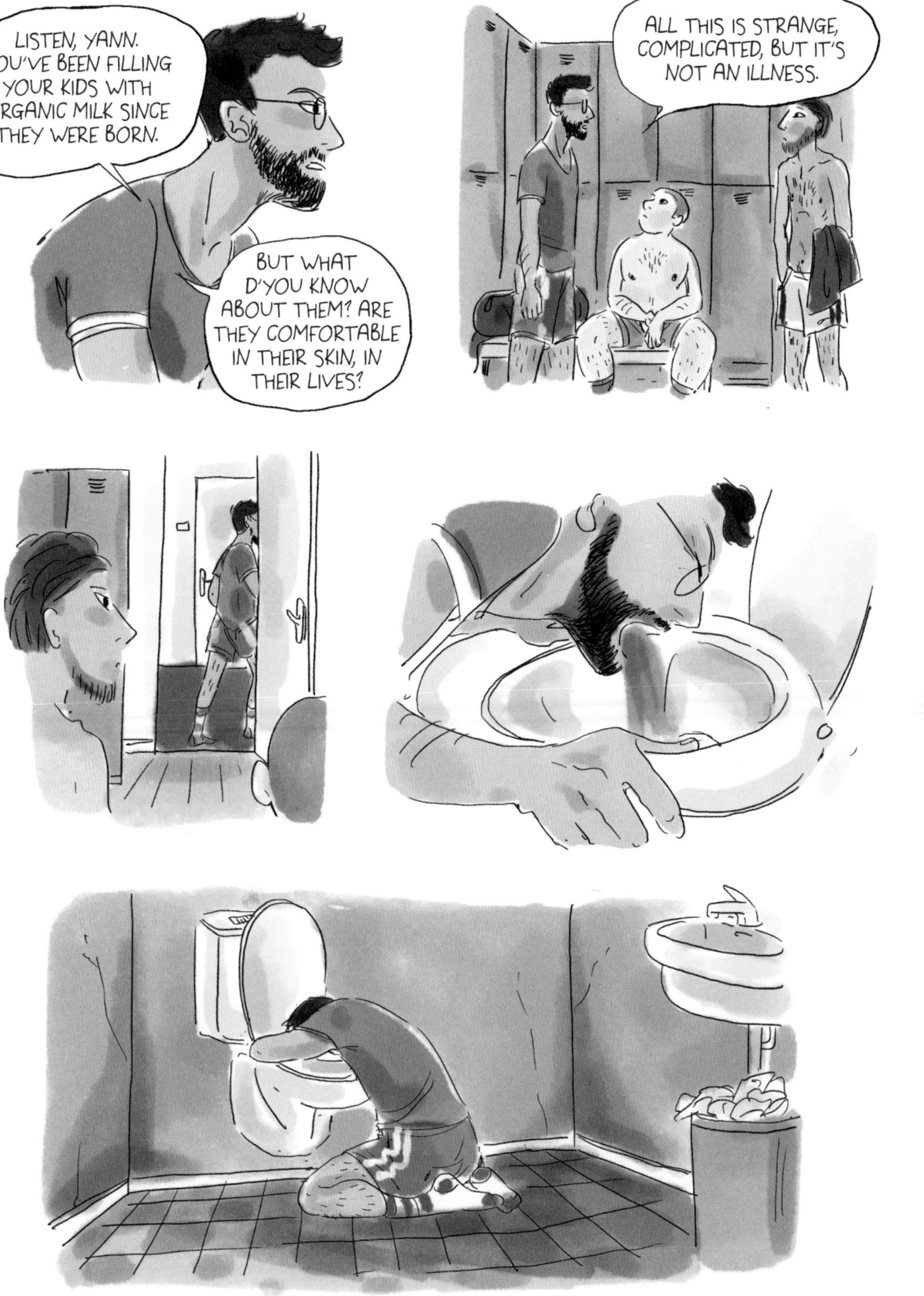
LISTEN, YANN. YOU'VE BEEN FILLING YOUR KIDS WITH ORGANIC MILK SINCE THEY WERE BORN.
BUT WHAT D'YOU KNOW ABOUT THEM? ARE THEY COMFORTABLE IN THEIR SKIN, IN THEIR LIVES?
ALL THIS IS STRANGE, COMPLICATED, BUT IT'S NOT AN ILLNESS.

I have two sons. Two sons! Is that so complicated? I don't have a daughter that I have to worry about when she's out at night. I have two sons. Nathan and Théo. Two sons.

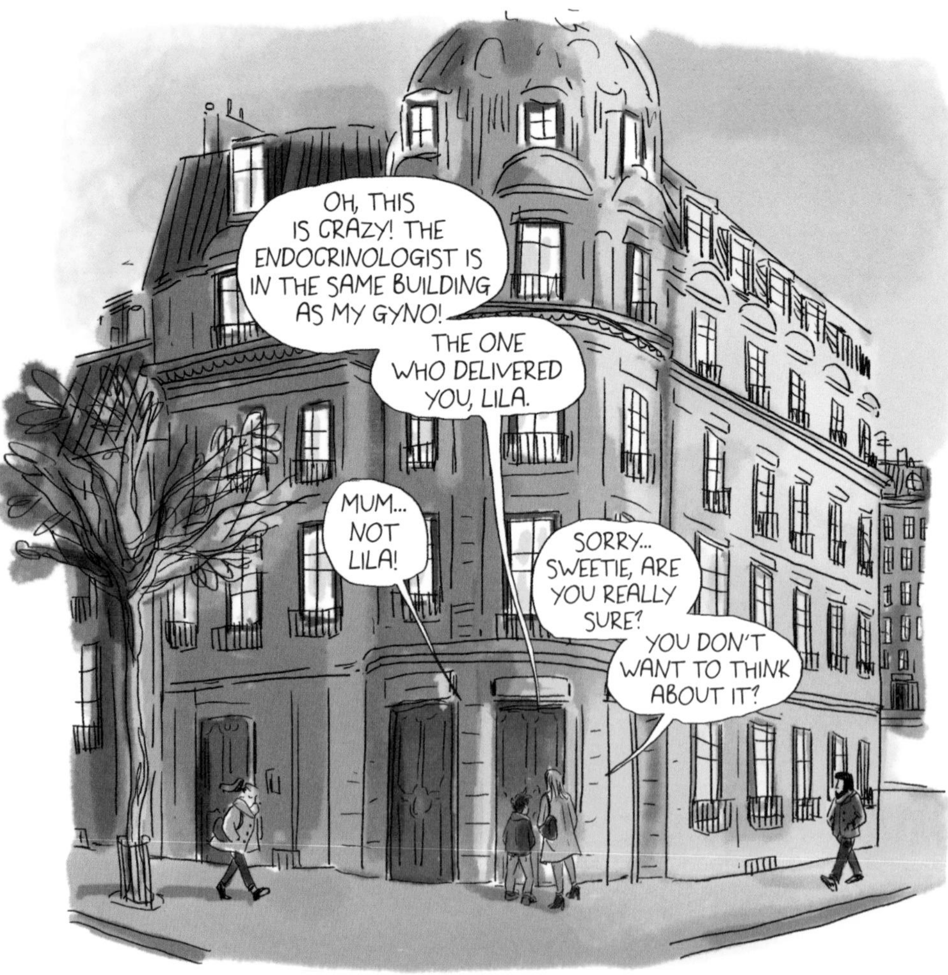
OH, THIS IS CRAZY! THE ENDOCRINOLOGIST IS IN THE SAME BUILDING AS MY GYNO!
THE ONE WHO DELIVERED YOU, LILA.
MUM... NOT LILA!
SORRY... SWEETIE, ARE YOU REALLY SURE?
YOU DON'T WANT TO THINK ABOUT IT?

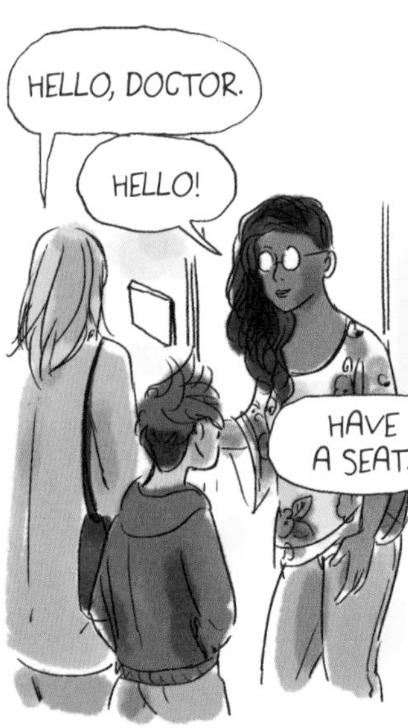
HELLO, DOCTOR.
HELLO!
HAVE A SEAT.

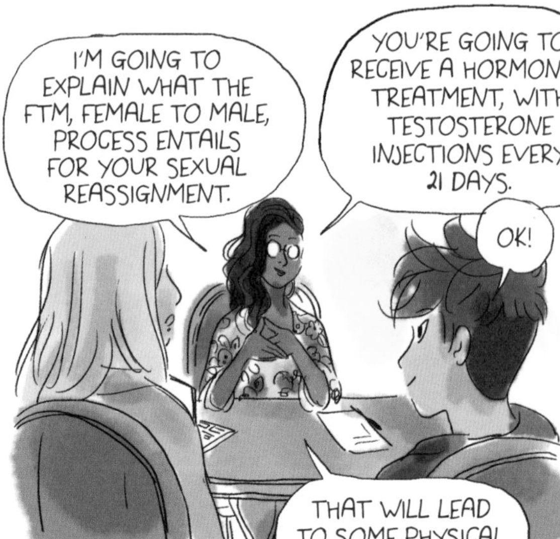
I'M GOING TO EXPLAIN WHAT THE FTM, FEMALE TO MALE, PROCESS ENTAILS FOR YOUR SEXUAL REASSIGNMENT.
YOU'RE GOING TO RECEIVE A HORMONAL TREATMENT, WITH TESTOSTERONE INJECTIONS EVERY 21 DAYS.
OK!
THAT WILL LEAD TO SOME PHYSICAL CHANGES.

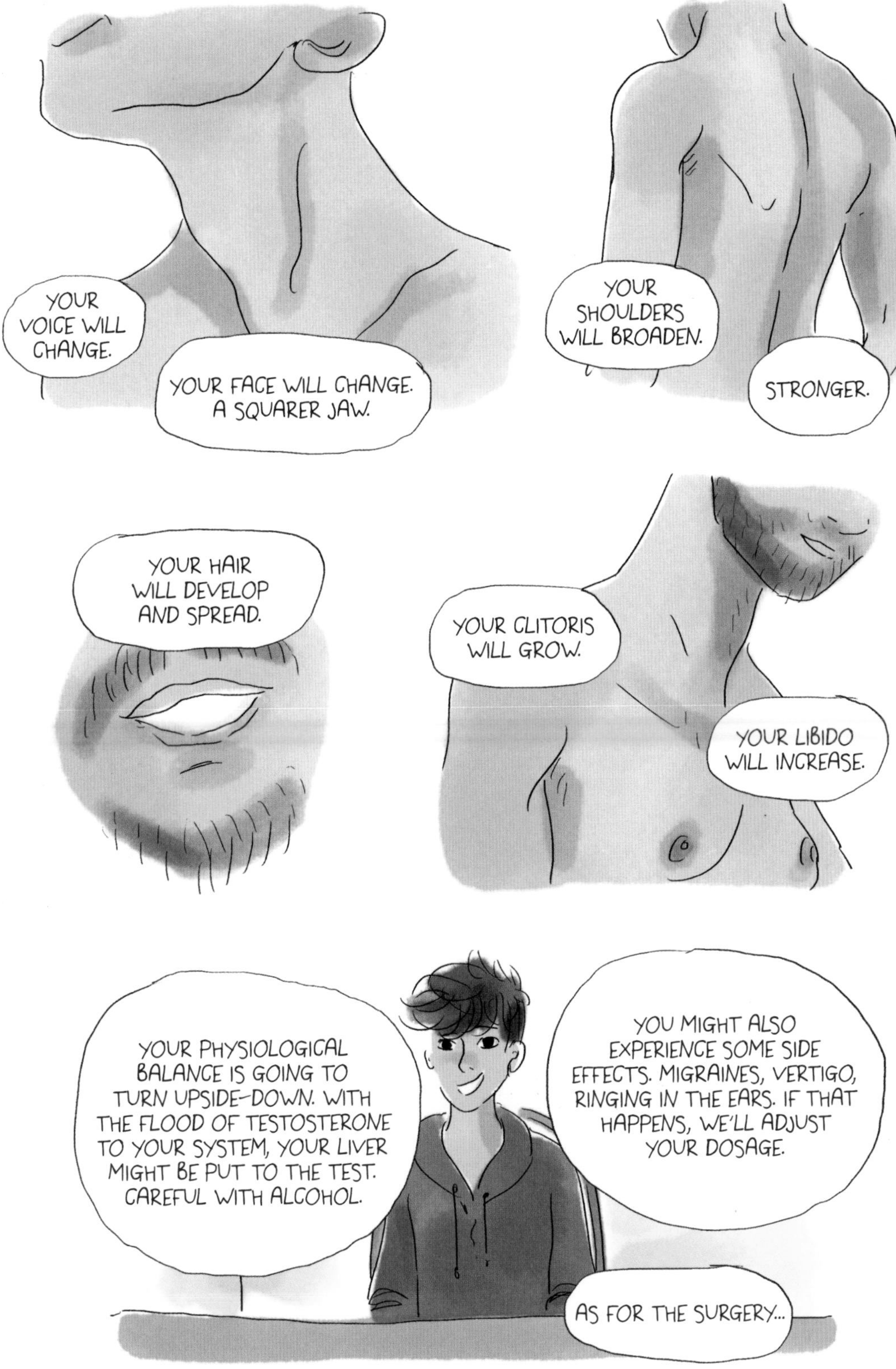
YOUR VOICE WILL CHANGE.
YOUR FACE WILL CHANGE. A SQUARER JAW.
YOUR SHOULDERS WILL BROADEN.
STRONGER.
YOUR HAIR WILL DEVELOP AND SPREAD.
YOUR CLITORIS WILL GROW.
YOUR LIBIDO WILL INCREASE.
YOUR PHYSIOLOGICAL BALANCE IS GOING TO TURN UPSIDE-DOWN. WITH THE FLOOD OF TESTOSTERONE TO YOUR SYSTEM, YOUR LIVER MIGHT BE PUT TO THE TEST. CAREFUL WITH ALCOHOL.
YOU MIGHT ALSO EXPERIENCE SOME SIDE EFFECTS. MIGRAINES, VERTIGO, RINGING IN THE EARS. IF THAT HAPPENS, WE'LL ADJUST YOUR DOSAGE.
AS FOR THE SURGERY...

THE BILATERAL MASTECTOMY IS THE REMOVAL OF THE BREASTS. THE FIBROUS AND FATTY MAMMARY GLANDS ARE EXCISED.
IT COSTS BETWEEN €1,000 AND €4,000, ONLY PART OF WHICH IS COVERED BY YOUR HEALTH INSURANCE. IF YOU WENT THROUGH AN OFFICIAL TEAM AT THE UNIVERSITY HOSPITAL, IT WOULD BE FREE.
THE HYSTERECTOMY IS THE REMOVAL OF THE UTERUS AND OVARIES. IT IS STRONGLY ADVISED.
WITH THE HORMONE TREATMENT, THE UTERUS ATROPHIES, RISKING THE FORMATION OF CYSTS.

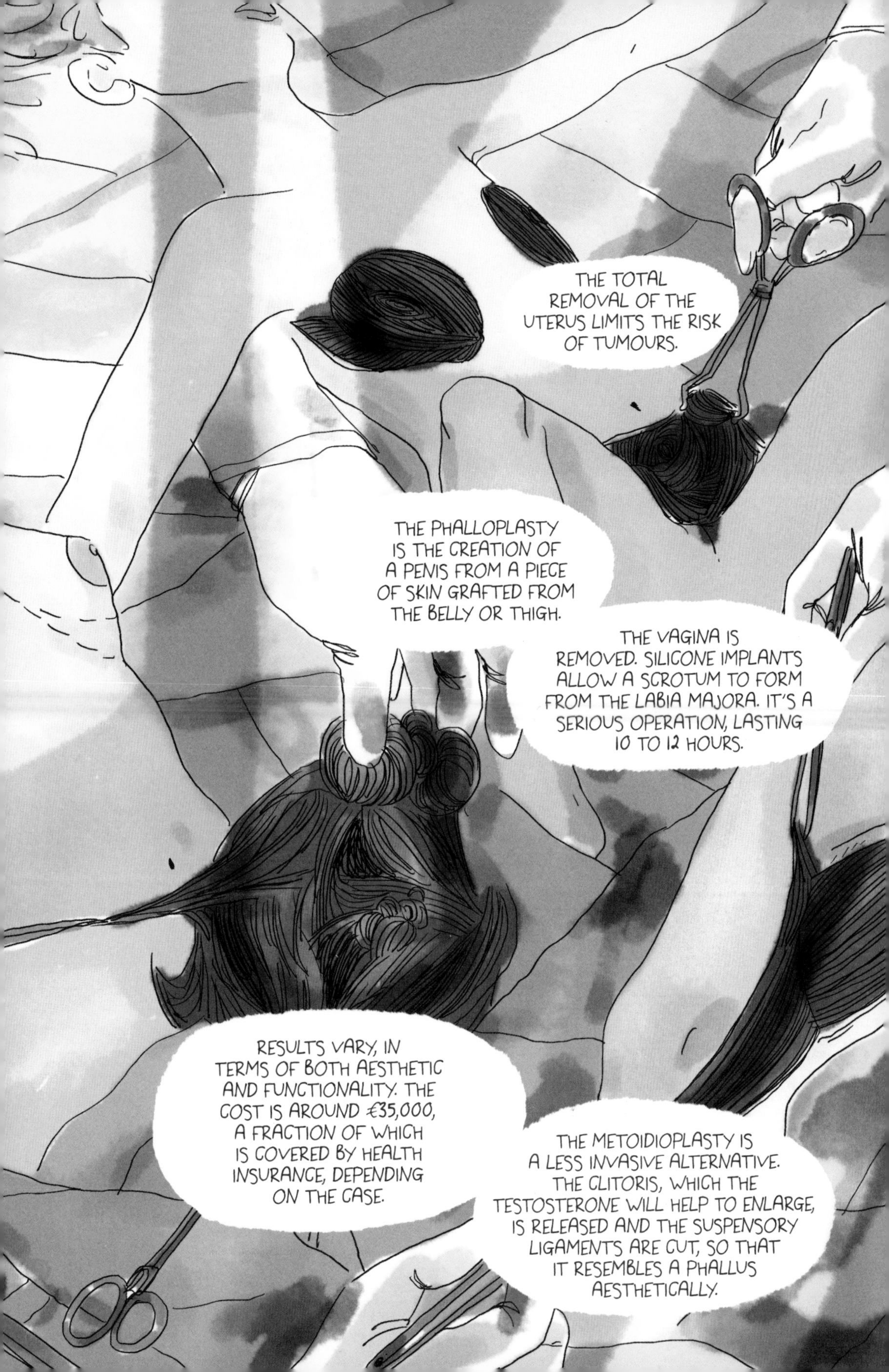
THE TOTAL REMOVAL OF THE UTERUS LIMITS THE RISK OF TUMOURS.
THE PHALLOPLASTY IS THE CREATION OF A PENIS FROM A PIECE OF SKIN GRAFTED FROM THE BELLY OR THIGH.
THE VAGINA IS REMOVED. SILICONE IMPLANTS ALLOW A SCROTUM TO FORM FROM THE LABIA MAJORA. IT'S A SERIOUS OPERATION, LASTING 10 TO 12 HOURS.
RESULTS VARY, IN TERMS OF BOTH AESTHETIC AND FUNCTIONALITY. THE COST IS AROUND €35,000, A FRACTION OF WHICH IS COVERED BY HEALTH INSURANCE, DEPENDING ON THE CASE.
THE METOIDIOPLASTY IS A LESS INVASIVE ALTERNATIVE. THE CLITORIS, WHICH THE TESTOSTERONE WILL HELP TO ENLARGE, IS RELEASED AND THE SUSPENSORY LIGAMENTS ARE CUT, SO THAT IT RESEMBLES A PHALLUS AESTHETICALLY.

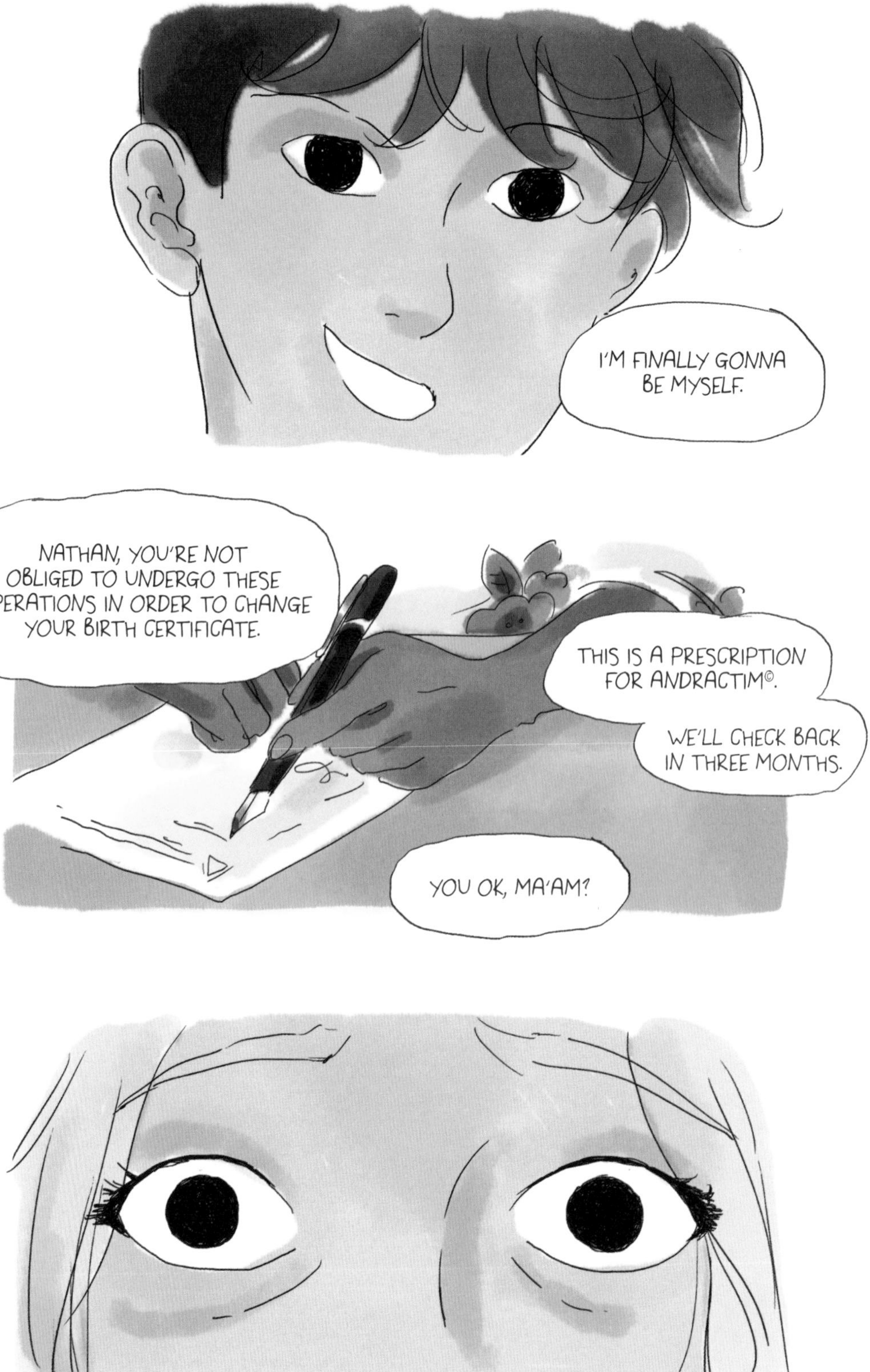
I'M FINALLY GONNA BE MYSELF.
NATHAN, YOU'RE NOT OBLIGED TO UNDERGO THESE OPERATIONS IN ORDER TO CHANGE YOUR BIRTH CERTIFICATE.
THIS IS A PRESCRIPTION FOR ANDRACTIM©.
WE'LL CHECK BACK IN THREE MONTHS.
YOU OK, MA'AM?

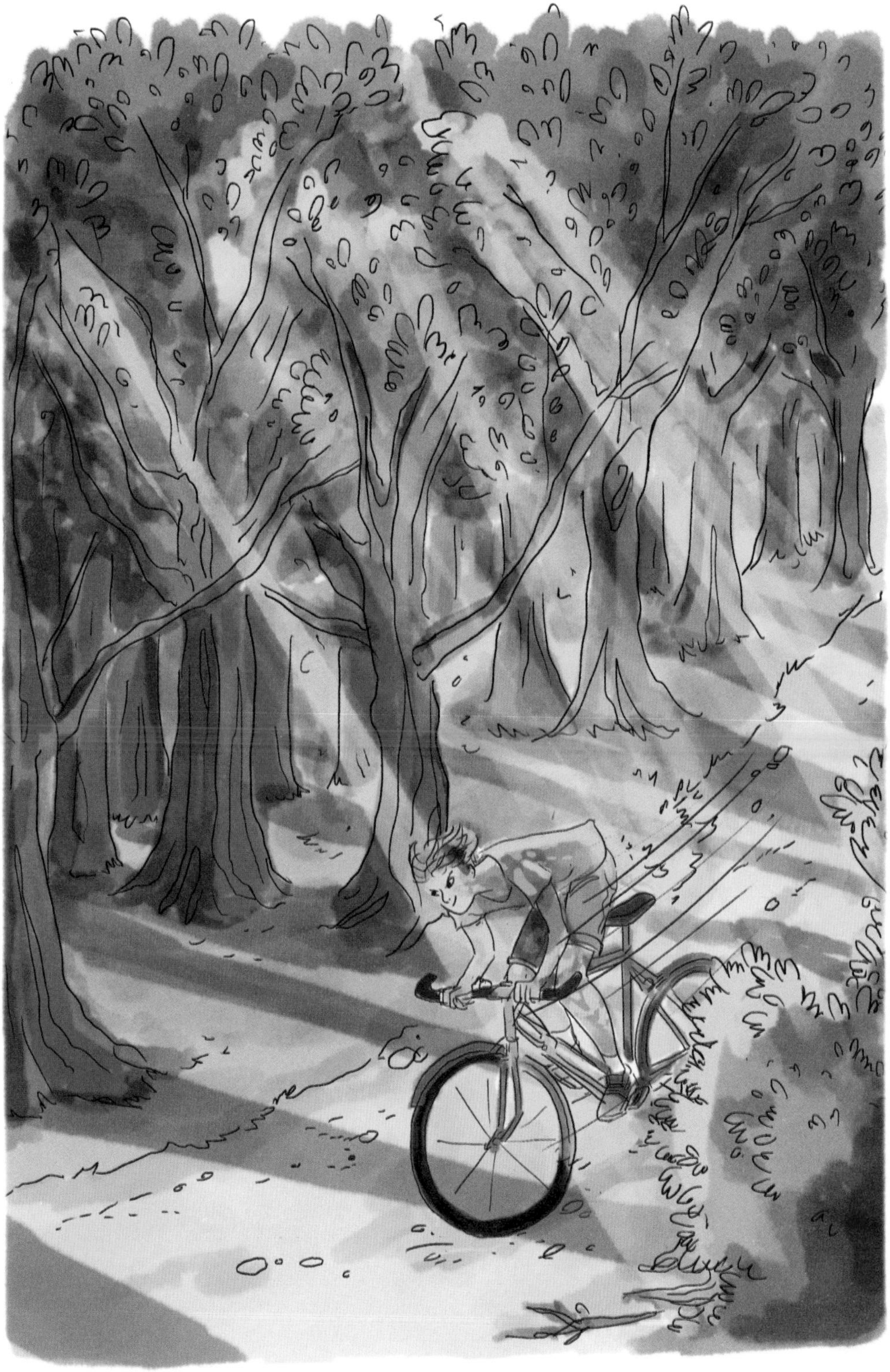

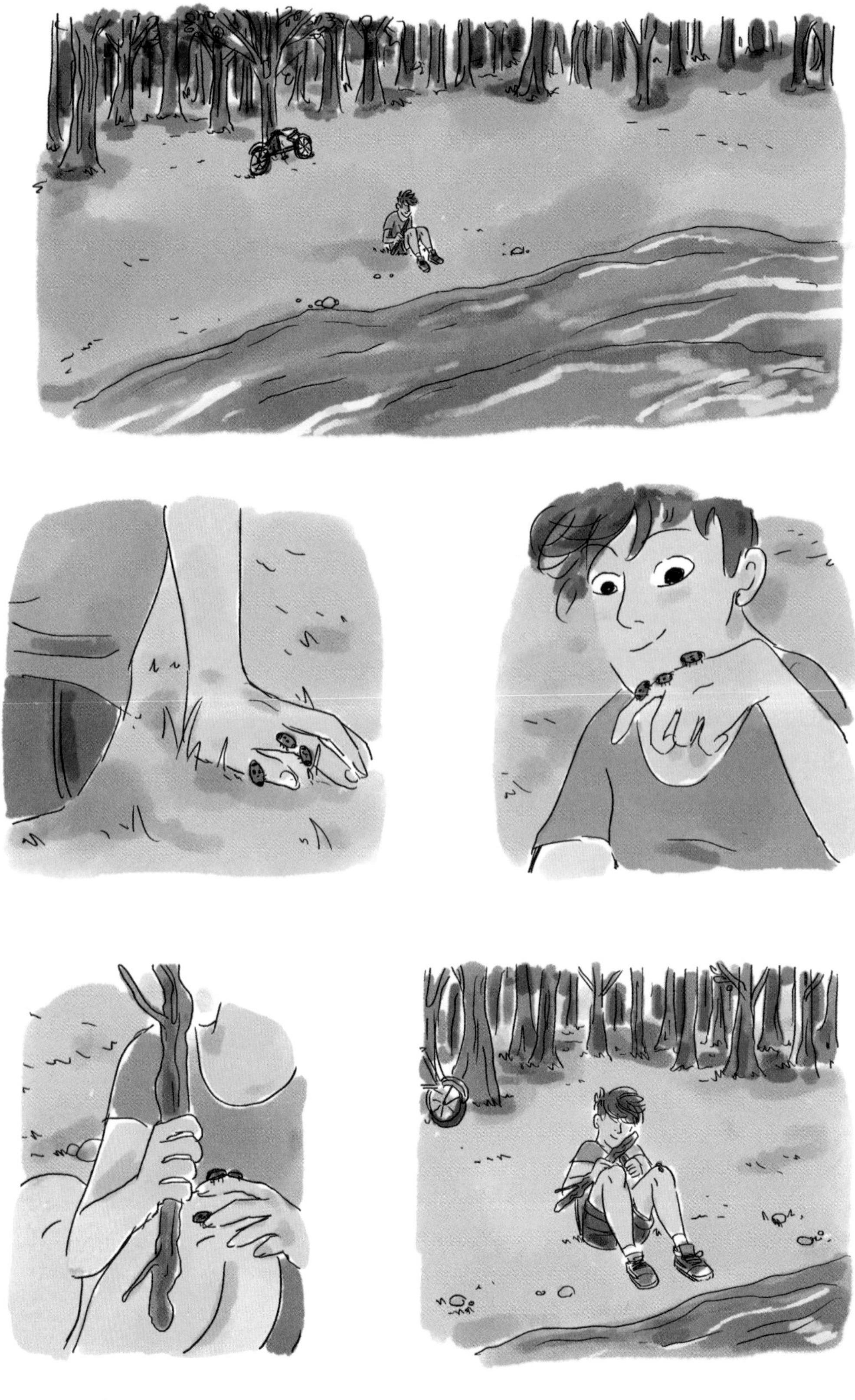

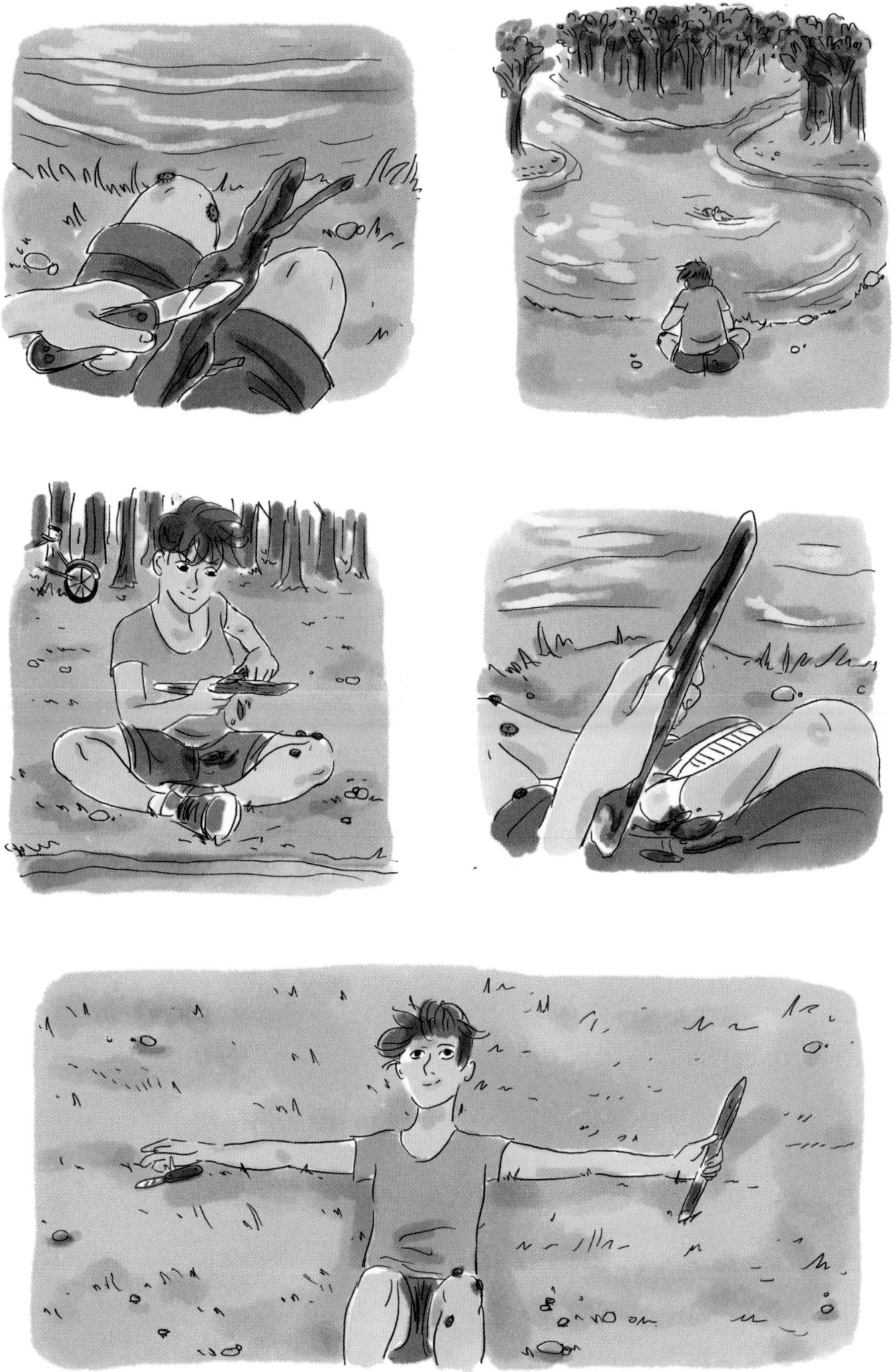

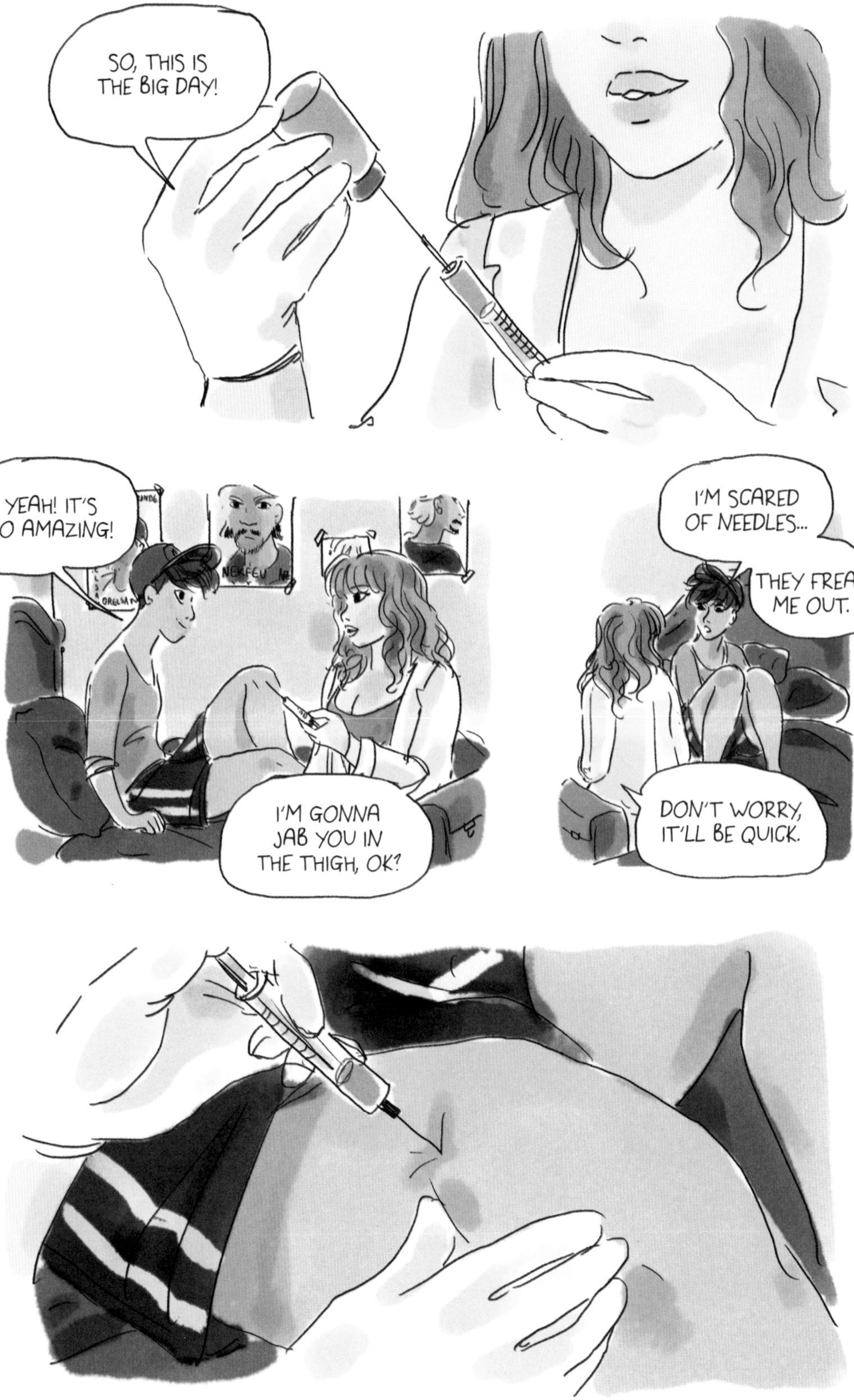
SO, THIS IS THE BIG DAY!
YEAH! IT'S SO AMAZING!
NEKFEU
I'M GONNA JAB YOU IN THE THIGH, OK?
I'M SCARED OF NEEDLES...
THEY FREAK ME OUT.
DON'T WORRY, IT'LL BE QUICK.

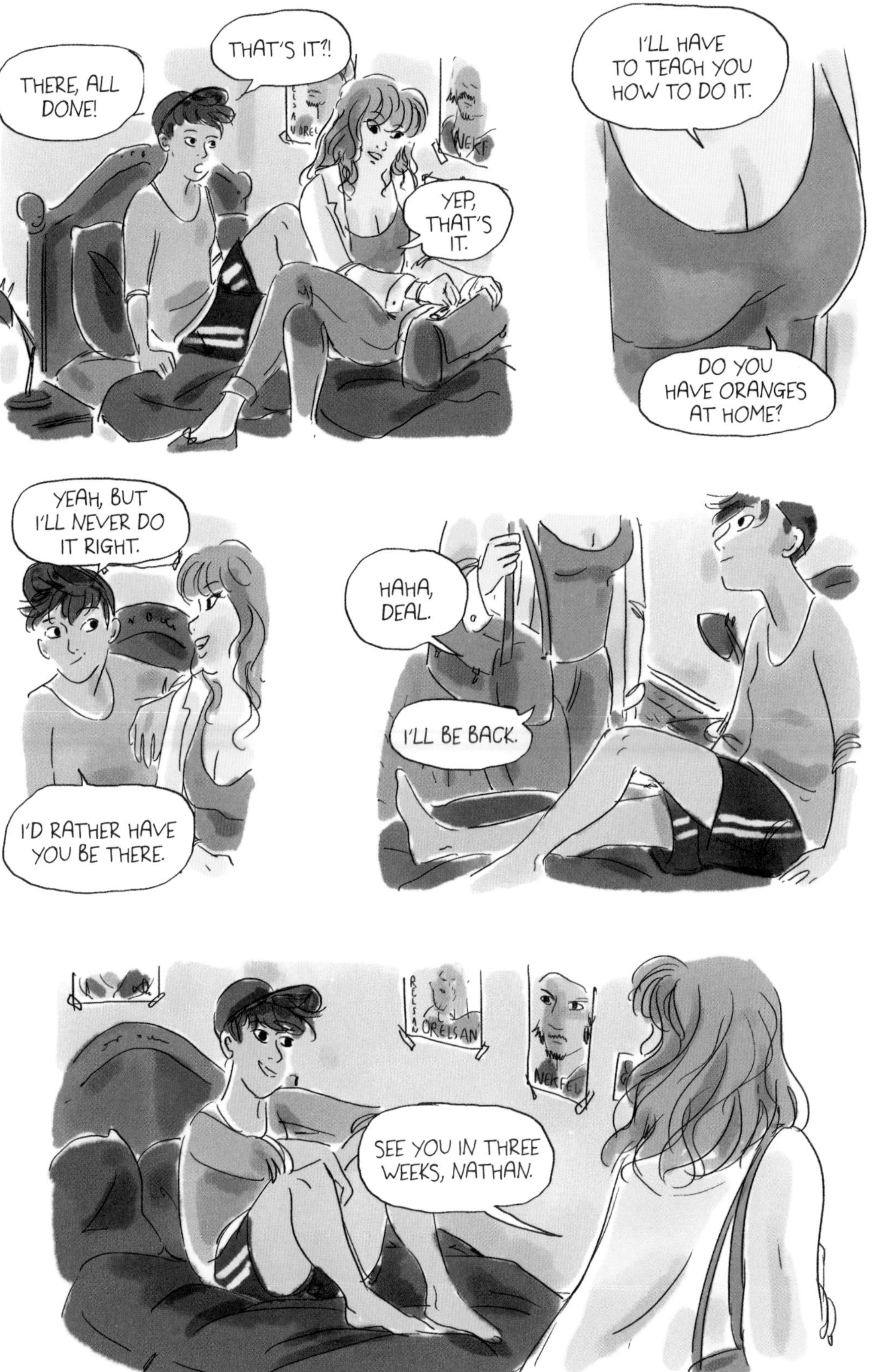
THERE, ALL DONE!
THAT'S IT?!
YEP, THAT'S IT.
I'LL HAVE TO TEACH YOU HOW TO DO IT.
DO YOU HAVE ORANGES AT HOME?
YEAH, BUT I'LL NEVER DO IT RIGHT.
I'D RATHER HAVE YOU BE THERE.
HAHA, DEAL.
I'LL BE BACK.
SEE YOU IN THREE WEEKS, NATHAN.

Being among people like me is awesome! No questions, no explanations, we're separate together. It feels like I'm on solid ground.

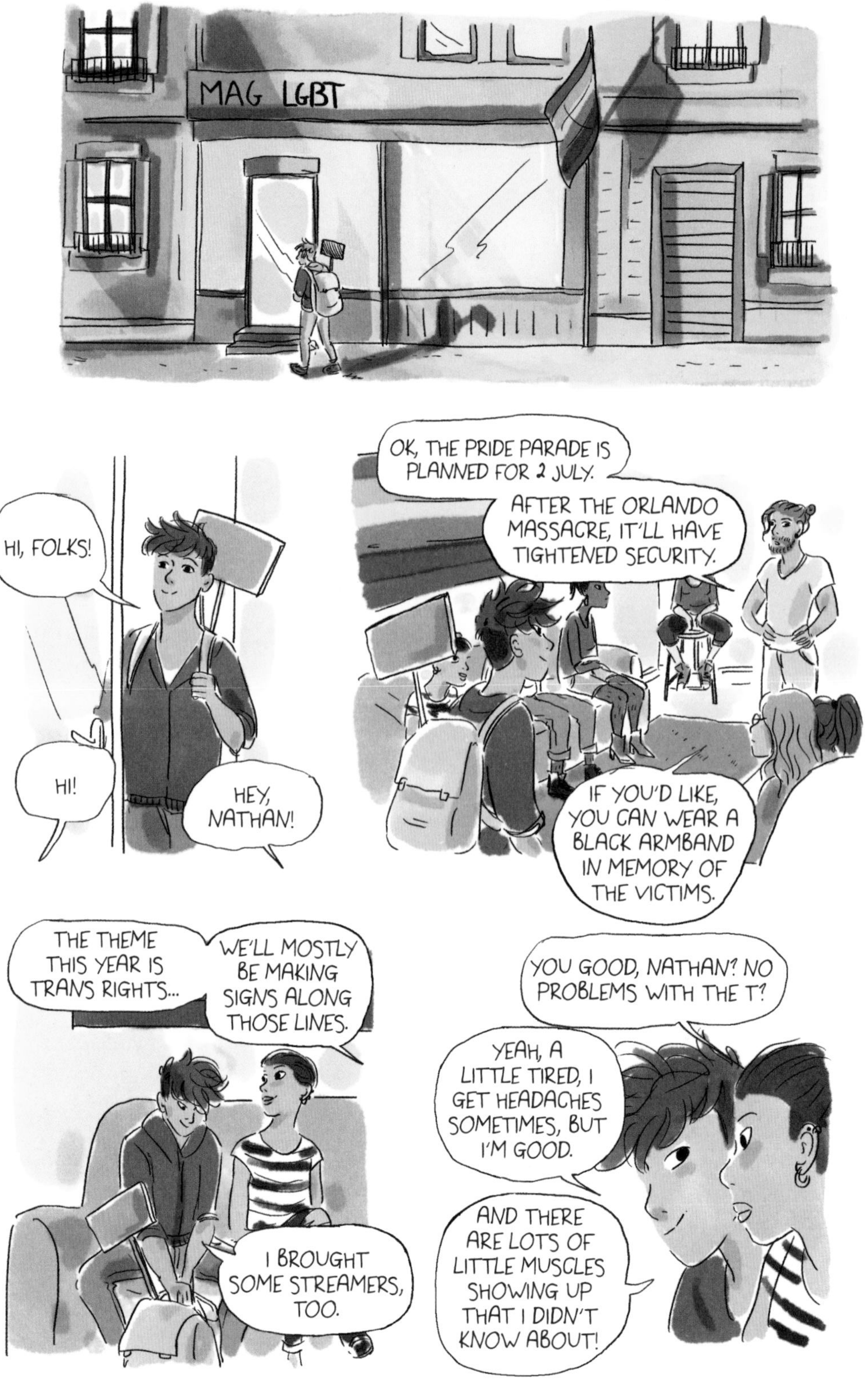
MAG LGBT
HI, FOLKS!
HI!
HEY, NATHAN!
OK, THE PRIDE PARADE IS PLANNED FOR 2 JULY.
AFTER THE ORLANDO MASSACRE, IT'LL HAVE TIGHTENED SECURITY.
IF YOU'D LIKE, YOU CAN WEAR A BLACK ARMBAND IN MEMORY OF THE VICTIMS.
THE THEME THIS YEAR IS TRANS RIGHTS...
WE'LL MOSTLY BE MAKING SIGNS ALONG THOSE LINES.
I BROUGHT SOME STREAMERS, TOO.
YOU GOOD, NATHAN? NO PROBLEMS WITH THE T?
YEAH, A LITTLE TIRED, I GET HEADACHES SOMETIMES, BUT I'M GOOD.
AND THERE ARE LOTS OF LITTLE MUSCLES SHOWING UP THAT I DIDN'T KNOW ABOUT!

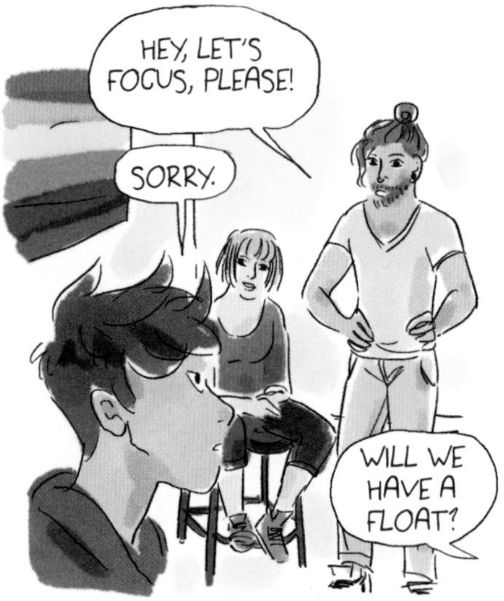
HEY, LET'S FOCUS, PLEASE!
SORRY.
WILL WE HAVE A FLOAT?

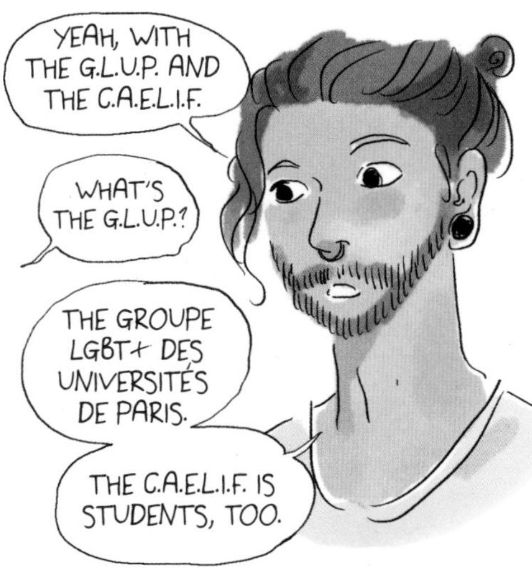
YEAH, WITH THE G.L.U.P. AND THE C.A.E.L.I.F.
WHAT'S THE G.L.U.P.?
THE GROUPE LGBT+ DES UNIVERSITÉS DE PARIS.
THE C.A.E.L.I.F. IS STUDENTS, TOO.

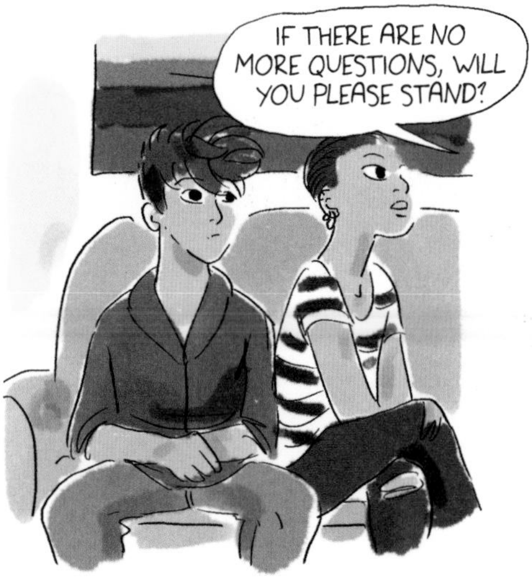
IF THERE ARE NO MORE QUESTIONS, WILL YOU PLEASE STAND?

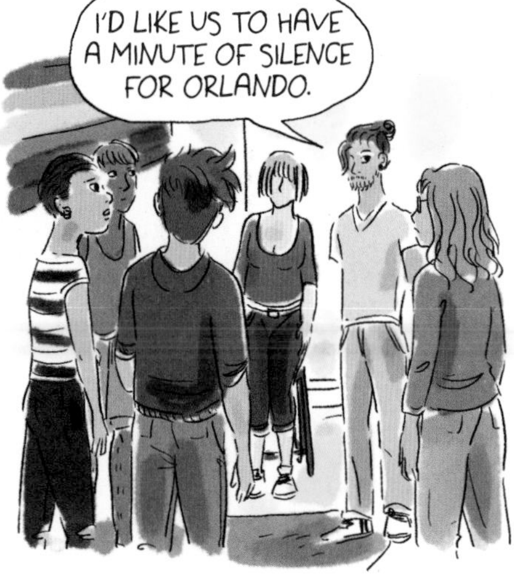
I'D LIKE US TO HAVE A MINUTE OF SILENCE FOR ORLANDO.

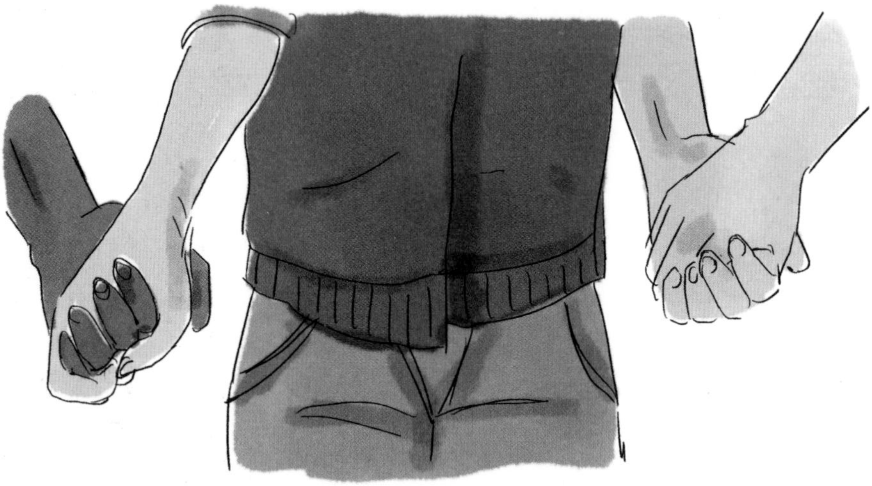

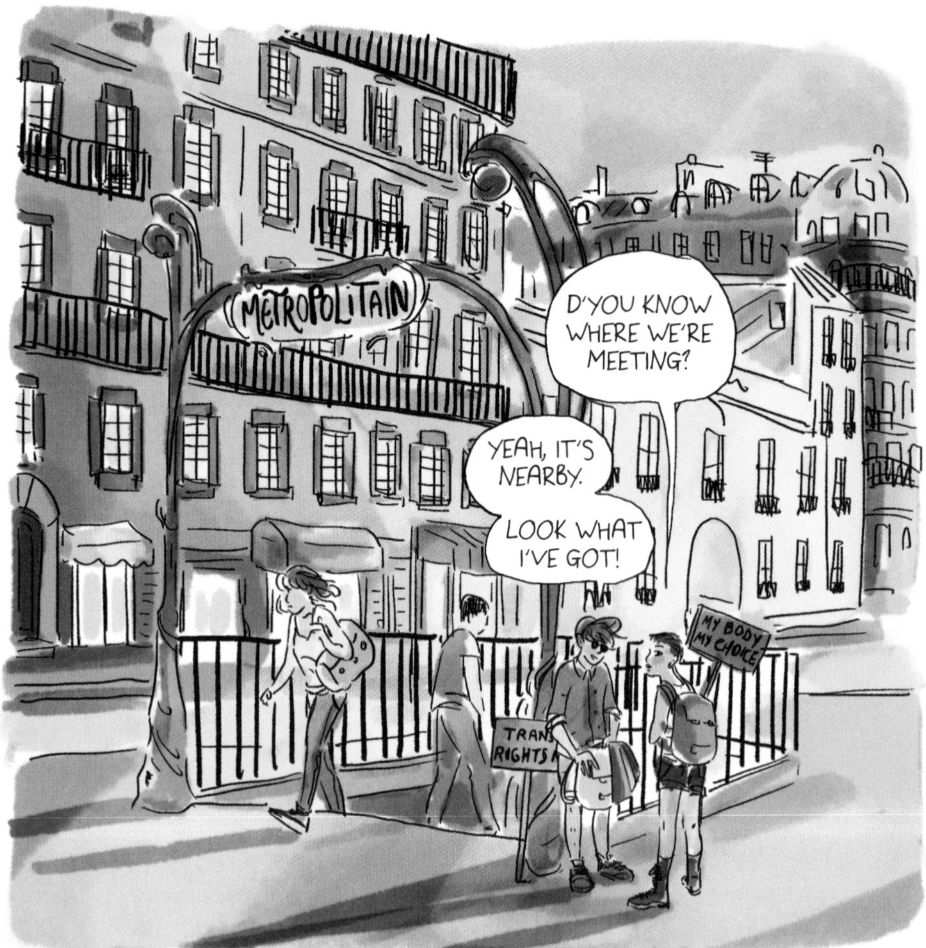
METROPOLITAIN
D'YOU KNOW WHERE WE'RE MEETING?
YEAH, IT'S NEARBY.
LOOK WHAT I'VE GOT!
MY BODY MY CHOICE

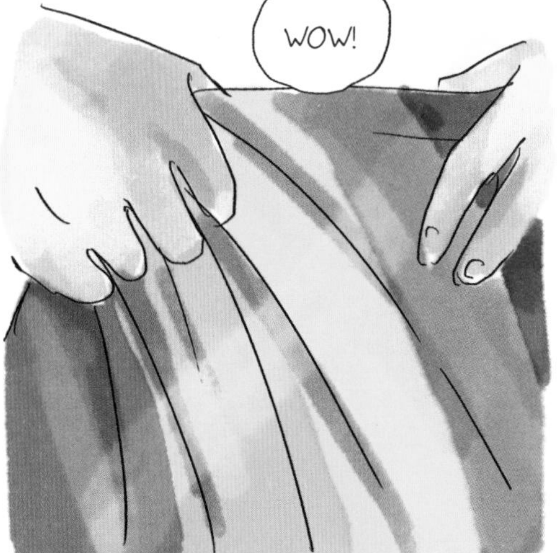
WOW!

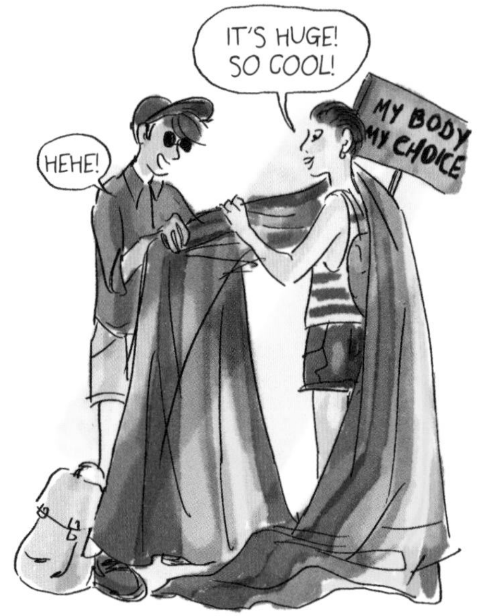
IT'S HUGE! SO COOL!
HEHE!
MY BODY MY CHOICE

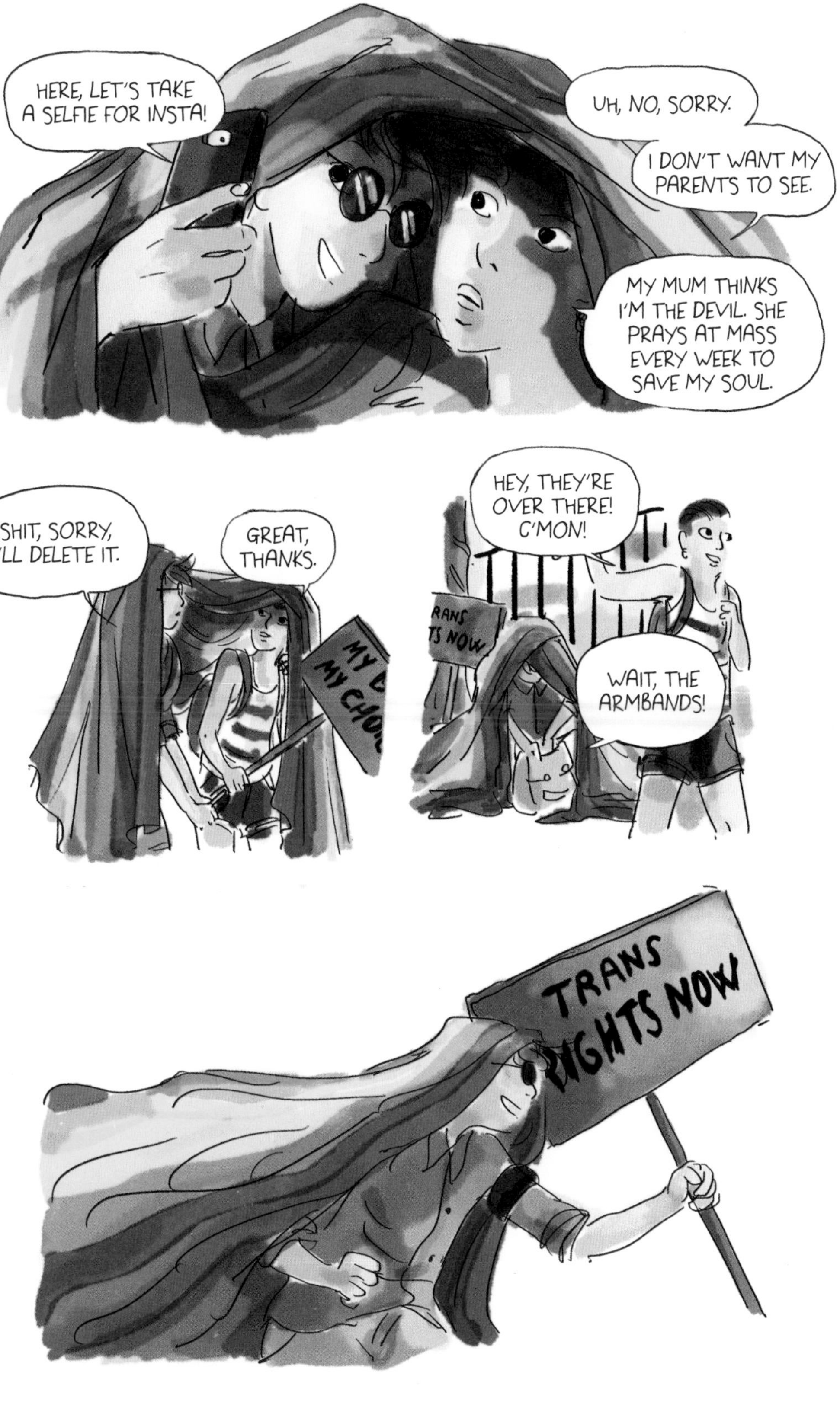
HERE, LET'S TAKE A SELFIE FOR INSTA!
UH, NO, SORRY.
I DON'T WANT MY PARENTS TO SEE.
MY MUM THINKS I'M THE DEVIL. SHE PRAYS AT MASS EVERY WEEK TO SAVE MY SOUL.
SHIT, SORRY, I'LL DELETE IT.
GREAT, THANKS.
HEY, THEY'RE OVER THERE! C'MON!
WAIT, THE ARMBANDS!
TRANS

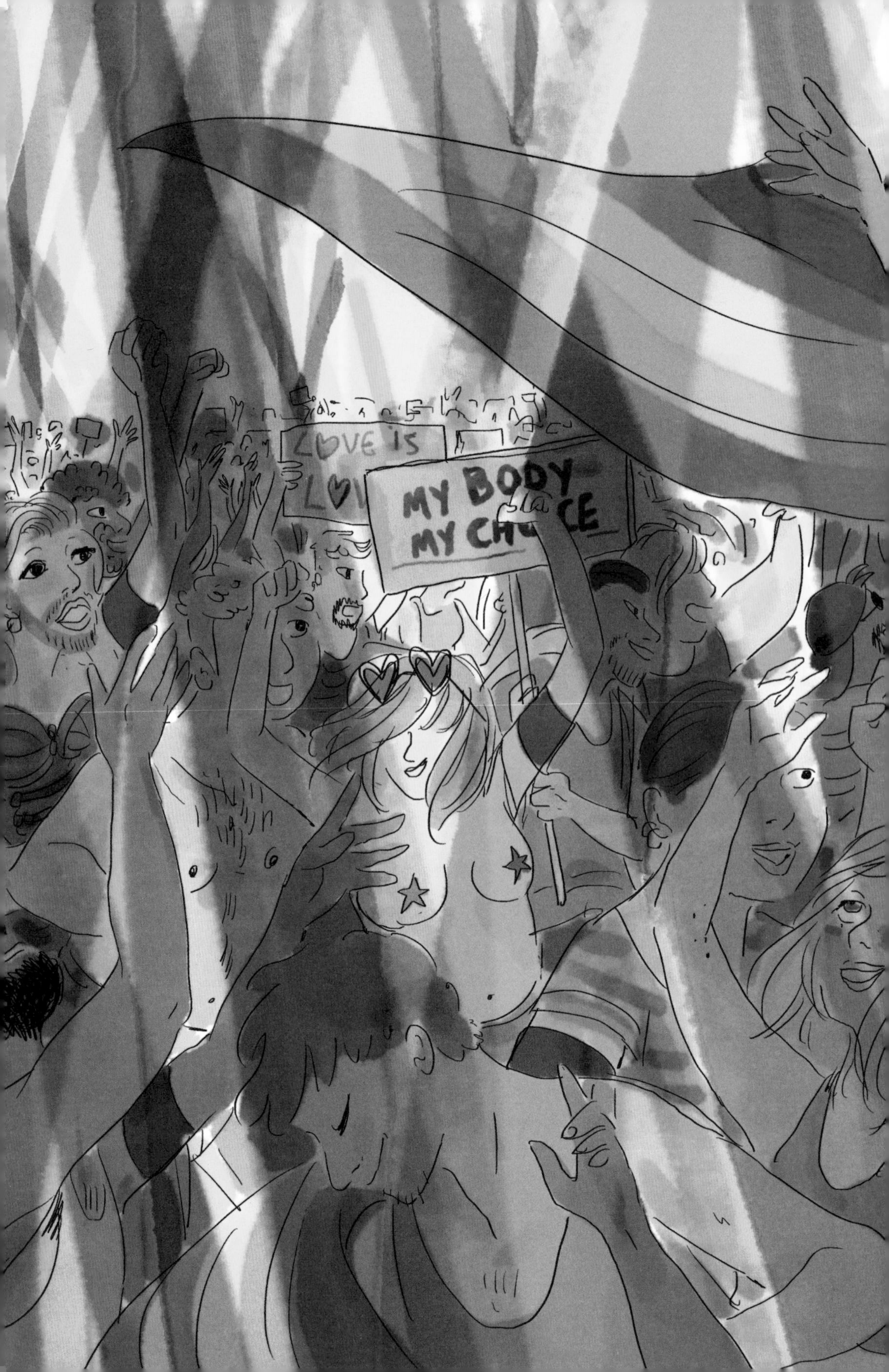

L♥VE IS
MY BODY

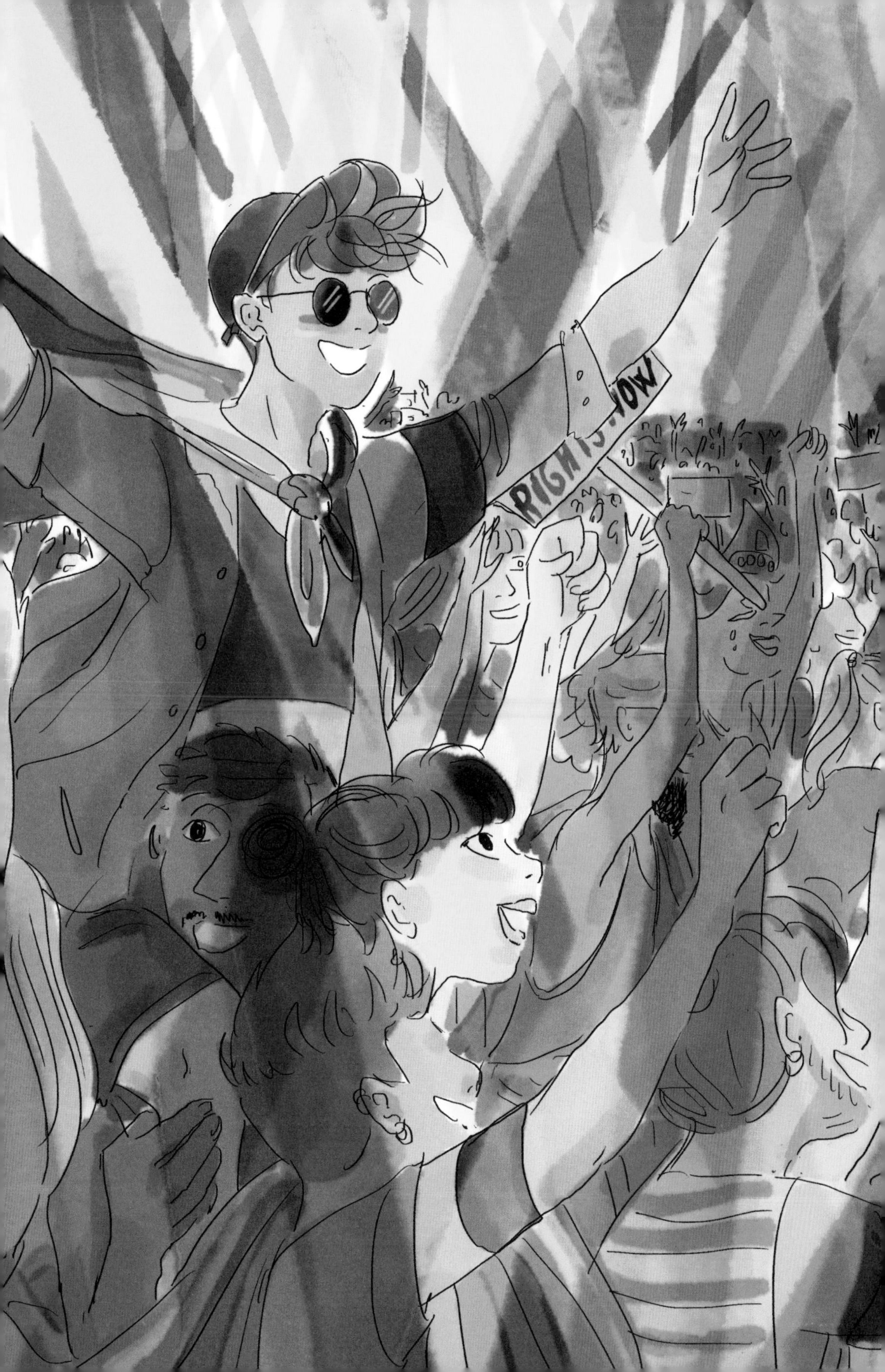
RIGHTS NOW

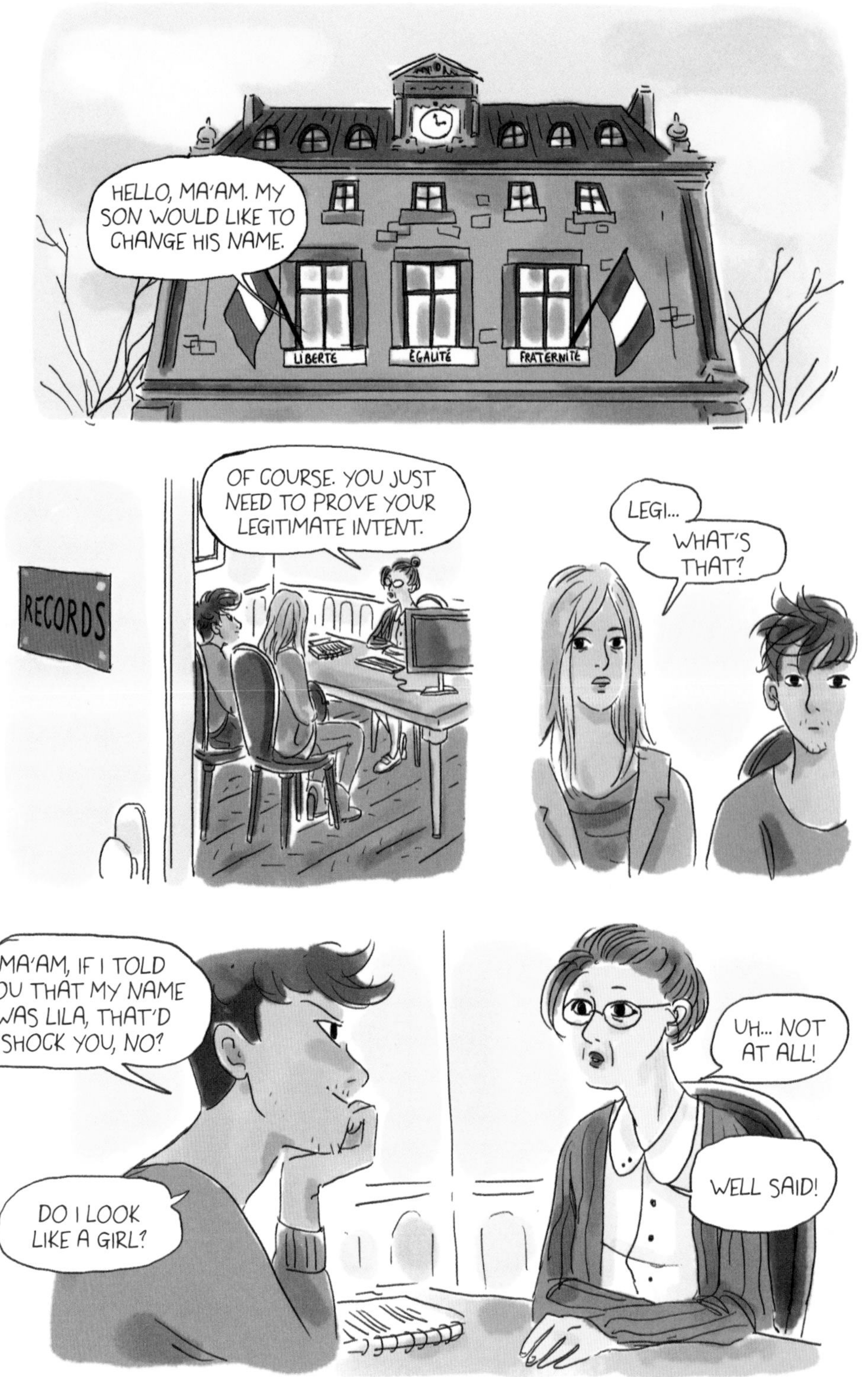
HELLO, MA'AM. MY SON WOULD LIKE TO CHANGE HIS NAME.
LIBERTÉ
ÉGALITÉ
FRATERNITÉ
RECORDS
OF COURSE. YOU JUST NEED TO PROVE YOUR LEGITIMATE INTENT.
LEGI...
WHAT'S THAT?
MA'AM, IF I TOLD YOU THAT MY NAME WAS LILA, THAT'D SHOCK YOU, NO?
DO I LOOK LIKE A GIRL?
UH... NOT AT ALL!
WELL SAID!

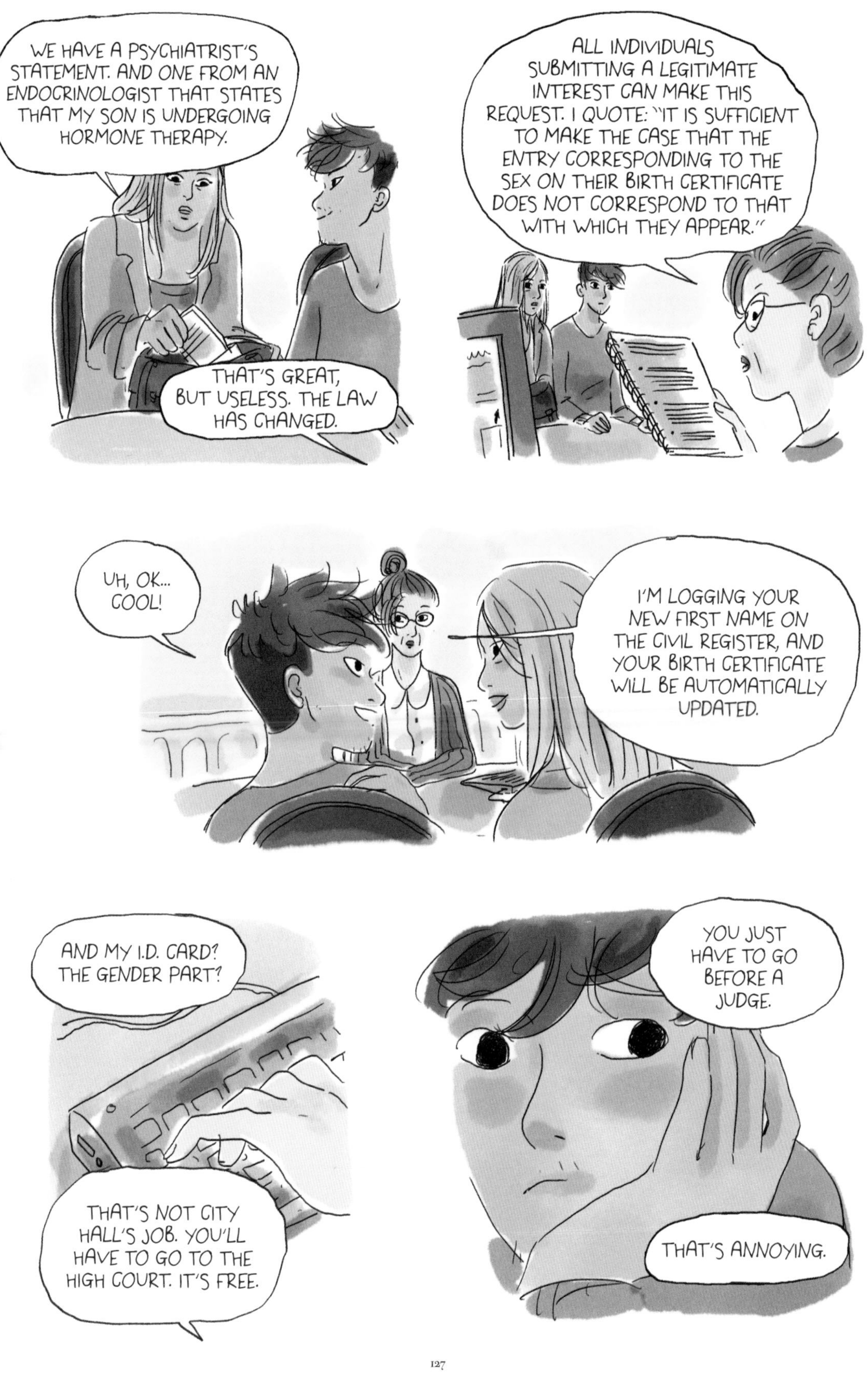
WE HAVE A PSYCHIATRIST'S STATEMENT. AND ONE FROM AN ENDOCRINOLOGIST THAT STATES THAT MY SON IS UNDERGOING HORMONE THERAPY.
THAT'S GREAT, BUT USELESS. THE LAW HAS CHANGED.
ALL INDIVIDUALS SUBMITTING A LEGITIMATE INTEREST CAN MAKE THIS REQUEST. I QUOTE: "IT IS SUFFICIENT TO MAKE THE CASE THAT THE ENTRY CORRESPONDING TO THE SEX ON THEIR BIRTH CERTIFICATE DOES NOT CORRESPOND TO THAT WITH WHICH THEY APPEAR."
UH, OK... COOL!
I'M LOGGING YOUR NEW FIRST NAME ON THE CIVIL REGISTER, AND YOUR BIRTH CERTIFICATE WILL BE AUTOMATICALLY UPDATED.
AND MY I.D. CARD? THE GENDER PART?
THAT'S NOT CITY HALL'S JOB. YOU'LL HAVE TO GO TO THE HIGH COURT. IT'S FREE.
YOU JUST HAVE TO GO BEFORE A JUDGE.
THAT'S ANNOYING.

To: info@jeanmonetschool.com   Cc Bcc

Subject: Lila Molina

Dear Sir,

My daughter Lila Molina is enrolled in tenth grade at your high school. I write "my daughter", but in reality my daughter is now my son. Allow me to explain. Last spring, Lila began an identity and gender change by means of hormone therapy. Supervised by a psychiatrist and an endocrinologist, he has become, in everyone's eyes (we his parents, but also his family and friends), a boy. So it is not a young woman who is attending your establishment, but a young man in the midst of a transition. His first name is henceforth Nathan, which has been registered at City Hall.

I would appreciate it if you would call him Nathan Molina, which corresponds with his true identity, even if he still needs to submit his request to the High Court for his identity card to be updated.

In anticipation of your understanding, we send our kindest regards,

Madeleine Molina

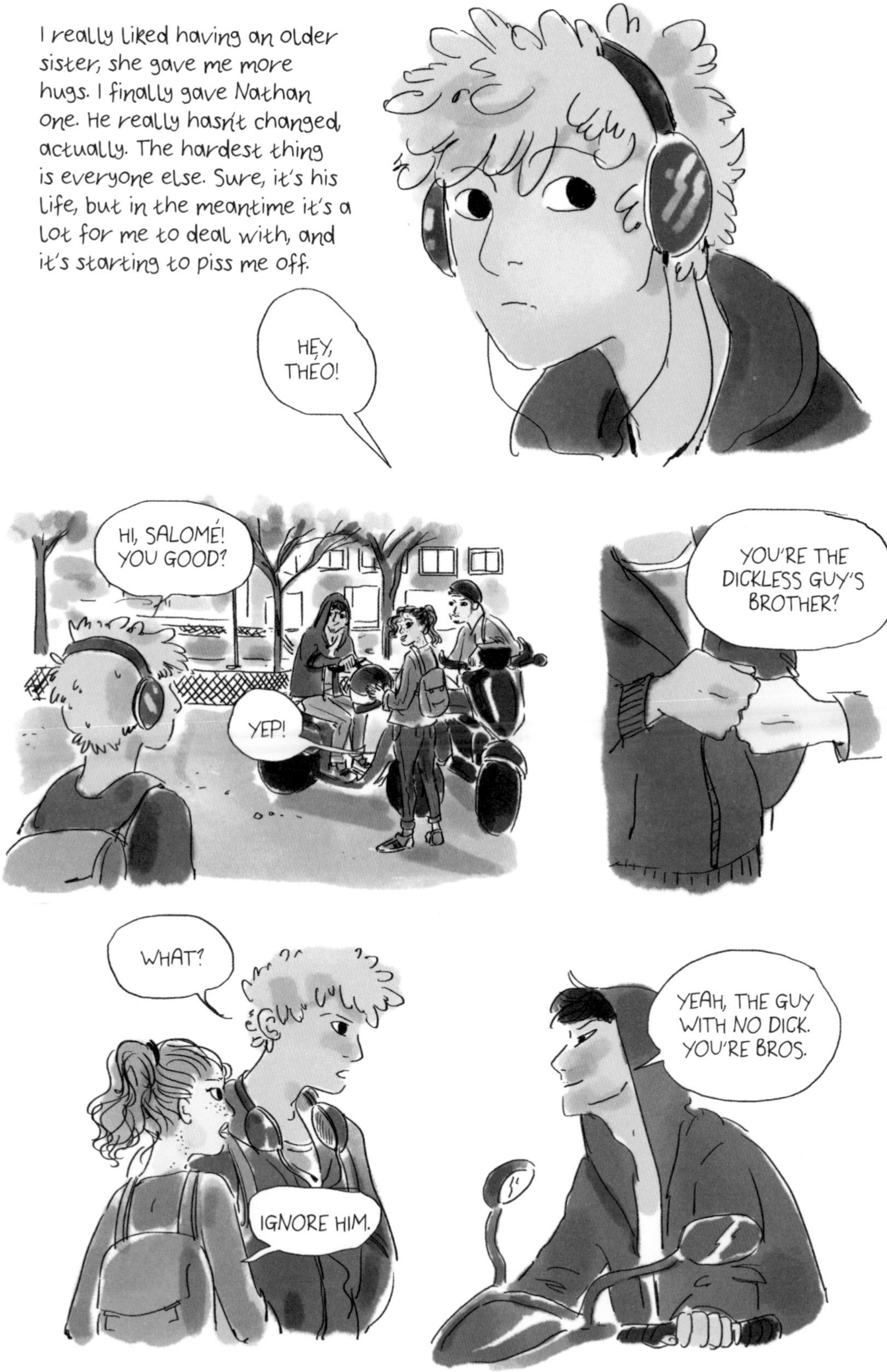
I really liked having an older sister, she gave me more hugs. I finally gave Nathan one. He really hasn't changed actually. The hardest thing is everyone else. Sure, it's his life, but in the meantime it's a lot for me to deal with, and it's starting to piss me off.
HEY, THÉO!
HI, SALOMÉ! YOU GOOD?
YEP!
YOU'RE THE DICKLESS GUY'S BROTHER?
WHAT?
IGNORE HIM.
YEAH, THE GUY WITH NO DICK. YOU'RE BROS.

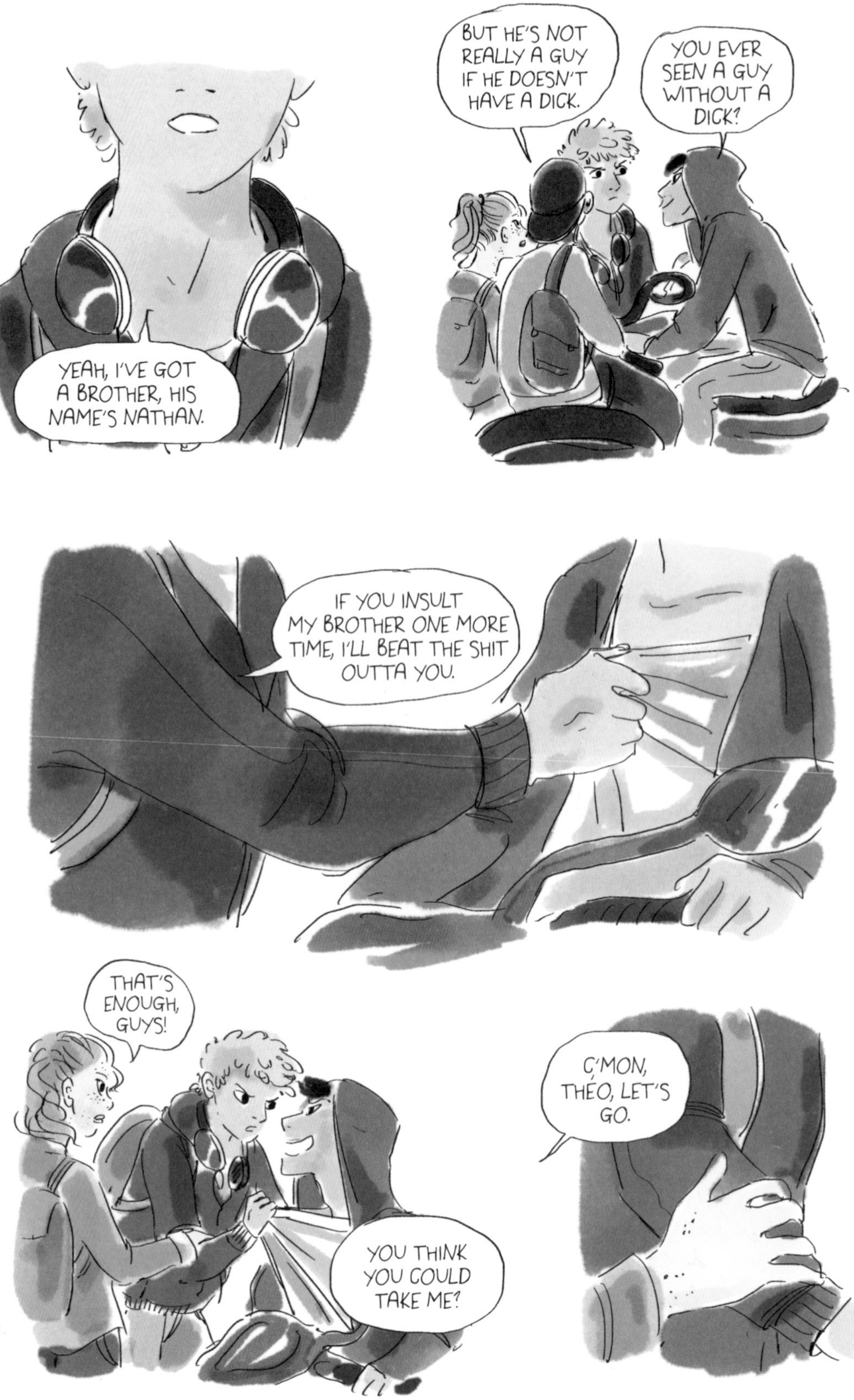
YEAH, I'VE GOT A BROTHER, HIS NAME'S NATHAN.
BUT HE'S NOT REALLY A GUY IF HE DOESN'T HAVE A DICK.
YOU EVER SEEN A GUY WITHOUT A DICK?
IF YOU INSULT MY BROTHER ONE MORE TIME, I'LL BEAT THE SHIT OUTTA YOU.
THAT'S ENOUGH, GUYS!
YOU THINK YOU COULD TAKE ME?
C'MON, THÉO, LET'S GO.

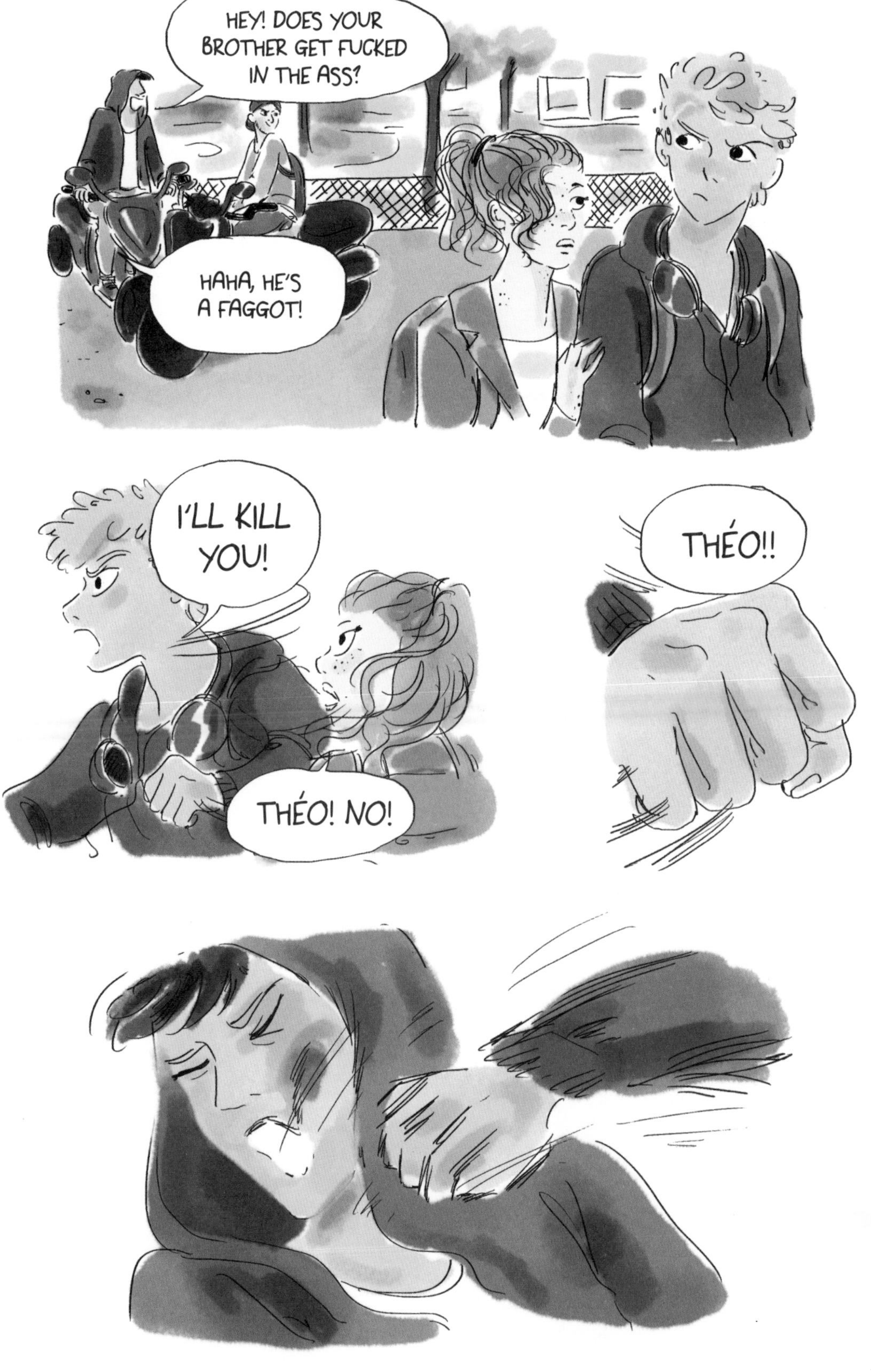
HEY! DOES YOUR BROTHER GET FUCKED IN THE ASS?
HAHA, HE'S A FAGGOT!
I'LL KILL YOU!
THÉO! NO!
THÉO!!

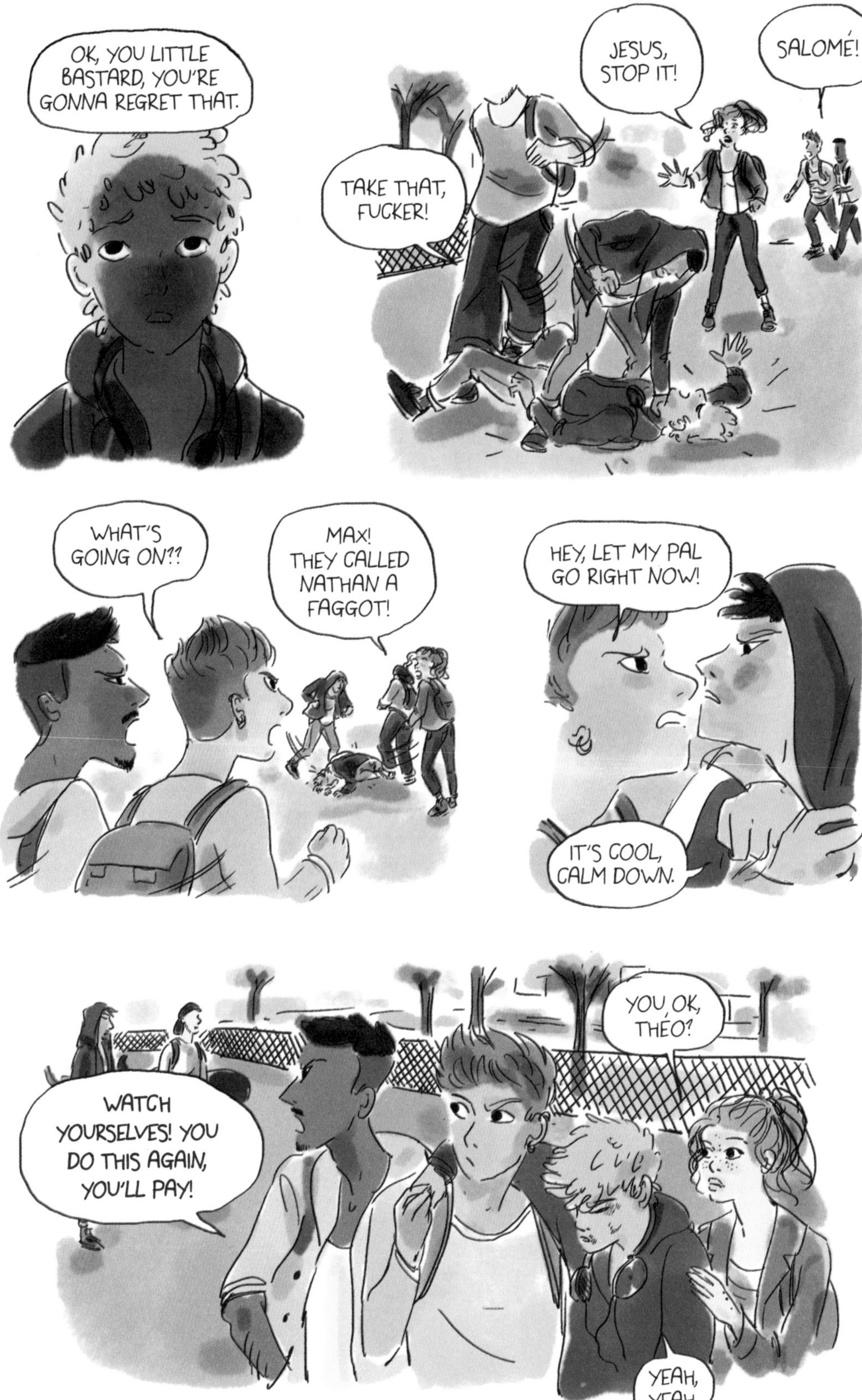
OK, YOU LITTLE BASTARD, YOU'RE GONNA REGRET THAT.
JESUS, STOP IT!
SALOMÉ!
TAKE THAT, FUCKER!
WHAT'S GOING ON??
MAX! THEY CALLED NATHAN A FAGGOT!
HEY, LET MY PAL GO RIGHT NOW!
IT'S COOL, CALM DOWN.
YOU, OK, THÉO?
WATCH YOURSELVES! YOU DO THIS AGAIN, YOU'LL PAY!
YEAH, YEAH.

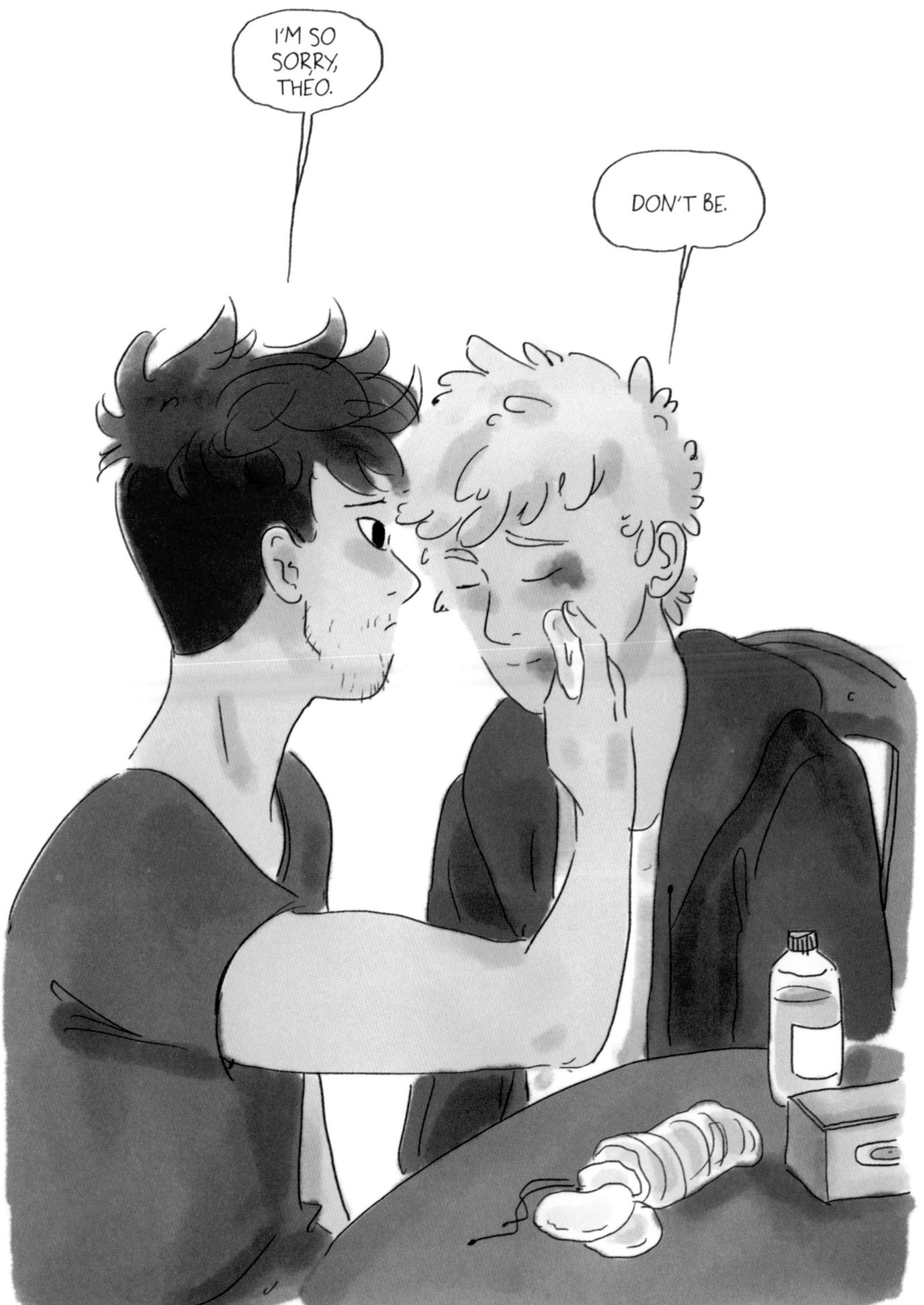
I'M SO SORRY, THÉO.
DON'T BE.

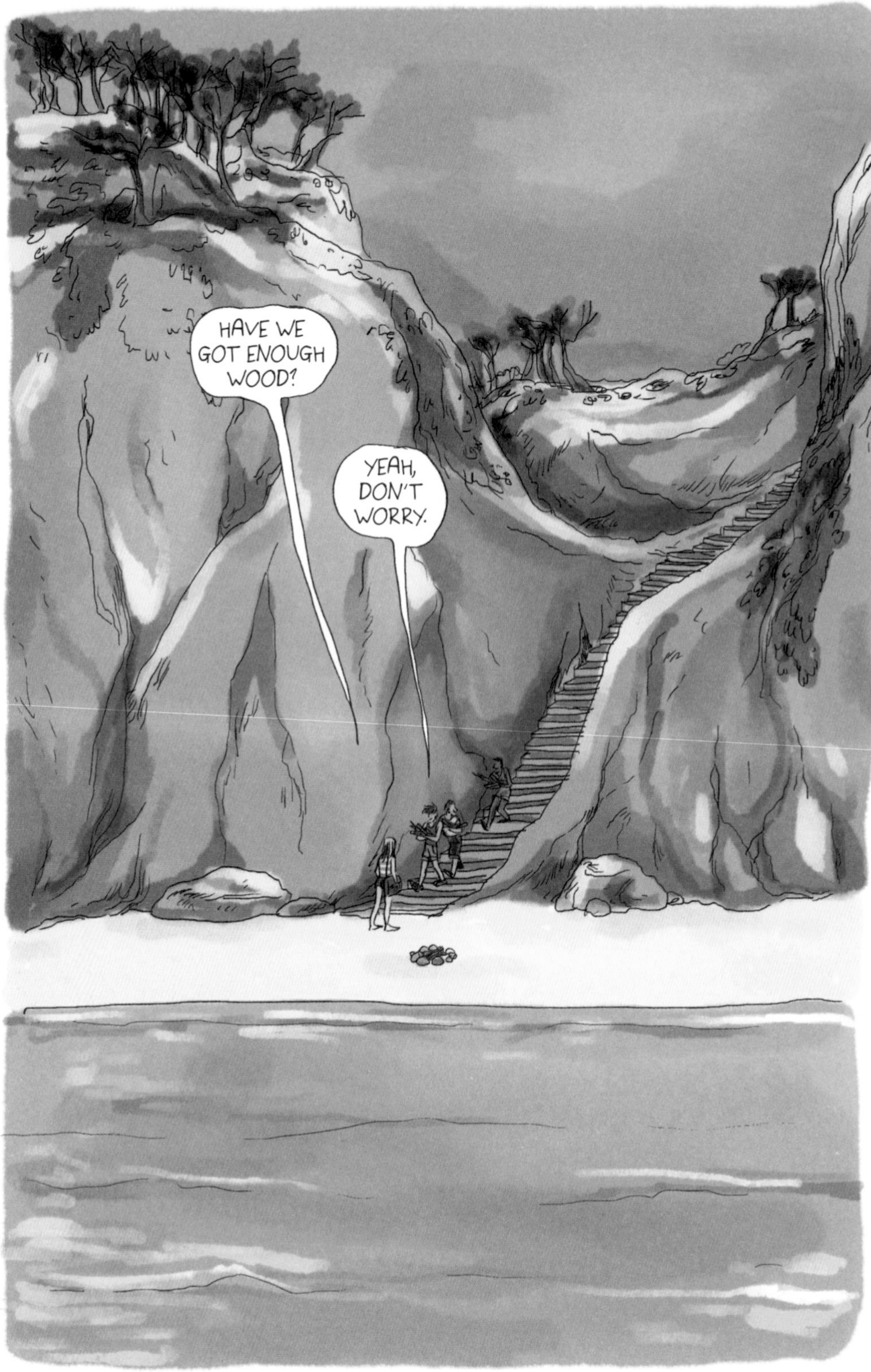
HAVE WE GOT ENOUGH WOOD?
YEAH, DON'T WORRY.

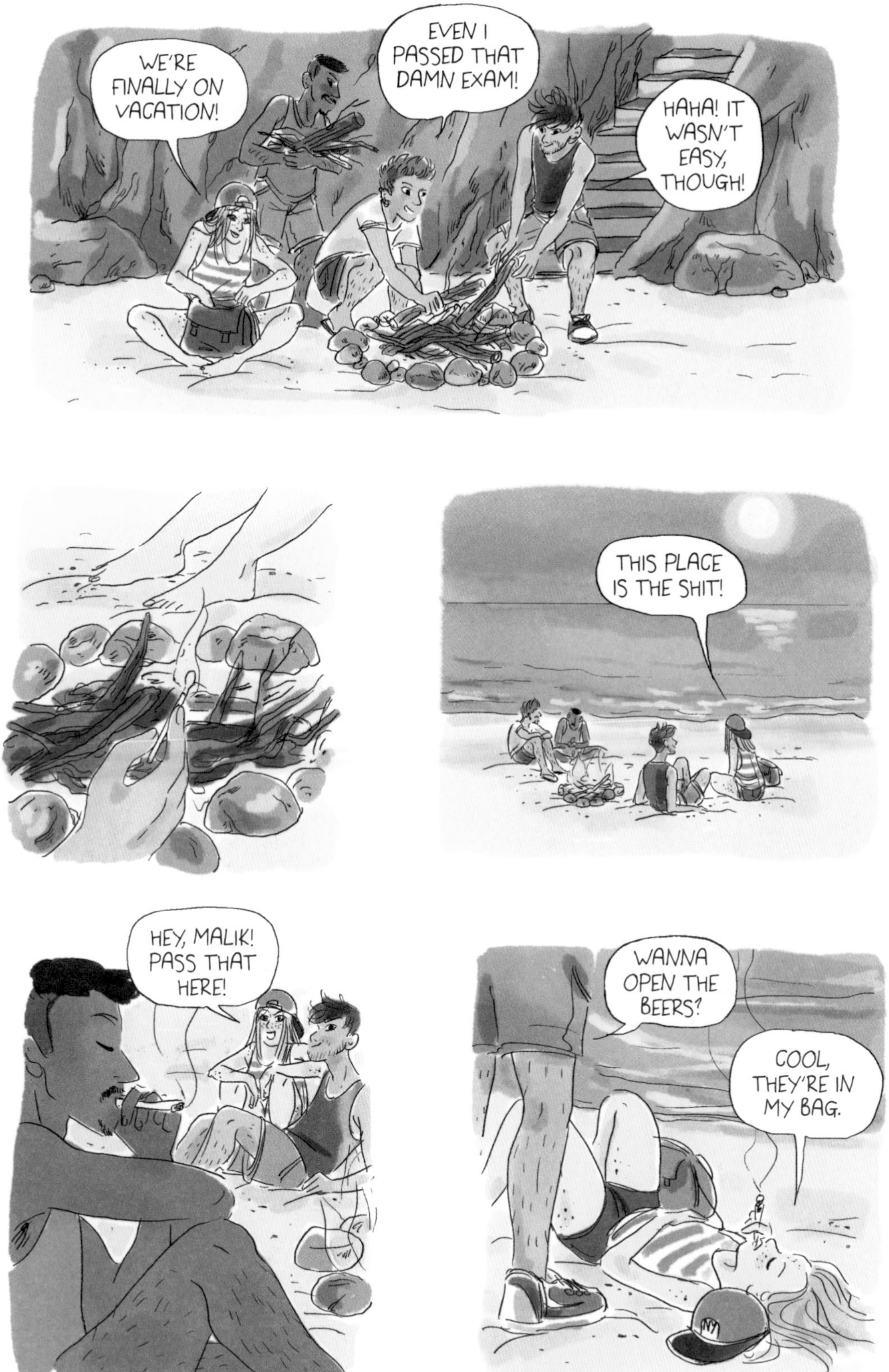
WE'RE FINALLY ON VACATION!
EVEN I PASSED THAT DAMN EXAM!
HAHA! IT WASN'T EASY, THOUGH!
THIS PLACE IS THE SHIT!
HEY, MALIK! PASS THAT HERE!
WANNA OPEN THE BEERS?
COOL, THEY'RE IN MY BAG.
NY

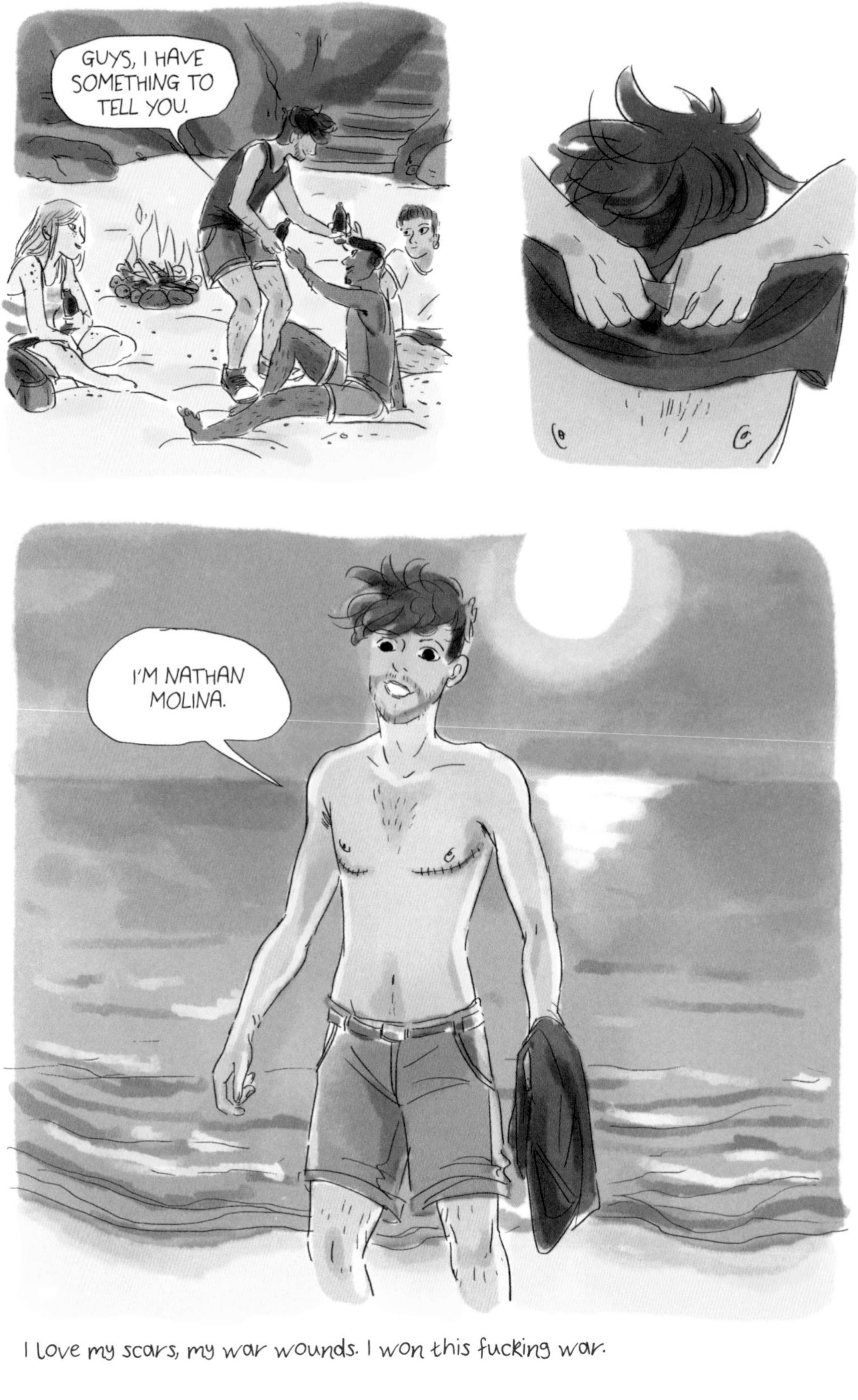
GUYS, I HAVE SOMETHING TO TELL YOU.
I'M NATHAN MOLINA.

I love my scars, my war wounds. I won this fucking war.

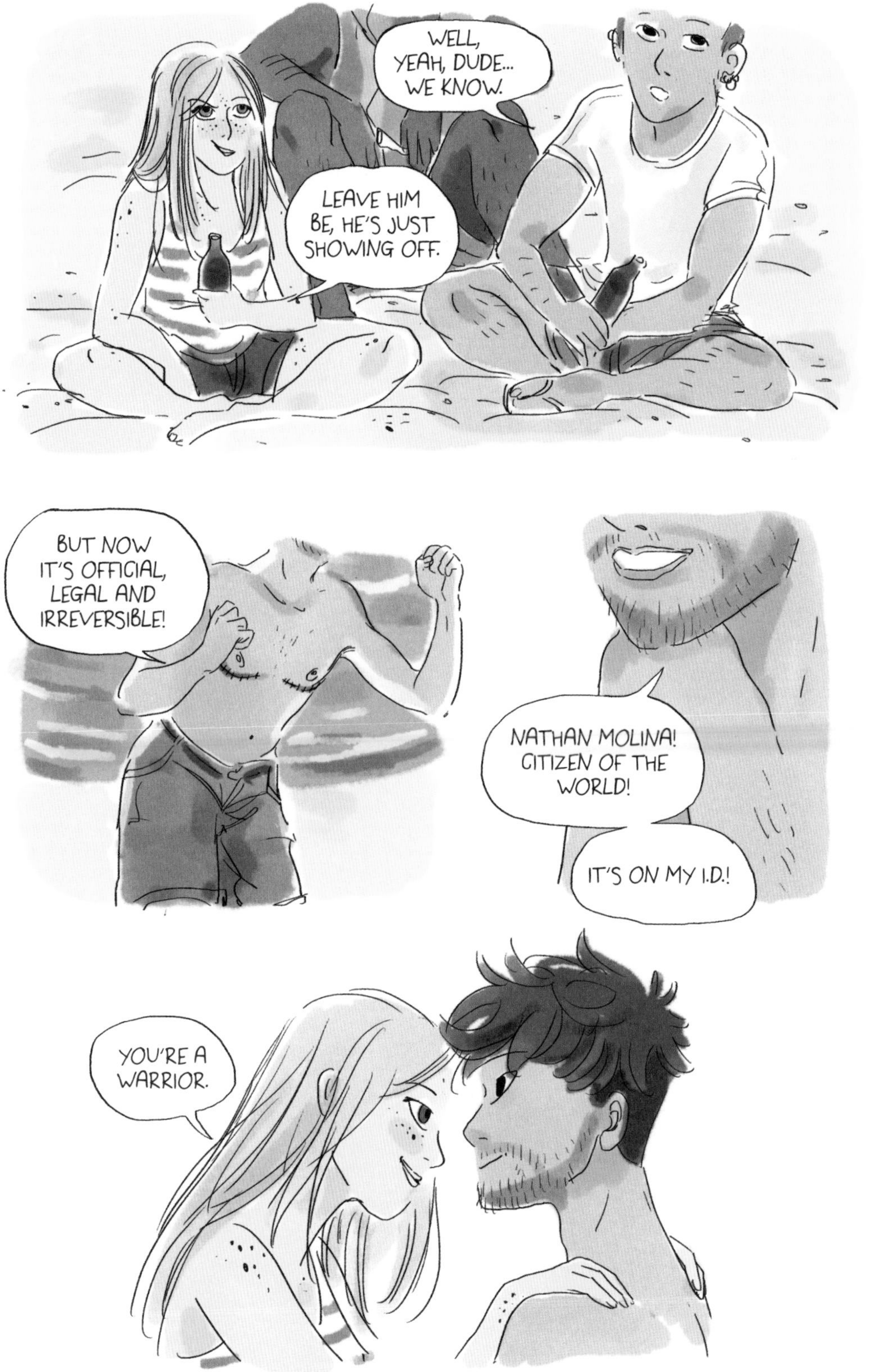
WELL, YEAH, DUDE... WE KNOW.
LEAVE HIM BE, HE'S JUST SHOWING OFF.
BUT NOW IT'S OFFICIAL, LEGAL AND IRREVERSIBLE!
NATHAN MOLINA! CITIZEN OF THE WORLD!
IT'S ON MY I.D.!
YOU'RE A WARRIOR.

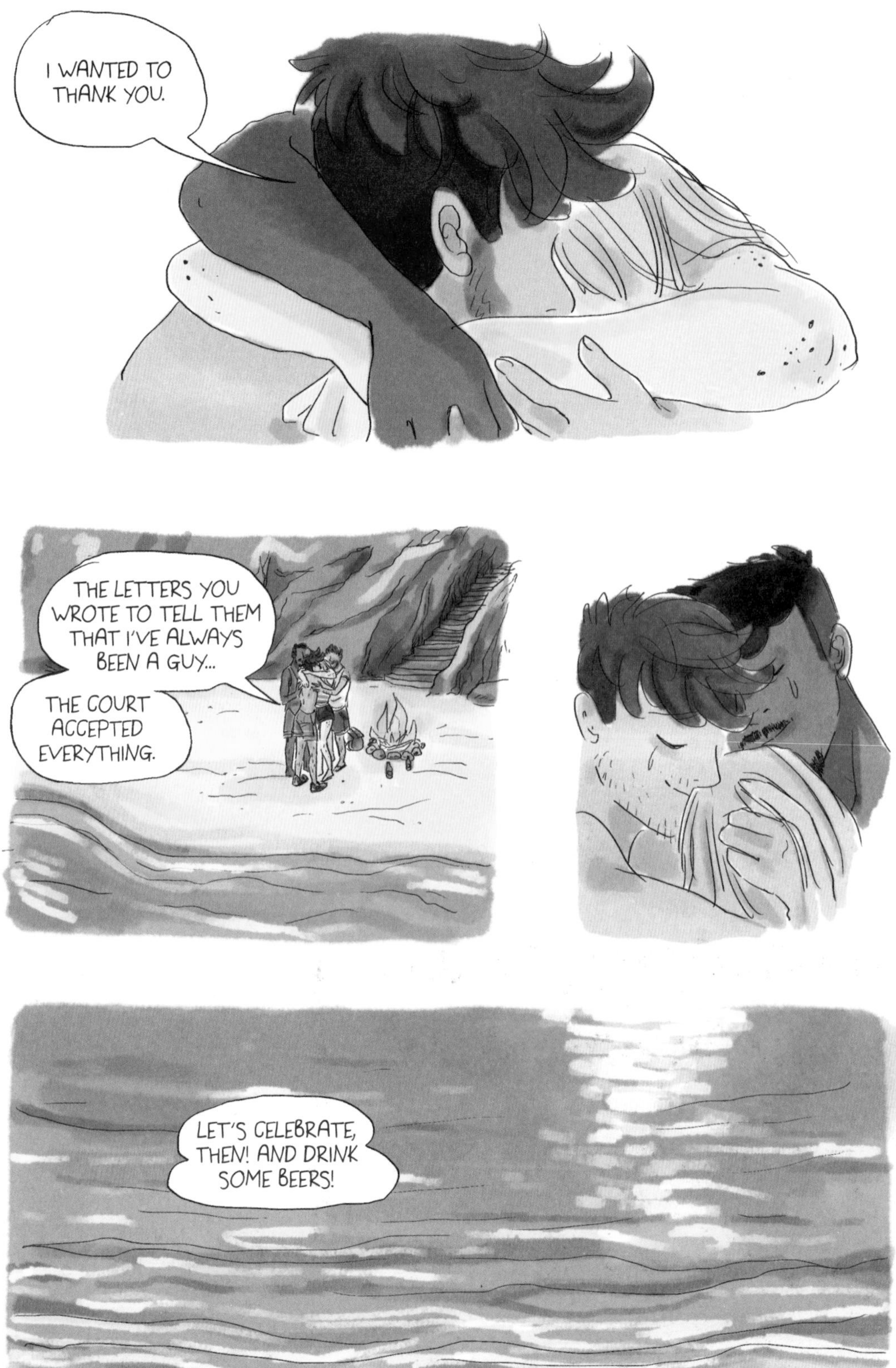
I WANTED TO THANK YOU.
THE LETTERS YOU WROTE TO TELL THEM THAT I'VE ALWAYS BEEN A GUY...
THE COURT ACCEPTED EVERYTHING.
LET'S CELEBRATE, THEN! AND DRINK SOME BEERS!

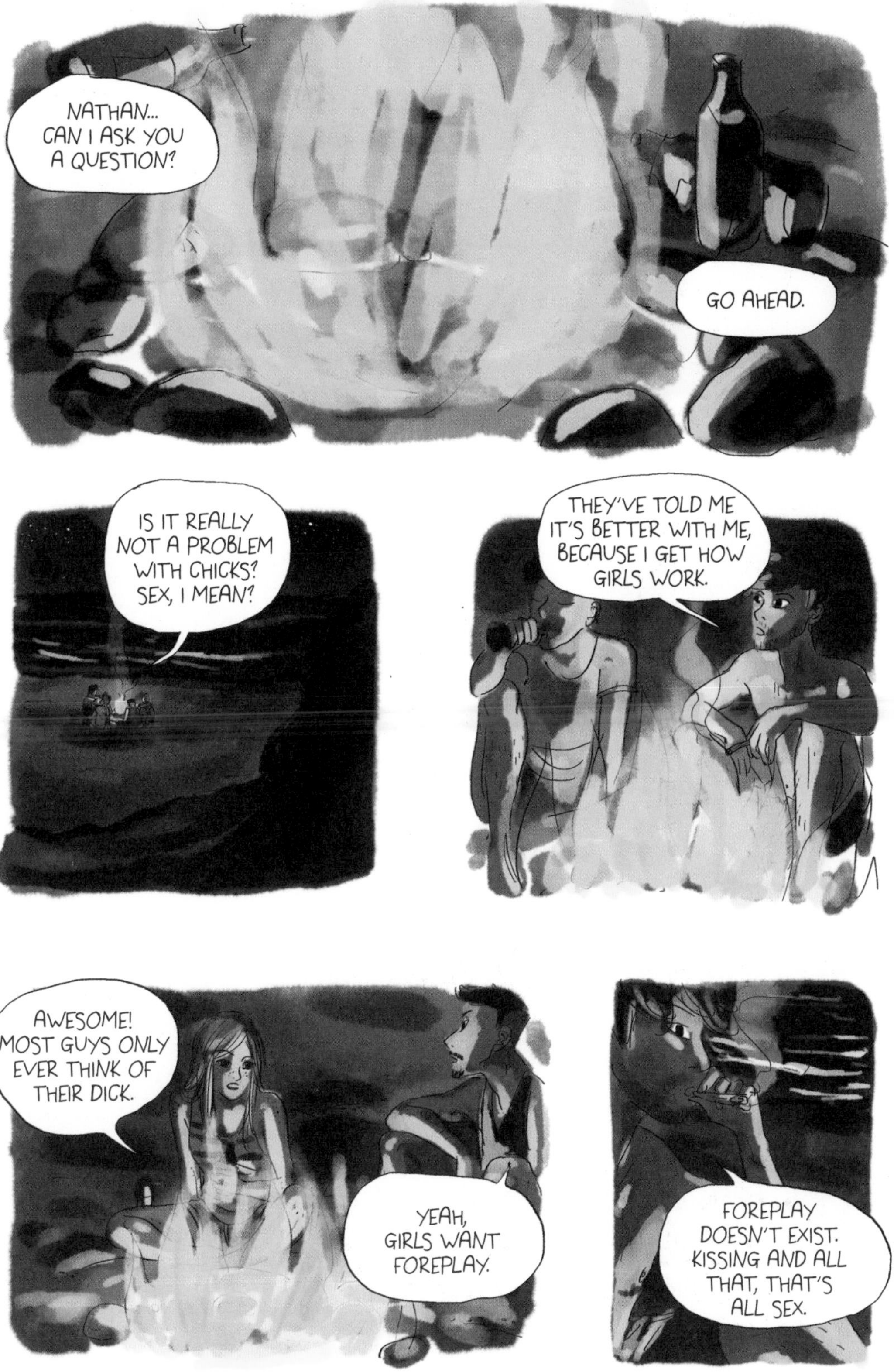
NATHAN... CAN I ASK YOU A QUESTION?
GO AHEAD.
IS IT REALLY NOT A PROBLEM WITH CHICKS? SEX, I MEAN?
THEY'VE TOLD ME IT'S BETTER WITH ME, BECAUSE I GET HOW GIRLS WORK.
AWESOME! MOST GUYS ONLY EVER THINK OF THEIR DICK.
YEAH, GIRLS WANT FOREPLAY.
FOREPLAY DOESN'T EXIST. KISSING AND ALL THAT, THAT'S ALL SEX.

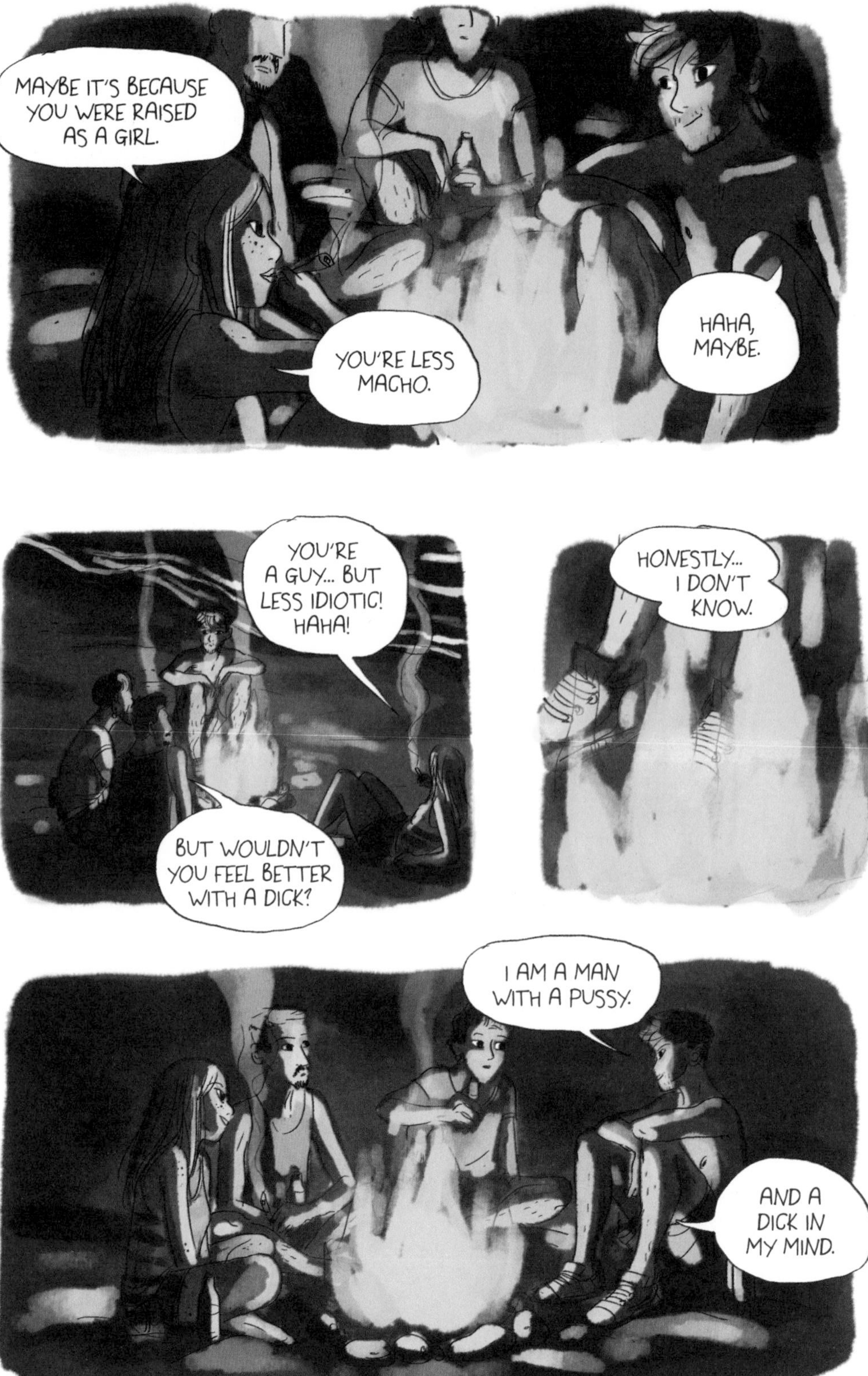
MAYBE IT'S BECAUSE YOU WERE RAISED AS A GIRL.
YOU'RE LESS MACHO.
HAHA, MAYBE.
YOU'RE A GUY... BUT LESS IDIOTIC! HAHA!
BUT WOULDN'T YOU FEEL BETTER WITH A DICK?
HONESTLY... I DON'T KNOW.
I AM A MAN WITH A PUSSY.
AND A DICK IN MY MIND.

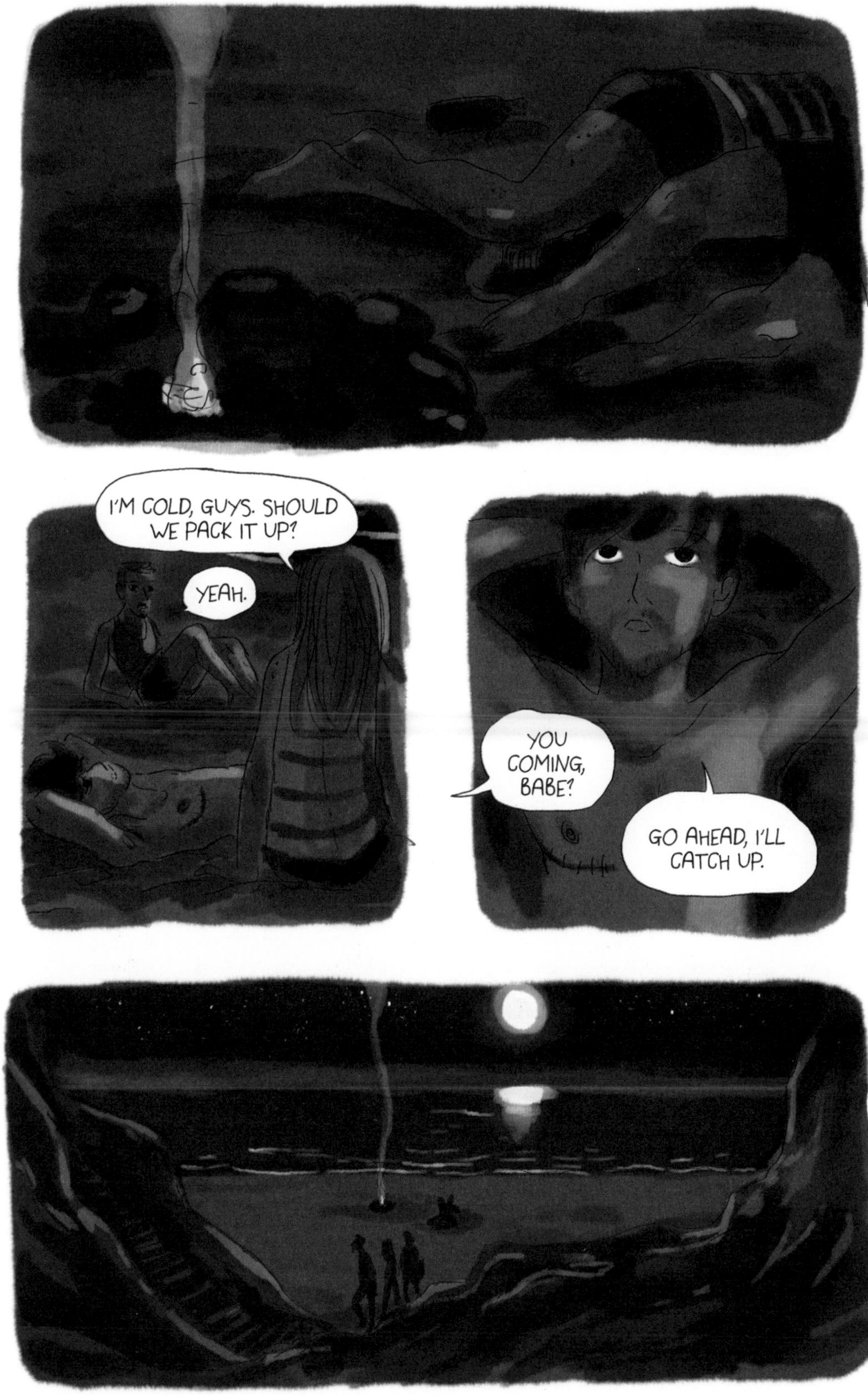
I'M COLD, GUYS. SHOULD WE PACK IT UP?
YEAH.
YOU COMING, BABE?
GO AHEAD, I'LL CATCH UP.

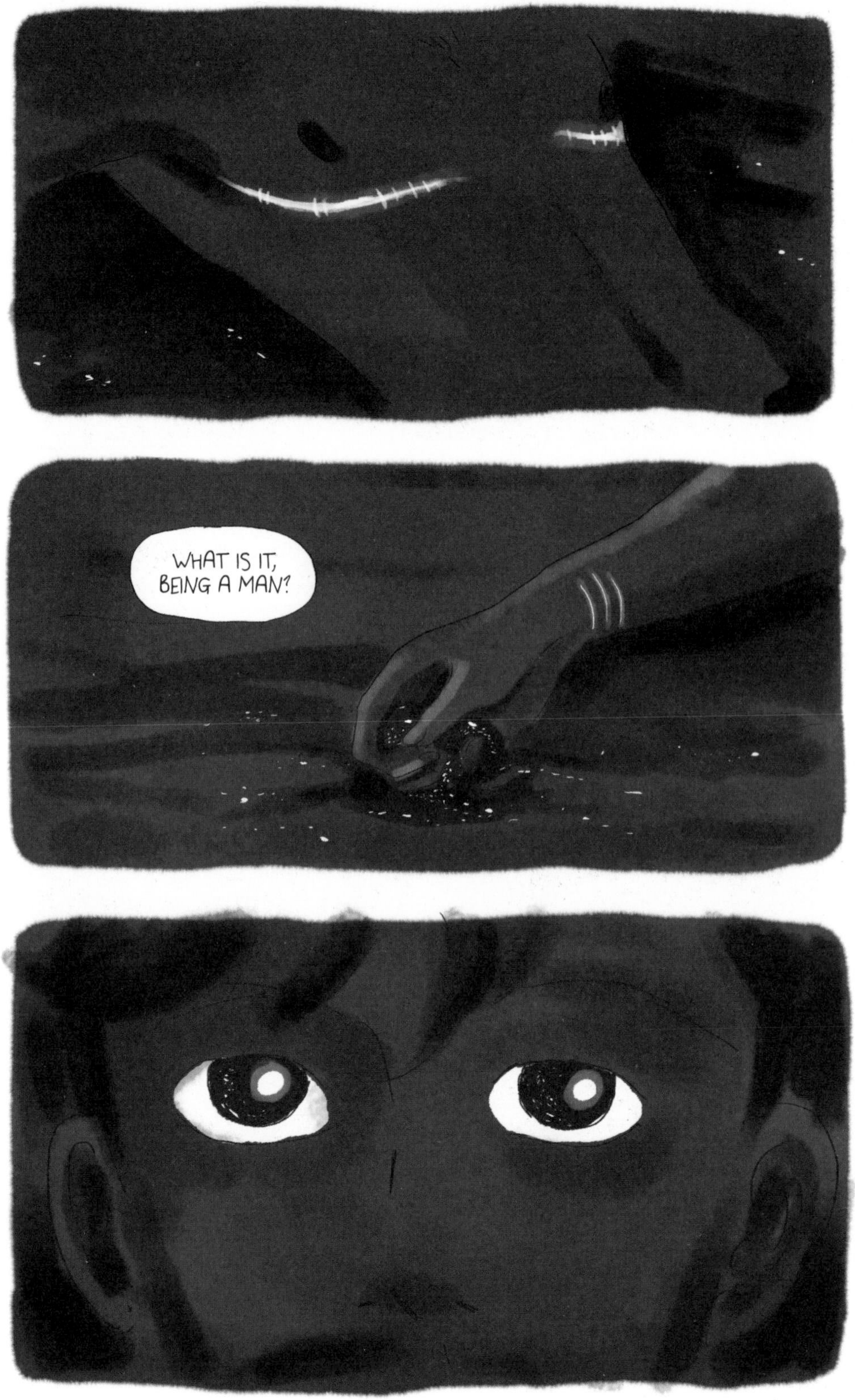
WHAT IS IT, BEING A MAN?

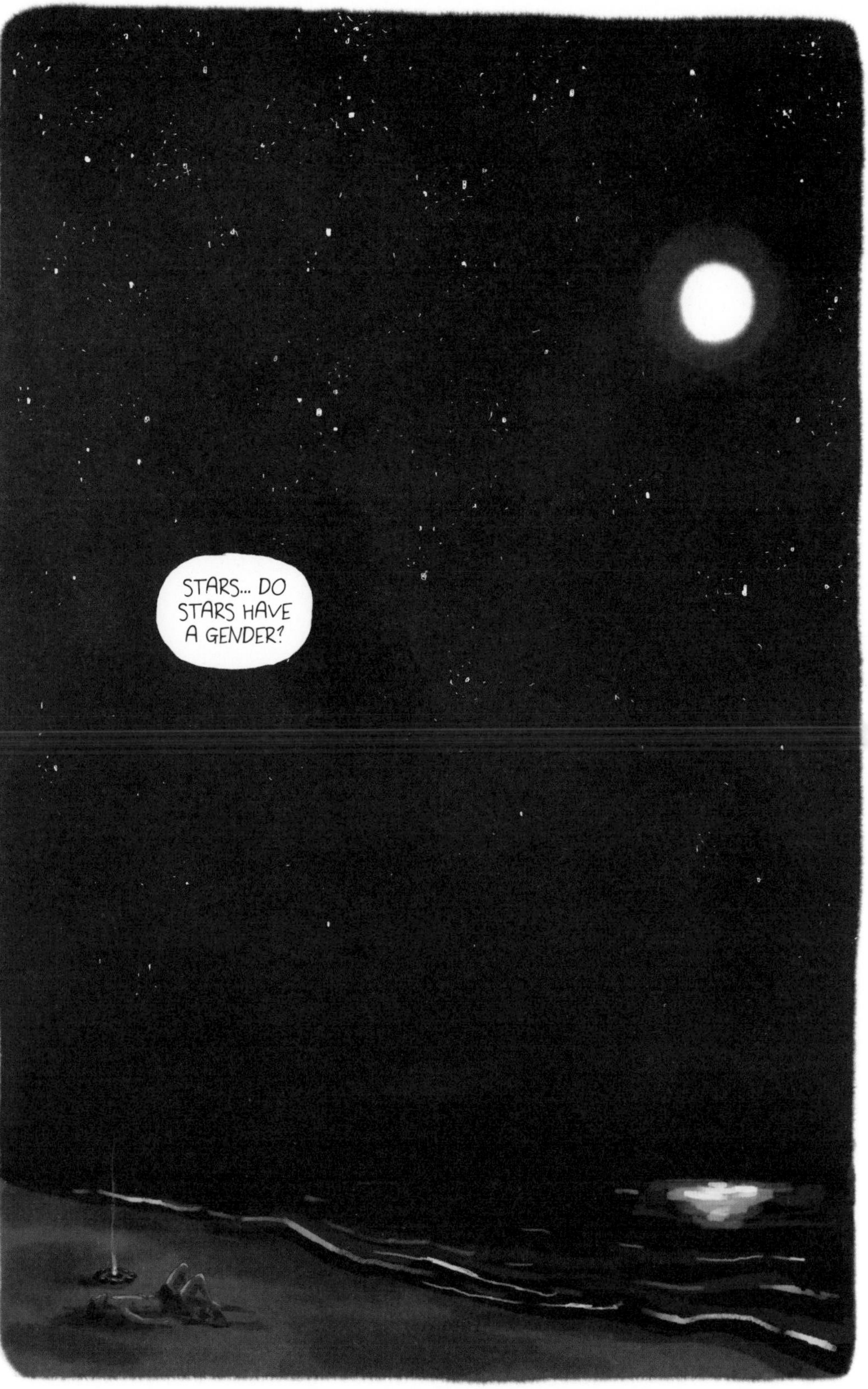
STARS... DO STARS HAVE A GENDER?

Thanks!

The real characters from this story wanted to remain mostly anonymous.
Thanks to you, Lucas, for your life and to your exceptional family for your trust.
Thanks to my co-author Quentin, for his infernal talent.
Thanks to Guillaume Prieur, the magical editor without whom this book would not exist.
Thanks to Hélène Fiamma for believing in me. Thank you, Pauline.
In short, you all prove that love is the only way to face anything.

Catherine Castro

Thanks to Mama Odile.

Quentin Zuttion

Translator's Note

I would like to dedicate the translation of this marvellous book to the trans
siblings who are no longer with us. In a world that strives to thwart trans rights
at every turn, being able to translate this journey to trans joy has electrified my
own gender euphoria and raison d'être. I am so enamoured with Catherine's
storytelling and Quentin's visceral, masterful images of trans life, a pairing
that brought me to tears through Nathan's highs and lows. Their
work transcends boundaries and binaries, and I am delighted that this
translation will help to enlighten and engage more readers around the globe.
Every trans experience is different, and the publication of *Call Me Nathan* adds yet
another touching, genuine stitch to the tapestry of trans literature. My thanks to
everyone at SelfMadeHero for their fearless passion to publish this inspiring story
in English. And a special thanks to Cleo, Lindsay, Jeffrey, Edward, Emma,
Dan, Guillaume and my loving, affirming friends and family.
Trans is beautiful. Trans is a superpower. No one is alone.

Evan McGorray